SOUTHBOUND

Southbound

Essays on Identity, Inheritance, and Social Change

Anjali Enjeti

The University of Georgia Press ⁓ Athens

Published by the University of Georgia Press
Athens, Georgia 30602
www.ugapress.org
© 2021 by Anjali Enjeti
All rights reserved
Designed by Erin Kirk
Set in ITC New Baskerville
Printed and bound by Sheridan Books
Illustration by Swati Gupta
The paper in this book meets the guidelines for
permanence and durability of the Committee on
Production Guidelines for Book Longevity of the
Council on Library Resources.

Epigraph to part 1, "Identity," from Audre Lorde,
"Learning from the 60s," in *Sister Outsider: Essays and
Speeches by Audre Lorde* (Berkeley: Crossing Press/Penguin
Random House, 2007), 137, © 1984, 2007 by Audre Lorde.

Epigraph to part 3, "Social Change," from Grace Lee
Boggs with Scott Kurashige, *The Next American Revolution:
Sustainable Activism for the Twenty-First Century* (Berkeley:
University of California Press, 2011), 47, reprinted with
permission.

Most University of Georgia Press titles are
available from popular e-book vendors.

Printed in the United States of America
25 24 23 22 21 P 5 4 3 2 1

Library of Congress Control Number: 2021930398
ISBN: 9780820360065 (pbk.: alk. paper)
ISBN: 9780820360072 (ebook)

for my three precious daughters—
may you always be true, to you

Either way, change will come. It could be bloody, or it could be beautiful. It depends on us.

—ARUNDHATI ROY, "How Deep Shall We Dig?"
My Seditious Heart

Contents

Author's Note

Southbound contains essays about racism, white supremacy, gun violence, vigilantism, police violence, lynchings, homophobia, suicide, 9/11, and slurs.

Much of this book is based on my memories. I've reconstructed them here to the best of my ability. Where possible, I've consulted with others present during the events to verify information.

Over the years, language about bigotry and white supremacy has evolved. In these essays I've tried to use the language that most accurately reflects the time period as well as my own understanding of these concepts.

SOUTHBOUND

What *Are* You? Where Are You *From?*

Questions about my identity have echoed in my mind for decades. They have been absorbed by the tympanic membranes of my eardrums and have traveled through the synapses of my brain. Shadows, they have followed me everywhere. They are most predictable words I've ever known.

Timing and intent make all the difference, of course. Other people of color who ask these questions are trying to determine whether I share their same culture or community. They are searching for a linked heritage in the diaspora, a bridge to forge an alliance. They wish to expand their circle, offer an invitation to their home. Others inquire after we've had time to get to know one another and our histories and stories. The questions are an olive branch, an effort to create space for a more intimate relationship. In either of these circumstances, I am grateful to respond.

But often it's complete strangers who abruptly ask what I am and where I'm from.

When I was younger, peers would scrunch their noses, as if the ambiguity of my racial and ethnic background brought with it a sour odor, the emphasis on *are* jarring, like a siren, a foregone conclusion that I am part alien.

What *are* you?

In the slightly less abrasive version, the speaker's voice drops to a lower key, the emphasis shifts to the last word, drawn out, as if multisyllabic. Where are you *fro-om?* And when the answer is less than satisfactory because it fails to meet the speaker's exotic expectations, there's the inevitable follow-up: *No, where are you really from?*

For others, my racial and ethnic identity is oftentimes a Rubik's Cube to be solved. I am half Indian, a quarter Puerto Rican, and a quarter Austrian. I am an immigrant's daughter and also a daughter of the Deep South. Despite an ever increasingly diverse United States, I remain a perpetual foreigner.

But wait a minute, a woman ahead of me in line says, *you look so much like the travel guide we had in Cairo!* In Philadelphia, during a law school mock mediation, one of the actors playing the role of an aggrieved party insisted I was Sicilian. *Come on, admit it,* he prodded. *What are you ashamed of? It's a lovely island.* A coworker once suggested that I take a DNA test. *You look exactly like my Lebanese girlfriend. I bet you're at least part Lebanese.* Apparently, others' confusion is partially my own fault. *That's why I couldn't tell that you were Indian—because you're only half!*

Violence, erasure, exoticism, appropriation—these forces can shape assumptions about identity. Beginning in 2014, when the plight of Syrians fleeing civil war blanketed the airwaves, a man working inside my home said, without prompting, that he could tell I was from Syria. When the United States denounces countries of the Southern Hemisphere, I am Venezuelan or Guatemalan or Mexican. Having ambiguously brown skin makes me an aberration, a visitor, or an intruder who can pose a threat to someone's safety, success, or security.

In *Mistaken Identity: Race and Class in the Age of Trump,* Asar Haidar, a Pakistani American born in central Pennsylvania and a child during 9/11, relays how his ideas about his identity were born out of the worst terrorist attack committed on U.S. soil: "My identity had become a matter of homeland security. But how could I respond to such a scenario? Should I proudly claim a fixed Pakistani identity, one that never felt quite like the right fit, that belonged to a place on the other side of the world? Or should I assimilate into the world of whiteness around me, even though it was racist and parochial and had never really welcomed me?"[1]

My own identity began to form after the 1982 racialized killing of Vincent Chin in Detroit, and was later shaped through the hostility toward brown people during the Persian Gulf War and after 9/11. For years my identity was a reactionary state of being. It has taken me time, reflection, and a lot of work to develop a sense of identity that is defined by my own parameters, that derives from an authentic self-concept, rather than a defensive posture born of stereotypes or suspicion.

The truth of the matter is that when I was growing up in the 1970s and 1980s, there was no accurate language to describe my identity, at least not any kind of language that resonated with me. In 1990, the year I began applying to college, racial categories on applications included *Asian, Black, Caucasian, Hispanic, American Indian,* and *Other,* and were accompanied with a request to check *one* of the boxes. Only one application offered the designation *Multiracial.* On the rest, I relegated myself to *Other.*

It was an accurate category. For seventeen years, I'd felt othered. College applications seemed to make it official.

In 2000, the United States expanded census categories so that respondents could select more than one race.[2] Soon thereafter, I heard the term *mixed race* for the first time and felt an affinity with it. After nearly three decades on this earth, my categories for identity finally started catching up to the very fact of my existence.

Of course, identity goes far beyond trauma, pain, othering, and exclusion. It is history, family, traditions, lore, and love. It is a celebration of the myriad ways in which we view and move throughout the world. These essays will focus on how identity, when it derives from a place of injustice, can transform itself into collective sociopolitical power. They will explore how an individual identity can lead to an exterior energy, one that brings awareness, agency, and community, one that acknowledges complicity and, by doing so, gives rise to activism and social change.

1 Identity

If I didn't define myself for myself, I would be crunched into other people's fantasies for me and eaten alive.

—AUDRE LORDE, "Learning from the 60s," in *Sister Outsider*

Southbound

In mid-March 1984, on my first day of fifth grade in a new school, a new city (Chattanooga), a new region of the country (the South), I stand before sixty apprising eyes, almost all white bodies huddled behind their desks. Fluorescent bulbs struggle to light the dim classroom. Outside there is ground. Green grass, dirt, pavement. I am used to Michigan winters that stretch long into spring, to pure white snow, to black ice, and mud slush, snow pants with bibs, calf-high boots that can't be removed unless one of my parents yanks them off me.

Today I am wearing a cardigan sweater—it's all I needed to leave the house.

My homeroom teacher introduces me as the *new student*. This is my fourth school since kindergarten—being new is nothing new to me. But I am vehemently opposed to this particular move. It's as if someone has ripped a bandage off the most tender part of my skin.

My Michigan is half a country away, more distant with each passing day. I picture my old school. At this very moment, Mrs. P is likely breaking the class up into reading groups. Who is my friend Lisa sitting next to now that my desk is empty? What would they have done with it? And how will I navigate life without my best friend Katy, who threw my going-away slumber party with all of my friends? We had been joined at the hip since the second grade. Her absence in my new life leaves a pit in my stomach.

At my teacher's prompting, I mutter a few words about myself. *Dad's new job. Younger brother. Living with aunt right now. Michigan. I'm from Michigan.*

My new teacher, Mrs. O., then poses a question. I've no recollection what it was. But I clearly remember my answer, "Yes."

Her correction arrives swiftly. "Yes, *ma'am.*"

My face goes hot. A muffled giggle echoes throughout the room. "Yes, ma'am," I reply.

After I'm dismissed, I find an empty plastic chair and sink deeply into its pocket. Until that moment, I'd only heard the word *ma'am* out of the mouths of characters in television shows and movies. I had presumed it was an antiquated term, a relic from the past, an honorific for very old women with permed hair.

The rest of the day is a blur. Several of my classmates ask if I'm a Yankee, a term I'd always associated with baseball. "I'm from Michigan, the state that looks like a mitten," I respond, as if this will somehow clarify my status. A girl whose desk abuts mine, her long stringy hair parted in the middle, a thick plaid headband framing her face, announces to the pod that my arms are too hairy and I need to shave them. "You've shaved before, haven't you?" she asks.

I may only be ten years old, but I understand this question for what it is—a challenge to gauge how far along I am in the process of becoming a woman. The night before, I had bleached my coarse, dark arm hair with the hope it would render it invisible. But my forearms appear as if they have been invaded by hundreds of blond caterpillars. Shame burns along my neck. When the girl turns away, I remove the cardigan from the back of my chair and thread my arms through the sleeves.

Later in the day, on the playground, students ask where my headdress is and what tribe I'm in. One child lights up when she learns my father is from India. "I know that country," she exclaims, as if answering a question in a game show. "I read about it in *National Geographic.*" I am a museum artifact missing a label. I make friends quickly with Ebony, the only Black student in the class, the only Black person I see in the building aside from our homeroom teacher. She doesn't make a single comment about my skin color, my body hair, or my long braided plaits. By the end of my first week, I realize that aside from the one white-passing Hispanic girl in my class, most of my classmates have never even seen a brown person before.

Brown. It is a color and a concept I had never used to describe or identify myself until the first bell rang to change classes, when in the crowded light blue hallways, a sea of sneakers squeaking across the linoleum floor, my arms loaded with textbooks, I realize that I am the only brown child as far as the eye can see.

The artery of Interstate 75 descends the entire length from Detroit to Chattanooga, and with every mile marker our maroon and wood-paneled Plymouth Volare station wagon crosses, I feel as if I am sliding down the chute in a game of Chutes and Ladders. Despite digging my heels in, I still reach the bottom.

On the drive, images flood my mind of Detroit's annual Grand Prix, race cars zooming around bends, colorful downtown festivals, the shores of Lake Erie that I bike to on my red ten-speed bike.

I know the bare-bones reason for my parents' decision to move. The previous year, while on vacation visiting my aunt, uncle, and cousins in Chattanooga, my mother fell in love with the tail end of the Appalachian range, how Lookout and Signal Mountains hugged the south and west sides of the city birthing a lush green valley, how the Tennessee River curled around Moccasin Bend. Those duo mountains in Chattanooga reminded my mother of the Alps of her mother's home in Linz, Austria. After years of the grind that is academic medicine in Detroit, my father finds solace in them too.

Mountains seem to beckon the matrilineal line in my family. Going back a generation earlier, my mother's Austrian mother, my Oma, found comfort in the Franklin Mountains when in the 1960s my Puerto Rican grandfather was stationed at Fort Bliss, in El Paso, Texas. Those mountains reminded my Oma of her Alps in Linz, the mountains of her childhood, where her parents, brothers, and entire extended family still lived. They were a boomerang in my mother's and grandmother's memories when they made homes in the long shadows their peaks cast across the Atlantic Ocean.

In our family station wagon, stuffed animals filling my lap, my forehead presses against the window in this liminal space between the North and the South. The Mason-Dixon Line is a porous border we permeate easily. The watchful gaze of the Appalachian range is fast approaching. Flowers that awaken at the tail end of February and yawn open by March dot the sides of the interstate. I am awash in something new.

Before we moved to the South, what little I knew about the Confederate flag came from our family's favorite television show, *The Dukes of Hazzard*. I was six years old when it premiered in 1979. That bright orange 1969 Dodge Charger with the flag painted on its roof rocketed Bo and Luke Duke to the clouds whenever they revved the engine. I built ramps with books and shot my own metal replica into the air. The flag, to me, symbolized Hazzard County, Georgia, and a show not based in reality.

When we arrived in Chattanooga in the spring of 1984, I had some scant understanding that the Civil War was about the South's insistence on keeping slavery. I knew, too, that white-hooded men were in the Ku Klux Klan, that Black and white people once had to go to different schools and drink from different water fountains, and that Dr. Martin Luther King Jr. led the civil rights movement.

Slavery and segregation, I believed, were buried deep in the past. My concept of time at age ten belied reality. The Civil Rights Act had been passed only twenty years earlier, the Voting Rights Act only nineteen. It wasn't until our family visited the Confederama,[1] a museum and gift shop built in 1957 at the foot of Lookout Mountain, that the sordid history of the flag and its present-day usage began to come into sharper focus.

The Confederama resembled a fort with two faux towers on either end, and a battlement roofline with apertures like gaps between teeth. Confederate flags were painted on either side of the building and hung from two flag poles at the entrance like erect soldiers. The castle-like exterior exuded triumph. Inside, miniature painted replicas of figurines dressed in rebel and union uniforms reenacted the battles of Chattanooga. Tiny little cannons dotted the landscape. In the gift shop, Confederate flag T-shirts, towels, and other apparel draped the walls and aisles.

I remember turning to one of my parents and saying *this place is weird*, though *weird* didn't quite capture the feeling that settled in my gut. I didn't have the precise language to describe it, but I began to understand that the flag symbolized white people's celebration of the South, and this celebration was rooted in its history of slavery. But what was particularly jarring to me as a young child was how unapologetic, misinformed, and prevalent this celebration felt. It was as if the South had won the Civil War, and the War had ended only yesterday.

Over the next several years, whenever we toured friends or family around the city, we'd hit up the same tourist traps, Rock City Gardens and the Incline, but I made sure we avoided the Confederama. I never wanted to set foot in that building again.

The Deep South is no more racist than any other parts of the country. We know this from gerrymandering and redlining and mass incarceration and the police killings of unarmed Black people and Flint's poisoned water, as well as the disappearance of Indigenous women, broken treaties with First Nations, the caging of people lacking lawful residency status in for-profit detention centers, and hate crimes that occur from sea to shining sea.

Our family's move to the South just so happened to coincide with my coming of age, my transition from a little girl whose utmost concern was the arrangement of stuffed animals on her bed, to an adolescent slowly awakening to the reality of racism. At the exact moment of our family's geographic upheaval, I had begun looking outwardly and critically at the world, had started to adopt opinions I'd formed on my own instead of inheriting them from my parents or other adults.

The racism in the South is blatant, open and obvious, and this kind of racism (even more widespread across the United States today) is what took me by surprise when I first moved here. What's more, some of the most racist comments I heard in my youth came from adults who held positions of authority—teachers, employers, or friends' parents. I trusted them and did not feel empowered to challenge them, and as a result I internalized their hatred of me. That may have been the worst part. Cathy Park Hong addresses this in her book *Minor Feelings*. "Racial self-hatred is seeing yourself the way the whites see you, which turns you into your own worst enemy."[2]

In the 1970s and 1980s, when my parents had a subscription, *National Geographic* was home to the white gaze, poverty porn, and colonialism. Famines erupted across the globe. Photographs of emaciated bodies filled the centerfolds of magazines to elicit shock, disgust, and pity to drive up circulation.

I was a rail-thin child. My bow legs seemed to accentuate this. The racism and xenophobia I experienced centered on both my skin color and my weight. My body was deemed the product of parental neglect and, to use the speakers' term, a Third World country.

You look like one of those starving kids in Ethiopia/India/Mexico. Does your mom ever feed you?

From about sixth grade until I graduated from high school I fielded such questions routinely. The aggressors' faces were wrenched during their observations, mouths twisted to one side. Their pronouncements were public, spoken at the beginning of class, when students slowly filtered in. Or at birthday parties. Or at my place of employment. Humiliation was the goal.

Worse, I often laughed along with the "jokes" to defuse the moment. At other times I made my eyes still as stone, lids raised, a feeble attempt to stave off tears. I did what I could to change my appearance. Despite the scorching summer heat, I cloaked my body in layers of oversized clothes and abstained from tank tops. I ate until I felt sick.

I had always loved the color of my brown skin, how it turned a deep bronze in the sun, how it glowed against peach or lavender. I'd never known such cruelty before, the kind that made me feel as if my body and skin color were so abnormal and abhorrent they belonged in a Ripley's Believe It or Not museum. The racism felt like a dissection. I felt conquered and colonized, as if I did not own my own body, as if my survival required silence or complicity. After a few months of racialized abuse, I longed to be like a white person, which is to say that I wanted desperately to possess a skin color that went unchallenged, to feel as if only *I* possessed myself. I did not desire white skin. I wanted to be treated as if I had white skin.

The fall of my freshman year in college, I learned that I was the only one of my close girlfriends (all of whom were white) who did not receive one of the beautifully embossed invitations to the city's debutante ball, the Cotton Ball (today called the Chattanooga Ball).[3] Like other debutante balls, the Cotton Ball is a coming-out party for young women of marriageable age, an elaborate celebration of the upper financial crust, of spheres of influence whose members could trace their family trees back several generations to the South's storied antebellum legacy—white people's glory days before the Civil War.

Debutante balls were not born of the South. Queen Elizabeth I began the tradition in England during her reign in the latter half of the 1500s. Lucky debutantes (from the French word *débutante*, meaning novice) in their late teens to early twenties curtsied before the queen with the hope of a prompt engagement. Four hundred years later, in 1958, Queen Elizabeth II banned the tradition, owing to corruption. Today debutante balls are still held all over the United States, though their popularity has waxed and waned over time.[4]

This formerly Eurocentric rite of passage, though, has evolved into something distinctly southern. Chattanooga's Cotton Ball, one of the oldest debutante balls in the southern United States, was started in 1933 by a woman named Zella Armstrong.[5] Ironically, Armstrong never married and, according to her gravestone, had a career as an author, editor, and publisher. Her father, Captain John McMillan Armstrong, served in the Confederate Army.

Slavery was barely in the rearview mirror in the South, and Jim Crow and the separate-but-equal doctrine ensured the continued subjugation of Black people. Though over the years a handful of Black women and other women of color have been presented, Chattanooga's ball remains largely a celebration of whiteness, of aristocracy and old money, of men's ownership of women, and an ode to the selective memory of a region's cruel and traumatic history.

The mere idea of the Cotton Ball seemed so absurdly racist, sexist, and classist, I could hardly believe it still existed in the early 1990s. "Belles" a year out of high school, with hair swept into elaborate updos, wore satin or silk gowns that swished as they waltzed and curtsied. The Queen, a recent former belle, was paired with a King, an older adult male at least twice her age. (The fact that few people seem bothered by the optics of this is still mind-blowing to me.)

But when all of my white friends received invitations to the Cotton Ball and I didn't, it hurt like hell.

Despite years of existing in an environment that glorified whiteness, of attempting to be seen in a landscape of whiteness, of incessant othering, I still longed to be included. After learning from my former high school classmates that the invitations had been mailed out, I remember calling my mother and tearfully asking if she could please double-check the mailbox and make sure my invitation wasn't hiding somewhere amid the junk mail.

I had no intention of actually attending the Cotton Ball. In fact, I had already composed a letter in my mind to accompany my RSVP declining the invitation, expressing my disappointment that the institution continued to serve almost exclusively white women.

But these conflicting emotions of disappointment and revenge barely scratched the surface of the forces at play. At age nineteen, I still wholly bought into white supremacy. I hated that I wasn't invited to the Cotton Ball. I also loathed myself for wanting to be invited. Around and around I went, disparaging the Cotton Ball while envying those lucky enough to be able to choose not to attend. The Cotton Ball confirmed every suspicion I'd ever had. White people would never see me as worthy, and it was my own damn fault for trying to prove them wrong.

In my teens and early twenties, I still lacked the clarity or the consciousness to reckon with the ways I was directly perpetrating harm against other brown and Black people. Vijay Prashad writes about this in his book *The Karma of Brown Folk*, utilizing the framework in W. E. B. Du Bois's *The Souls of Black Folk*. He asks "how we can live with ourselves as we are pledged and sometimes, in an act of bad faith, pledge ourselves, as a weapon against black folk. What does it mean . . . for us to mollify the wrath of white supremacy by making a claim to a great destiny?"[6]

Longing for a white supremacist goal while complaining about racism is about much more than hypocrisy. The centering of my own individual injustice actively marginalized other brown and Black people. It also fed right into the model-minority myth. I "deserved" a Cotton Ball invitation because other brown and Black women weren't as "deserving." Though I did not possess the lens to understand it, my hurt and humiliation were rooted in racism and the deep-seated belief that after white women, I was the next best thing.

The brown desire for white benefits has historical roots in the US. In 1927, in *Gong Lum v. Rice*, the Supreme Court upheld the decision of the Mississippi School Board to exclude nine-year-old Chinese American Martha Lum from a white public school because she was "colored." Certainly, Chinese Americans faced and have always faced racial discrimination. But the Lum family believed that their Asian American identity made them superior to Black families and entitled them to white rights.[7]

My desire for a Cotton Ball invitation was a desire born of a social contract that I, and I imagine Martha Lum, had subconsciously signed at birth. In exchange for years of conformity, silence, humiliation, abuse, and erasure, white people and white institutions would reward us with eventual acceptance and inclusion. Or so we thought.

But that's not how whiteness works.

One of the biggest injuries of racism in a very white environment is the mask. I projected a fake, false front to everyone, including my own family. (My mother is white passing. My brother, my father, and I are brown.) I pretended that I was confident, strong, and secure. I never cried and almost never complained. I buried the anger. I isolated myself from myself. I attempted to laugh off my own experiences with racism in order to neutralize or defuse them. I did this to attempt to minimize my trauma, but I also did it because I thought (I hoped) it would be met with white approval. That I might receive a gold star in return.

The problem with masks is that it's very hard to see out of them. My mask made me a terrible ally. The few times other brown people, particularly other Indian American teenagers, confided in me about their own experiences with racist bullying, I was so badly triggered that I found myself incapable of adequately supporting or consoling them. I stayed relatively silent, nodding my head, mumbling "That's terrible" or some other empty sentiment, and then quickly changed the subject.

Secretly I believed that because I could carry my own trauma, I was stronger than they were, that my shield to protect myself from racism was more durable. This response was more harmful than any white person's. Because there's nothing more cruel than when a person from the same community seeks comfort only to have their trauma minimized or dismissed.

About a year after the Cotton Ball, my relationship to white supremacy, and the ways I contributed to it, slowing began coming into focus. While home from college, I came across an Indian woman on our television screen. A few minutes later, I realized the setting was Mississippi. I couldn't believe what I was watching. I grabbed the remote control and turned up the volume.

It was Mira Nair's 1991 feature film *Mississippi Masala*.

The film is about an Indian family cast out of Uganda by Idi Amin. The family immigrates to Greenwood, Mississippi, to run a motel. The prodigal daughter, Mina, played by Sarita Choudhury—who happens to be one-half Indian like me—falls in love with a Black man named Demetrius, played by Denzel Washington. The Indians exiled from Uganda are heartbroken over leaving their African homeland, and yet they are racist against Black people in Mississippi. Colorism is also in play. Mina's mother fears her daughter is too dark for a good marriage.

The film forced me to look inward, particularly at how the ways I moved through the world directly impacted Black people. It shined a light on my own internalized racism, and it forced me to see my non-invitation to the Cotton Ball in a new light.

Anti-Black racism and colorism carried out by brown people is pervasive, though for years I didn't even notice it. Or, more accurately, I probably *did* notice it and brushed it under the rug. In this sense, *Mississippi Masala* was my reckoning. The fact that I endured racism myself didn't exonerate me from being anti-Black or from perpetuating colorism.

Brown people (myself included) are racist. As it turns out, after more than a decade of calling the South my home, of criticizing Confederate flags and Civil War memorials, I was also very much a product of it.

"Southern pride" is a pugnacious and antagonist term meant to erase slavery, Jim Crow, and present-day racism from the South's narrative in order to elevate whiteness and white supremacy.[8] There's no way around this, and even as a child I caught on pretty quickly. "That flag simply cannot be divorced from the white-supremacist, pro-slavery doctrine of the Confederacy," wrote Tyler Bishop for the *Atlantic.*[9] The South's resistance to the Union was based on its desire to bond human beings in order to fill its coffers.

I learned virtually nothing about slavery until high school, and even then it was glossed over in favor of a more rigorous understanding of the kind of farming that existed in the South in the 1700s and 1800s—the type of soil, the crops planted. This hasn't changed all that much for the next generation. According to Nikita Stewart, a *New York Times* journalist and contributor to the 1619 Project, "there is no consensus on the curriculum around slavery, no uniform recommendation to explain an institution that was debated in the crafting of the Constitution and that has influenced nearly every aspect of American society since."[10] When my own children reached this era in their social studies class late in elementary school, I had to explain who did much of this work— enslaved Africans who had been kidnapped from Africa, sold to slave masters, and placed in bondage—and that their children and grandchildren and great-grandchildren were born slaves in the South, and that all non-Black people benefited directly or indirectly from slavery because the South's entire economy, and much of the U.S. economy, was built upon it.

Their history curriculum about this era was told in the passive voice. There was never any obvious actor in slavery. *It just happened.* Slavery and the Civil War have remained, especially in the Deep South, an ahistorical chapter with a cultural context that borders on fantasy, a nostalgia rooted in race-based oppression and violence.

The Walnut Street Bridge was built in Chattanooga in 1891. It crosses the Tennessee River, connecting two banks that once belonged to the Cherokee Nation. In the shadow of the bridge, just west, lies Ross's Landing, where in 1838 some fifteen thousand Cherokee were forcibly relocated to the West pursuant to the Indian Removal Act.[11]

While I was growing up in the 1980s, the Walnut Street Bridge was an eyesore, a blight on the city's then meager skyline. It had sat unused and rotting since 1978 and avoided demolition only because the city couldn't afford it. In the late 1980s a resurgence of interest in the bridge led to its inclusion in the National Register of Historic Places. It underwent a major renovation and reopened in 1993 to become one of the longest pedestrian bridges in the world.[12]

It's now spectacular. Graceful turquoise struts and bracings crisscross against the sky like Paul Klee's 1938 painting *Heroic Strokes of the Bow.* One can picture the wheels of old-time cars crawling across its wood planks as pedestrians with sunhats and parasols pause to catch their breath and peer over the railings to the river below.

Today the Walnut Street Bridge is an ecosystem. Walkers and joggers become one with skateboarders and scooter riders. Couples hold hands and sip from paper coffee cups while teenagers flash peace signs and pose for selfies. The community of the bridge ebbs and flows as the river's gentle waves lap at the cement-and-stone foundation, and the setting sun bleeds across the horizon. When our children were small, we became a part of this ecosystem. While visiting my parents, we'd take them to ride the carousel in Coolidge Park, which sat just below, and then chase them across the bridge.

It's the history of this bridge, which I discovered only recently, that brings to light my most harrowing feelings about the South. Two men were lynched on it, Alfred Blount in 1893 and Ed Johnson in 1906.

After a white woman named M. A. Moore accused Blount of rape, he was swiftly arrested and jailed. A mob of some five hundred men used sledgehammers and other weapons to break into his cell. They beat him, hung him from the bridge, and shot him more than a hundred times. On Wednesday, February 15, 1893, the all-caps headline in the *Chattanooga Times* read: "LYNCHED." And below it: "Alfred Blount, a Negro, Suffers Death. He Ravished a Woman and Swift and Sure Was the Vengeance of the People. Taken From the County Jail to the County Bridge, Strung Up Under an Iron Girder and His Body Riddled With Bullets. THE HIDEOUS CRIME." It was reportedly Chattanooga's second of what would be at least four lynchings during the Jim Crow era. Mrs. Blount, Alfred's widow, sued the city for not protecting her husband from the mob. She received no justice for his killing.[13]

In 1906 a white woman named Nevada Taylor accused Ed Johnson of raping her (though she could never decisively identify him). He was convicted and sentenced to death despite having an alibi: a dozen or so persons claimed he was with them at the time of the alleged crime. The U.S. Supreme Court stayed the execution until an appeal could be heard. But the following night, a mob descended upon Johnson's jail cell. Before he was lynched at the bridge, he said: "God bless you all. I am innocent." Johnson was cleared of the conviction in 2000.[14]

A local committee recently unveiled artist Jerome Meadows's rendering of a future memorial for Ed Johnson.[15] I don't know why the memorial wasn't built when the Walnut Street Bridge was restored in 1993—it was already well past due. (At Ross's Landing, a water memorial to the Cherokees' removal called the Passage was opened in 2005.) The delay of the memorial is emblematic of the South's stubborn refusal to reckon with its racist history until it's good and ready.

Like places, we too must take responsibility for our relaxed complacency and intentional obliviousness. We can be targets of racism while also upholding and benefiting from white supremacy. We can enjoy a long stroll along Walnut Street Bridge and the breezes coming off the river when our ignorance of its complete history makes us complicit in its crimes. The lynching memorial, still largely in the imagination, reminds me of this: Like the South, I too have much to learn and a long, long way to go.

Fraught Feminism

The first time I came to understand the words *feminist* and *feminism* was in the early 1990s, when I was a college student in North Carolina. Until then my knowledge of women's rights was downright provincial. My parents raised me to be strong and independent and encouraged me to work hard to achieve my goals. Success in life could be summed up in a line from the iconic 1985 feature film *Back to the Future*. "If you put your mind to it you can accomplish anything."[1]

This is as deeply as I probed, especially as a child. If I failed or if I wasn't treated fairly, it was because I didn't try hard enough. During my teens, I spearheaded efforts to raise thousands of dollars for charities in the community—without once considering the larger forces that intentionally deprived people of financial stability or food security. My privilege afforded me the luxury of living in my own bubble. Which is to say that I had little understanding about the locus of control and institutional oppression, and how this meant that success and agency correlated with privilege.

Certainly, geography was complicit in my ignorance. My landscape was narrow, sheltered, shallow, the points A and B a stone's throw away. I lived in a small southern city in southeastern Tennessee, a proud notch in the Bible Belt, where residents identified one another by family name, church, or high school (and sometimes all three).

A *right* was a direction, or a check mark next to a math problem. Not freedom, liberation, or claim. History was a relic of the past. Slavery began and ended. The Holocaust began and ended. The

British colonization of India began and ended. The decimation of First Nations began and ended. Apartheid began and ended. Afterward, everything was restored to "normal." Trauma evaporated into thin air. Human suffering was finite, self-contained, dutifully indexed, and summarily forgotten. It's not as if I never questioned these postures or this framework, I was simply saturated in this way of thinking. It was hard for me to find my way out of it.

In my town, divorce was shameful, as was being gay (gender nonconforming or not heterosexual), nonwhite, disabled, low income, "alien" (undocumented), or non-Christian. Virginity was a gift from God that women and girls bestowed upon one lucky man. Those who "lost" their virginity before marriage were sluts that should be discarded like chewed-up pieces of bubble gum. In the eighth grade one of my dearest childhood friends, who came from a "good" Christian family with old money and lived on one of the illustrious mountains in town, where other "good" monied Christian families lived, told me she was an atheist. I didn't even know what this was. She had to explain it to me. And when she did, it was one of the most scandalous things I'd ever heard.

I attended an all-girls private school from seventh through twelfth grade, and though I roamed the hallways with some six hundred (mostly white) young women, I did not once hear the word *feminist* or *feminism*. The philosophy of the school centered on instilling self-confidence in young women and teaching them to be leaders. I read widely, but not diversely, and didn't possess the sensibility and awareness to critique books like Ayn Rand's *The Fountainhead* or Nathaniel Hawthorne's *The Scarlet Letter* with a feminist lens.

Which is to say that while I had a few questions, thoughts, and suspicions about how the world worked and for whom, I lacked the language and the imagination to examine them more deeply.

Besides, who would I even talk to?

Dr. Jean Fox O'Barr, a short woman with a shock of white cropped hair and a soothing voice, was the catalyst for my enlightenment. At Duke University, she taught what was then called Introduction to Women's Studies, a class I enrolled in during the fall semester of my sophomore year. I didn't know what women's studies was, but I was game. The previous year I had taken Introduction to Sociology, which demonstrated to me how little I knew about human beings and socialization. I craved more of this kind of knowledge that challenged and deconstructed the very foundation of what I thought I knew to be true.

Every women's studies class brought an avalanche of epiphanies. Endless lightbulbs flicked on in every crevice of my brain. Patriarchy! *There is a patriarchy!* I had the immense urge to rush out of the classroom into the quad and scream this fact so loudly the sound would echo off the gargoyles. It was as if I had been stranded in a desert, feet burnt, throat parched, and had suddenly come upon a cool spring to throw myself in.

Adrienne Rich, Nikki Giovanni, Angela Davis, and Audre Lorde appeared to me like archangels. Every verse of their wisdom converted me to a religion, a faith, that I had been seeking without knowing it. Suddenly there was a language and a vocabulary to express my feelings. In her book *Talking Back: Thinking Feminist, Thinking Black,* author and activist bell hooks describes it this way: "Moving from silence into speech is for the oppressed, the colonized, the exploited, and those who stand and struggle side by side a gesture of defiance that heals, that makes new life and new growth possible. It is that act of speech, of 'talking back,' that is no mere gesture of empty words, that is the expression of our movement from object to subject—the liberated voice."[2] Her use of the word *silence* in this passage astonished me. It was a word that up until then I had known only to mean the absence of sound, the quiet in a library or a movie theater, that eerie lull when even crickets surrender to slumber, the stillness of the phone when the boy who says he likes you never calls. I had not considered the fact that silence also embodied spaces where some people had the power to speak and others didn't.

My best friend from high school attended the University of North Carolina at Chapel Hill, just ten miles down the road. Our discovery of feminism occurred almost simultaneously. It was as if we'd just figured out the combination to a safe. During late-night conversations over the phone, we'd share the shock of our newfound awareness. *Isn't it something? All those years of girls' school. How did we not know about feminism? How did we not know there was a patriarchy? How come they didn't tell us?*

Few students pursued women's studies beyond the survey course, but a small cohort of us charged forth to the more advanced, upper-class seminars, comrades now in activism. Our in-class discussions were animated, dramatic, soulful, searing, unlike any of the other classes I'd taken in college. In between, while roaming our leafy campus, we flashed one another knowing glances, as if to say, *Doesn't the world look different now that we know about feminism?*

In my final semester of senior year, in my last seminar class, after months of rigorous critical thinking and debate, we took a break to share snacks, listen to the soulful voices of Sweet Honey in the Rock, and talk about our plans after graduation. Our time at Duke was coming to an end, and we, the class of 1995, would be the second class to graduate with a women's studies major. (I would be one of the first women of color to do so.)

Dr. O'Barr, our fearless leader, our lighthouse, our guide, posed a final question we hadn't expected: How should we grade our efforts this semester?

We exchanged confused glances. Grade? Wouldn't *she* give us our grades?

No, she said plainly. We should grade ourselves.

We were off again, turning over our thoughts, weighing pros and cons, wrestling with questions like: What is a grade? What does it represent? What does it mean to have an A, B, or C? How are we qualified to judge our individual contributions in work that has been largely collaborative all semester? What role does the patriarchy play in how we value our work, our worth, our value as human beings?

In the end, we decided to give ourselves A's. We'd worked hard. We'd earned it.

Besides, fuck grades. And fuck the patriarchy that required them.

The idealism through which I viewed feminism, though, had begun to unravel the summer before my senior year in college, in 1994, when one of my fellow women's studies scholars and I decided to intern and share an apartment in Washington, D.C. We struggled to find something affordable and finally signed a lease for a place just inside the northeast rim of the Beltway, far away from the flood of summer interns who crashed in tony neighborhoods like Dupont Circle and Foggy Bottom. Nevertheless, we were thrilled. She would intern at the State Department, and I'd spend my six weeks at the National Organization for Women.

I was one of the interns with the latest starting dates that summer. On my first day, by the time I drove and parked my car at Greenbelt station, transferred to the red line at Takoma Park, and exited at Farragut North, I was more than eager to throw myself into the real, grassroots work of feminism. Here is where I'd put theory into practice at one of the greatest feminist organizations in the country. The twenty or so interns I joined had already spent a few weeks working with their mentors and had forged robust bonds with one another at local bars during happy hour.

The summer of 1994 was a turning point in women's rights. It was the summer immediately preceding the passage of the Violence Against Women Act, championed by the then junior senator from Delaware, Joe Biden.[3] When members of Congress held press conferences on the steps of the Capitol, I would stand in their shadows, proudly thrusting one of several "NOW rounds" (those iconic circular posters) into the air.

The mid-1990s breathed new life into the notorious "welfare queen," a caricature that originated two decades earlier when presidential candidate Ronald Reagan vilified a grifter named Linda Taylor who had, in fact, committed crimes.[4] But in the 1990s the welfare queen loomed large in the minds of both Republicans and Democrats. She embodied the racist and mythical portrayal of Black mothers who seemed to magically convert paltry government checks and food stamps into BMWs.

President Bill Clinton, hell-bent as ever on fulfilling his campaign promise to end what was then known as Aid to Families with Dependent Children (AFDC), began revving up his war on poor women that same year. Two years later, he would sign the Personal Responsibility and Work Opportunity Act, dumping AFDC and creating the Temporary Assistance for Needy Families program, which, among other things, capped how long benefits could go to recipients and promptly kicked off those who hit the limit, regardless of their circumstances.[5]

At NOW that summer of 1994, I was assigned to work with a man named Faith Evans, a former member of the Black Panther Party, a former board member of the National Welfare Rights Organization, and a single father to six children. Faith headed the department then known as Welfare Rights at NOW.

At the time, I did not appreciate his greatness. Faith had spent much of his life as an activist organizing for the rights of poor Black women. "He was an excellent collaborator," Loretta Ross told me in an interview. Ross worked for NOW in the 1980s, though her tenure there did not overlap with Faith's. As fellow organizers for issues that affected women of color, she and Faith bumped into each other often. "He always delivered on what he said he was going to do. And was there to back up anything I needed."

The rights of poor women featured prominently in NOW's agenda largely because of Faith's efforts. Soon after NOW brought him on board, he organized a meeting between then-president Patricia Ireland and other welfare rights activists and organizations to formulate an action plan for low-income families.[6]

Whatever reservations I had about working with a man at a feminist organization evaporated within minutes of our first conversation. Faith was kind and sensitive, and in between his explanations about the dangers facing poor mothers he regaled me with stories of his three heart attacks, his refusal to quit smoking, and his love for dogs. He was funny, warm, and generous. He had a swirl of salt-and-pepper hair and a neatly trimmed mustache and beard. When he thought deeply, his face tilted toward the ceiling. His daily polo shirts were permanently untucked as he moved throughout NOW headquarters.

Faith insisted on handwriting all of his correspondence rather than having me type it up on a computer, and he closed every letter with "Bread & Justice, Faith." It was a nod to the final point in the Black Panther Party's ten-point program. "We want land, bread, housing, education, clothing, justice, peace, and people's community control of modern technology."[7] It also reflected the words of Cesar Chavez, cofounder with Dolores Huerta of the National Farm Workers Association, who had passed away the year before my internship: "We shall pursue the revolution we have proposed. We are sons and daughters of the farm workers' revolution, a revolution of the poor seeking bread and justice."[8]

I was a naïve and extremely privileged college student—my parents paid for my apartment and living expenses for the six weeks of my unpaid internship in D.C.—and did not deserve any serious attention from anyone in activist circles, let alone someone as experienced and devoted to the cause as Faith. He likely had no choice but to have me as his intern, but I hope he at least got in a good eye roll behind my back when I first walked through his door.

We spent much of that summer organizing a conference on poverty and homelessness. I would meet activists from across the country, including Cheri Honkala, cofounder of the then Philadelphia-based Kensington Welfare Rights Union (now known as the Poor People's Economic Campaign), organizers from the National Coalition for the Homeless, and others.

The vast majority of interns at NOW that summer were white. There were two Asian American women besides me, and one Black woman. The NOW national office was also very, very white. Black women and other women of color mainly served as support staff. Three of the four national officers were white. Patricia Ireland had been reelected as president, Kim Gandy was executive vice president, Rosemary Dempsey was vice president of action, and Karen Johnson, a Black woman, was national secretary.

My co-intern under Faith helped show me the ropes. A local Asian American woman whom I shall call Eva had already been interning for several weeks. Opinionated and outspoken, Eva would win every debate she entered into with other interns. She was years, if not decades, ahead of any of us in her understanding about social justice and the liberation movement. She was also one of the brightest people I had ever met.

Though I respected the hell out of her, I could tell by the end of my first day at NOW that the other interns didn't like her and had written her off. Here they were, raising their feminist voices against the patriarchy, but barely tolerating the one woman whose incisive critiques of not just patriarchy but feminism itself went far deeper than discourse about body hair and bras.

Toward the end of the summer, NOW organized an intern lobbying day. Eva and I visited different congressional offices. I didn't see her again until late in the afternoon, when she tossed her bag down on a table in the intern room. She didn't say much to anyone, and after placing a phone call, she stormed out. Another intern who had lobbied with Eva sheepishly began relaying that Eva had interrupted the Virginia congressman multiple times when he spoke. Voices were raised; the atmosphere had been tense.

I had never seen Eva act rudely to anyone. She was blunt and direct, but never rude. I could only imagine what went down at the congressman's office. A young woman of color challenged a white man's talking points, and his ego was bruised. He had expected courtesy and sweetness. He was doing this young constituent of his a *favor* by giving her his time. But Eva had never been interested in platitudes. She deserved and demanded to be heard. I expected nothing less of her. I was proud.

What happened next happened swiftly. The congressman, a member of NOW (and I'm guessing a donor), phoned headquarters. He was furious. Soon thereafter, most of the NOW staff and all of the interns aside from Eva were assembled in the conference room. There we learned that NOW had decided to expel Eva from the internship program. We were not told the specifics of the exchange in the congressman's office. We were not told what justified Eva's termination, only that she had offended him. They led us to believe this severance of a woman of color, one of only four in the intern room, who had worked for two months without pay, was the only possible resolution. Their hands were apparently tied.

I searched others' faces for disgust. Instead, slight nods reverberrated throughout the room. Faith stood against the wall, his face grimacing, arms crossed, his chin tilted downward. It became clear to me that he had been warned about this announcement and that he disagreed with it wholeheartedly.

When a senior staff member asked if we had any questions, I wanted to raise my hand and protest the decision. But I was afraid. Here was a wall of mostly white women unanimously condemning an Asian American woman at one of the most powerful feminist organizations in the country.

Still, I have regretted not standing up for Eva in that moment ever since.

Beth, the intern coordinator, excused herself from the room. She had been our mother hen, our nurturer, our consoler. She had listened patiently to our endless dramas about lovers and hangovers. I jumped up from my chair, followed her out, and rushed down the hallway.

She was crying in her office. I told her how upset I was with NOW's decision, that what had happened to Eva was unfair. She said she was sorry. But if she agreed with me, she didn't let on. Her refusal to side with Eva broke my heart.

Faith was waiting for me when I walked out. He took me to another part of the floor to see Eva, who I assumed had already been sent home. Instead she was quarantined in Patricia Ireland's corner office. The irony did not escape me. To my knowledge, Ireland had stopped by NOW headquarters only once during my six weeks there. I had never met her. My only contact with her (a visit to her office) would occur when her organization turned on one of its few interns of color.

Eva and I talked for a few minutes. I hugged her tightly before she left for good.

On the long Metro ride home, and in the months that followed, I would come to understand that feminism didn't fit me quite the way I once thought it did, that patriarchy and white supremacy had a strong hold on feminism, too. Solidarity in the feminist movement, as it turned out, was not a circle, it was a refraction. And the light that burned bright when I first discovered feminism two years earlier had dimmed in the wake of NOW's betrayal of Eva.

A few days before I headed back to Tennessee, Faith took Eva and me out to lunch. We sat outside. In the scorching heat, the three of us crowded under an umbrella's shade. I wanted to apologize to Eva for not having the guts to openly condemn NOW's termination of her. But instead I chewed my pizza quietly. When I left D.C., though, I left NOW for good. I never renewed my membership, and I dumped all the mailers pleading that I do so straight into the recycling bin.

Eventually I lost touch with Eva. I have tried to find her several times to no avail. What I owe her today is an appreciation for modeling what feminism is and could be. Whenever I hesitate to publicly call out systems of power, I reflect upon Eva's courage at NOW. It shores me up and I press on.

By the time I graduated from college in 1995, I knew a few things. Feminism was too white, and white feminists controlled feminist narratives and feminist spaces. (I had not yet heard the term *white feminism*, which was coined by Indigenous activist and scholar Paula Gunn Allen in 1986.)[9] I also knew there had to be a different way to think about feminism, one that was more inclusive. I just didn't know what that looked like.

Black women have provided this framework. In 1974 a coalition of Black feminist lesbians called the Combahee River Collective drafted a manifesto declaring that feminism must address and rectify the multiple and "interlocking" forms of oppression that affect Black women, including racial, sexual, heterosexual, and class oppression. "We believe," they wrote, "that the most profound and potentially most radical politics come directly out of our own identity, as opposed to working to end somebody else's oppression. In the case of Black women this is a particularly repugnant, dangerous, threatening, and therefore revolutionary concept because it is obvious from looking at all the political movements that have preceded us that anyone is more worthy of liberation than ourselves."[10] This CRC statement would later serve as a building block for critical race theory scholar Kimberlé Crenshaw's singular 1989 paper, which introduced the term *intersectionality* and declared: "Because the intersectional experience is greater than the sum of racism and sexism, any analysis that does not take intersectionality into account cannot sufficiently address the particular manner in which Black women are subordinated."[11]

When I finally did come across the CRC and Crenshaw's scholarship, feminism burst wide open for me. It enveloped a far more comprehensive notion of equality and justice and a rigorous inclusivity that centered the communities, particularly Black communities, that should be centered. This kind of feminism, intersectional feminism, was one I could embrace more fully. And though Eva and Faith didn't use this term to describe their own understanding of feminism, this was the kind of feminism they believed in and practiced.

More than forty years after the publication of CRC's statement, feminism as a movement is still very white and very anti-Black, and it still struggles to implement authentic intersectionality. In movement spaces, non-Black women, femmes, and non-Black nonbinary and trans folks tend to rebuild the very same white patriarchal hierarchy that silences or excludes Black women, femmes, and Black nonbinary and trans folks.

It's a vicious cycle, one the feminist movement can't seem to eject itself from. In the spring of 2020, following the brutal police killing of George Floyd, white-controlled institutions, including feminist organizations, have been forced to reckon with their white supremacy. Several former staffers have come forward to expose NOW for its racism.[12] Though NOW was cofounded in 1966 by Black civil rights activist Pauli Murray, ten out of the organization's eleven presidents have been white, and twelve of seventeen current board members are white.[13] More than twenty-five years after my internship, NOW still has a huge race problem.

That fall after I returned to college, Faith and I exchanged a few letters. His neat, square penmanship filled the pages to the margins.

By the gentle tone of his letters I could tell he knew that I was struggling, that I was still shaken by Eva's unjustified termination and my own silence in it. He probably knew, too, that the incident at NOW had recalibrated something in me that I was still trying to process.

Not long after his last letter, he had another heart attack. This time it was fatal. I learned about his death a few weeks after the funeral from a former fellow intern. "It was a beautiful service though very sad," she wrote. "All of his children were there. Hundreds attended." I was absolutely devastated.

In the years that followed, I became a different kind of feminist and wished so desperately that I could thank him for putting me on that path. When I figured out how to do research online, I tried in vain to find out more about the work he did in the many years before I knew him. His name popped up here and there, but on the World Wide Web there were only scant traces of him.

Not long ago, to my complete surprise, I stumbled across an interview with Faith from a five-part PBS special titled *America's War on Poverty: Untold Stories from the Front Line*. It began airing in January 1995, shortly before his death. The interview largely focused on his work in the 1960s and 1970s with the National Welfare Rights Organization.[14]

In one excerpt Faith talks about how he learned to be a better advocate for poor single mothers when he realized how much harsher judgment they faced for receiving the very same benefits he received as a poor single father.

This was classic Faith, keeping his eyes open, looking at where injustice falls and who is affected the most, and centering and uplifting those voices. It's a lesson I learned from both him and Eva that I continue to hold close today. Feminism, for it to be feminism at all, must be radically inclusive. Only then can there be bread and justice for everyone.

Anger like Fire

Bitterness is like cancer. It eats upon the host.
But anger is like fire. It burns it all clean.
—MAYA ANGELOU

The mirrored room swims with the sour odor of sweat and aging rubber mats. I sit crossed-legged during the final minutes of yoga, my chest rising and falling in pranayama. My eyes are fixed on the instructor's round face, desperate for her to call an end to this last, tortuous pose, so that I can hop up, speed home, and collapse over one of the dozen or so ice packs I keep in the freezer.

I am thirty-nine years old, have been practicing yoga for several years, can twist myself any which way, but my tailbone pain, also known as coccydynia, has only worsened over the years. Even sitting is painful, as is savasana or corpse pose. Many people diagnosed with coccydynia have experienced a fall or other injury that bruises or fractures the tailbone. But for some, like me, there is no known cause.

The pain ranges from a moderate radiating ache to a piercing stab, and I can never predict how or when it will worsen. What I do know is that any pose of rest is painful. The only way for me to reduce or rid myself of this pain is to stand on two feet all day and all night or to keep ice packs pressed against my tailbone. The cold distracts me from the pain, at least until the ice pack starts to thaw.

Doctors, physical therapists, acupuncturists, herbalists, and friends advised me to practice yoga.

Yoga will help make the pain go away.

Yoga will keep you from spiraling into depression from pain.
The pain is from stress. Try yoga.

In the class, I make one last-ditch effort to forget about the pain. I picture a white sandy beach, waves lapping at the coast, sea water turning into white foam, dragging fragments of shells in its retreat. Tears escape my lashes, drip down my cheeks. Yoga has never worked. It has made me more limber, and stronger. But if anything, my chronic pain has only worsened.

After the class ends, I blow past the instructor, break for the door. I weave through exercise equipment I want to kick and knock to the floor. When a personal trainer smiles, I grimace in return.

My tailbone is on fire.

On the car ride home, a wall inside me crumbles, releasing a flood of fury. I am angry about having chronic pain for more than half my life, furious that it will likely never go away, enraged that I listened to others' advice about how to alleviate it instead of listening to myself. Each year, my world with chronic pain has grown smaller. Each year, I give up more and more activities I enjoy and turn down events I'd love to attend to accommodate my pain.

I can no longer downward-dog or breathe this rage away.

We are angry. We have always been an angry, seething, smoldering species, and though Darwin may not have tracked anger as a characteristic in his study of natural selection, I feel certain that *Homo erectus*, the ancestor to *Homo sapiens*, outlived *Homo habilis* and *Homo rudolfensis* because it was far more pissed off. Surely anger fueled its quest to overcome, to persist, to survive.

The anatomy of anger is complex. And the goal of anger is liberation. Feel it move from the pit of the belly, across the diaphragm, to scale the esophagus, seize the vocal cords, and burst audibly out of the mouth, escaping even the tight clutch of teeth.

Once released, anger must avoid attempts to silence it or shut it down. It must have a space and a place to go. Society (God damn it) rewards stoicism, poker faces, civility. It lauds those who swallow their rage like a bitter pill. Women, femmes, and nonbinary folks, especially Indigenous, Black, and other women, femmes, and nonbinary folks of color, are deemed rude, selfish, hysterical, a cross between Salem witches and the green-skinned wart-dotted Wicked Witch of the West.

Something special happens in the fifth decade of life, those roaring forties, when we blossom in our rage. It is the age of rage enlightenment. Rage flows unencumbered from our pores, a clear, clean mountain stream. Our fury is freedom. We are crocodiles lying in wait, our beady eyes cresting the surface of the water, ready to snap at the next person who hints that we should shut the hell up.

Literary comrades continue to guide us in our anger salvation. These women characters of a certain age, who have raised children, who have decades of work or relationships (or both) behind them, who watch as their male counterparts get ahead while they flounder—they are fountains of unrepentant anger.

Take Tillie Olsen's wrenching story "I Stand Here Ironing," a model of domestic rage. It drips with fury. Here the narrator despairs over the emotional needs of an adult child and the ways she may have failed her: "She has lived for nineteen years. There is all that life that has happened outside of me, beyond me. And when is there time to remember, to sift, to weigh, to estimate, to total? I will start and there will be an interruption and I will have to gather it all together again. Or I will become engulfed with all I did or did not do, with what should have been and what cannot be helped."[1]

In August Wilson's play *Fences*, Rose tears into her husband, Troy, when he tells her he has had an affair and is going to be a father. This seething sermon extends beyond Rose's feelings of betrayal. It captures her rage about not being seen as an individual with her own wants or needs. It is dazzling, a master class on pent-up anger. "I gave everything I had to try and erase the doubt that you wasn't the finest man in the world. And wherever you was going . . . I wanted to be there with you. 'Cause you was my husband. 'Cause that's the only way I was gonna survive as your wife. You always talking about what you give . . . and what you don't have to give. But you take, too. You take . . . and don't even know nobody's giving!"[2]

And when Celie abandons Albert in Alice Walker's *The Color Purple*, after years of raising his children, of keeping his house, of enduring his abuse, of his lying and stinking ways, she executes a curse to end all curses, which she describes in a letter to her sister Nettie: "Until you do right by me, everything you touch will crumble. . . . Until you do right by me, I say, everything you even dream about will fail. . . . Every lick you hit me you will suffer twice, I say."[3]

Love and rage intertwine in the friendship at the heart of Elena Ferrante's Neapolitan novels. In the fourth and final installment, *The Story of a Lost Child*, successful author Lenu reflects in her old age on the toxicity that was always at the heart of her relationship with Lila, her best friend and enemy. "Sometimes I hate her for this decision to cut me off so sharply right now, in old age, when we are in need of closeness and solidarity. She has always acted like that: when I don't submit, see how she excludes me, punishes me, ruins even my pleasure in having written a good book. I'm exasperated."[4]

Long live enraged midlife literary women. Long live our queens.

A few years ago, I spawned a Rage Fest to an exponential degree, a swirling dervish equal parts exasperation and ire. The tenth circle of hell, if Dante had dared to imagine one. During a four-month period in 2018, I was stalked by a local man. At the same time, I was routinely harassed by white men while passing out literature for Democratic candidates for the midterm election. *You don't know what you're talking about. You're trying to ruin our country.* In the background of this hellscape was Brett Kavanaugh's testimony before the Senate to determine his fitness to serve as a U.S. Supreme Court justice. His whiny ode to beer served as his asinine defense to Dr. Christine Blasey Ford's very credible accusation of sexual assault.[5] It worked. Kavanaugh was confirmed to the highest court of the land.

A younger version of me might have curled up into a ball in the center of my quilted bed, formed a protective shell over my gaping, bleeding wound. Waited out the pain. Hid away from the world for a much-needed hibernation.

But in my forties, this black hole of agony led to an awakening I can only describe as otherworldly, adrenaline with limitless reserves. Alliances rooted in collective trauma sprung up from the earth, fed and fortified me. Every part of my brain was ablaze, every lobe ignited in scorn. I was a volcano, lava erupting and gliding down the mountainside, smothering and charring everything in its wake. I shredded paper for hours to self-soothe. It was beautiful.

As the weeks wore on, the rage didn't dissipate. It divided and multiplied like cells, swelled and stretched and morphed into a force larger than myself. I schemed and planned. And then I acted.

On Facebook I posted a several-paragraph screed about being stalked and harassed. Though I didn't reveal the perpetrator's identity, I spelled out in great detail his modus operandi. It was enough to give away who he was to those who had endured or heard about his abuse. The next several weeks, dozens of women messaged me with similar and far more horrifying stories. They had been suffering, alone, in silence, and had no idea others were being harmed.

We formed a support network, checking on one another via text, phone calls, or emails, tallying up and documenting our grievances against him, researching legal action, warning others who we feared might cross his path.

There is no clear retribution for the routine mocking I endured from men for being a proud progressive brown woman volunteering for Democratic candidates. But I doubled my volunteer efforts. *For every asshole I encounter on the street, I'll knock on dozens more voters' doors.*

I was a pressure cooker with no steam release. So I had no control when I unexpectedly lost it.

A month before the 2018 midterm elections, our high school held a debate for local candidates. An Asian American man who'd been aggressive toward Asian American women at Democratic events for the past two years showed up. I knew him well. The first time we met, at a large event I organized in 2017 for Jon Ossoff, he wouldn't leave me alone, he disparaged undocumented immigrants, and when I walked away multiple times, he cornered me to insult Asian Americans who supported Jon Ossoff. He harassed at least three other Asian American women at this particular event, leaving one nearly in tears.

A friend kicked him out. The following year at another event for a different candidate, *I* kicked him out.

After the debate, I stood outside the auditorium chatting with neighbors. I spotted him making his way to the exit. I had no intention of going anywhere near him. But then we briefly made eye contact as he cut through the crowd. It set me off.

I wanted him to know that I remembered him. That he could no longer push Asian American progressive women around. I sprinted over and put my body between him and the door. "So nice to see you again," I said.

And then?

I was Mount Vesuvius in 79 AD. He was Pompeii.

I tore into his support of the Trump administration and then Representative Karen Handel. I reminded him of their string of atrocities—family separation, the Muslim ban, open threats to journalists, bold-faced bigotry. For every piece of garbage he tried to counter with, I lobbed a clever, concise comeback. His voice crescendoed, but I doubled down on my calm, continuing to bat away his every lie with hard facts.

During my years as an attorney, I had been a terrible litigator, jumbling words, fumbling my arguments before the judge, dropping papers, panic coursing through my veins. Yet here I was now, measured, quick, unrelenting, fierce, unflappable, controlled. Counsel arguing before the U.S. Supreme Court. In my forties, I finally knew exactly what to say and how to deliver it.

Audre Lorde succinctly and forcefully argues for the power of anger in her essay "The Uses of Anger: Women Responding to Racism": "But anger expressed and translated into action in the service of our vision and our future is a liberating and strengthening act of clarification, for it is in the painful process of this translation that we identify who are our allies with whom we have grave differences, and who are our genuine enemies."[6]

In my forties, my anger has transformed into the kind of coalition-building that Lorde envisioned. There is no more efficient friend-filter than rage. There is no quicker method to determine who will put themselves on the line and go to bat for you. Collective anger is the shortest path to an enduring and nurturing community, one that elevates and amplifies the fierceness that fuels us. I have met some of my closest friends because we have banded together in rage to fight injustice. We see one another. We see red together.

This collective anger can birth something beautiful—direct political action. The 2013 acquittal of George Zimmerman for the murder of seventeen-year-old Trayvon Martin brought Alicia Garza, Opal Tometi, and Patrisse Cullors together to form Black Lives Matter. The federal government's plan to reroute the Dakota Access Pipeline through Standing Rock led to a mass protest of water protectors from all over North America. The anger of millions of people across the globe after the election of Donald Trump erupted in the form of the 2017 Women's March. The #MeToo movement, started by civil rights activist Tarana Burke, empowered survivors to call out their sexual abusers publicly.[7] After Kenyette Barnes and Oronike Odeleye demanded that the music industry #MuteRKelly, multiple sexual abuse charges were filed against singer Robert Kelly.[8] And the police strangulation of George Floyd in Minneapolis led to months of protests, rallies, and vigils for Black lives.

Anger *expression*, of course, is a privilege that poses an urgent question. Who gets to display their anger publicly, outside the safety of their own communities, in such a way that it doesn't get them fired from a job, evicted, imprisoned, deported, or killed?

Black people have always paid an enormous price for expressing every kind of emotion, from joy to curiosity to fear, let alone anger. For the Black community, anger expression and stereotypes about anger expression (the Angry Black Woman) can be dangerous or deadly. In her book *Eloquent Rage: A Black Feminist Discovers Her Superpower*, Brittney Cooper puts it this way: "Angry Black Women get dismissed all the time. We are told we are irrational, crazy, out of touch, entitled, disruptive, and not team players. . . . If you have the nerve to be fat and angry, then you are treated as a bully even if you are doing nothing aggressive at all."[9] My brown skin privilege protects me from many of the dangers and consequences that

Black women and femmes face. Having said this, I am routinely gaslit, threatened, insulted, harassed, trolled, infantilized, and targeted for expressing anger.

After Trump was elected, white *Clinton* voters came after me online. *You're so divisive. Your outrage is out of control. You're making this much worse than it has to be.* I heard these refrains dozens of times from people who supposedly held the same positions on politics and understanding of justice as I did. But in their eyes I had committed the greatest offense—I had rejected their notions of civility. Apparently this was a worse crime than casting a vote for Trump.

"Allies tend to crowd out the space for anger with their demands that things be comfortable for them," Mikki Kendall writes in *Hood Feminism.*[10] Indeed, I refused to carefully shape the expression of my anger into a medium that let others sleep at night, and this seemed to be a much more serious infraction than the underlying cause of my anger.

Why do I continue to express my unfiltered anger as loudly and unapologetically as I do? I feel I simply have no other choice. "Inherently, having privilege isn't bad," said Tarana Burke in an interview, "but it's how you use it, and you have to use it in service of other people."[11] With my brown, cishet, abled privilege comes a great responsibility. If I'm not leveraging my rage to challenge harmful points of view, policies, or laws, what exactly am I doing with it?

The expression of anger is certainly a necessary emotional release, but ultimately it's the fuel to get from point A to point B. It is a portal to our political power, agency, and legacy. It's the force and the fever behind identifying oppression and working toward a more just society.

What can we draw upon to find the strength to express our anger? The knowledge that we are not the first. Others came before us, still others work alongside us. We are not a single stream, but many. We cascade down mountains and eventually join together into a river. This river flows fiercely, over boulders and branches, before it spills out into a great wide ocean. And the ocean—have you seen its waves during a storm? They would knock you flat.

We are not alone. Our mothers, our sisters, and our ancestors, literary and otherwise, are our guides. They show us how to convert our anger into power. We can draw our courage from them, and their anger will nurture and sustain our own.

Virtual Motherhood

When the plane hits the first tower, I am on a conference call with a judge in Washington, D.C., trying to settle a case before trial. I sit on a leather chair opposite my cocounsel, my pregnant belly so rotund it's difficult for me to lean forward. After we conclude the call, I waddle to the other side of the floor, back to my office. The hallways are quiet, deserted. I think nothing of it.

The east-facing windows of our federal agency overlook Philadelphia's Independence Hall and the Liberty Bell. The sky is bright blue, practically cloudless, a summer that stretches past Labor Day, one that has left the humidity behind it. When I get back to my office, I will compose an email to my colleagues to see who wants to join me for lunch today outside in Washington Square.

As soon as I reach my desk, the phone rings. My brother is shouting. "Get out, get out, get of your building, Anj! Run as fast as you can! You have to get out of your building!"

His voice twists in on itself. *A plane. Twin towers.*

I picture a single-engine prop plane with a young, twenty-something pilot losing control and slamming into one of the towers. I remember thinking about the strength of that building, glass like steel, how likely it is that the only casualty is the pilot. I assure my brother that everything is okay. I assure him, though his sobs, I'll be fine.

I exit my office to seek out confirmation of my story. Instead I'm greeted with gaping mouths, wide eyes. Tears. A frightening possibility emerges, something so horrible we have no words for it. We gather, hands clasped to our chests. Radios blare the news from our desks, a conjoined chorus of chaos echoing through the hallway. The truth struggles to emerge amid a hurricane of confusion.

Then the unthinkable happens. A plane strikes the second tower. *Terrorism*, we whisper. *This is terrorism.* This is no accident. The death toll will be unimaginable.

An explosion at the Pentagon. A bomb. No, wait, another plane. An airplane has flown into the belly of the Department of Defense. A federal agency. Our own federal agency is housed next to Independence Mall. The targets straddle either side of us, New York City to the north and Washington, D.C., to the south. My mind slides into quicksand as my brother's panic takes shape in a narrative. Death feels near.

I pick up the phone to call my brother, to tell him that I now understand, that I will stay safe. I fumble with the receiver, press it to my ear. It is silent. I punch the button repeatedly. Nothing.

Our director closes the office and sends everyone home. *Terrorism*, I hear blaring on my office radio, just before I shut it off and head out the door. We are told to forgo the elevator, which I rode to the fourth floor just two hours earlier. Instead we take the stairs down, down, down. My palm slides along the cold metal railing.

Thousands stream out into the streets and make their way to the nearest regional rail station. I waddle as quickly as I can, the straps of my bag digging into my shoulder. Sweat gathers at my lower back. I am wearing a long-sleeved maternity shirt. Much too hot for this weather.

At the station, I join a swarm that fills the platform. Passengers check watches, fiddle with cuffs, stare out over the vacant track. Thirty minutes have passed when the R3 to Elwyn pulls up. I join the riders that pile into the cars, cram into every inch of space, sardines in a can. Bodies upon bodies fill the aisle, sweat lathered onto skin.

When the train groans to a start, I want to look out the opposite window to see if we're leaving anyone behind. But my view is blocked by a lattice of arms grasping the racks above, the tops of seats. At the very next stop, Suburban Station, 16th and Pennsylvania Boulevard, there is hardly room to breathe, much less to take on any more passengers.

But it doesn't matter. The lights have dimmed. We are no longer moving. The engine has gone quiet.

The train car is silent aside from a cleared throat, a cough, a shift, a sigh. We catch each other's stares, avert. The baby floats under my right hand but hasn't moved since my brother's phone call. I press one side of my belly, wait. I hold my breath, wait. Nothing.

Please, darling. Please move for Mommy.

I bled a few times during the first trimester, when the baby was the size of a walnut. *There's still a heartbeat,* my obstetrician cheerily assured me with each visit. *The baby's doing fine. You have nothing to worry about.* I remember thinking about those words, *nothing* and *worry,* how they seemed so ill-suited to be together in the same sentence.

My head tilts toward the ceiling. There is a building above the station itself. Several floors of steel beams and bricks, ceramic tiles, and concrete. What would happen if a plane hit? Would my child and I be buried alive? Would my husband ever find my body? Who would sense the impact first, the baby or me? Which one of us would be the first to go?

A woman is standing nearby. She is wearing a yellow blazer. Her damp bangs cling to her forehead. She glances down at my belly. Her face softens. "What a scary time to be pregnant," she says.

I nod and turn away.

It is on this day—a stalled underground train, seven months pregnant with my first child, forehead pressed against the passenger window, the moisture from my breath painting a circle on the glass that disappears seconds later, the odor of nervous sweat from hundreds of passengers joining my own—that I become a mother. It is in this moment that the abstract, swirling, incandescent ideas I have about motherhood begin to crystallize into something more tangible and focused, more real, and I realize that someday this sweet babe will emerge from the protective shell that is my womb and move about the world, uninsulated, unprotected. I now understand that all the preparation beforehand, the prenatal vitamins, the ultrasounds, the collection of baby gear, will not protect my child once it leaves my body.

Forty-five minutes later, the air conditioner kicks on. The lights brighten. The train's engine groans to a start and lurches us forward. A collective sigh echoes throughout the cabin. We creep west, emerge from underground, the bright sunshine shimmering off the surface of the Schuylkill River. We ease our way to the southwest suburbs, emptying what feels like thousands of passengers at each stop. I disembark in Morton, crawl into my car, and drive the one mile home.

Our street is eerily quiet, empty. I throw open the screen door, jam my bronze key into the hole. As I turn to unlock, the baby kicks so hard under my ribs that I gasp. A sign of life at last. *Safe*, I think. *My baby is safe.*

That night, after hours of watching the towers collapse over and over again, of people jumping from a hundred floors up, of the fire enveloping the Pentagon, of newscasters breaking down in tears, I dream a dream I will have over and over again for the next few years, of running barefoot through the streets of New York City, a baby whose face I never see swaddled in my arms, a black dust and ash cloud chasing us through an alley, encircling us, before swallowing us whole.

Two months later, I give birth. New motherhood is a tsunami when it hits. Its giant waves wash away everything I ever knew to be true, including the language to describe it. Like Rachel Cusk in her memoir *A Life's Work: On Becoming a Mother*, I had little understanding of what being a mother entailed before I became one myself. As Cusk puts it, "I arrived at the fact of motherhood shocked and unprepared, ignorant of what the consequences of this arrival would be, and with the unfounded but distinct impression that my journey there had been at once so random and so determined by forces greater than myself that I could hardly be said to have had any choice in the matter at all."[1]

Fear and feelings of insecurity are forces I hadn't counted on. But in those early months, I am always afraid of failing to keep my daughter alive. The world has turned upside down. I can no longer take care of myself, let alone a new baby. Perhaps if 9/11 never happened, I would feel more capable and less terrified. But on that horrible day a hard knot formed in my chest. After my daughter's birth, it only tightened its grip.

My daughter and I have a rough start. She is born with a vacuum suction after more than four hours of pushing, and a few days later her skin turns gold. Severely jaundiced, she wears a sheet of bilirubin lights wrapped around her once chubby and plump body. She is too weak to nurse. The fat falls off her. Her pediatrician explains that if she doesn't gain weight soon, she'll be classified as *failure to thrive*.

When we go for blood work to monitor her jaundice, I spend my time in the waiting room crying. My sweet baby girl is in danger. I am the only one who can save her. The 9/11 nightmare evolves over the first weeks of early parenting but the ending is the same.

I'm a failure of a mother. We can never outrun the black clouds.

The crisis, our first, subsides. My breasts soon overflow with milk. After a few weeks my daughter becomes a nursing champion, packs on the pounds. The dark cloud lifts, at least temporarily. I bond with her in a way I didn't think humanly possible. I no longer know where my newborn ends and I begin. It is a feeling Louise Erdrich captures in *The Blue Jay's Dance: A Memoir of Early Motherhood*: "It is twinned love, all absorbing, a blur of boundaries and messages. It is uncomfortably close to self-erasure, and in the face of it one's fat ambitions, desperations, private icons, and urges fall away into a dreamlike *before* that haunts and forces itself into the present with tough persistence."[2]

I am feral. The love is all consuming. It carries the oxygen through my blood. Her needs are my needs. They consume me completely those first few weeks when her body is so small it looks as if she's been stripped from the womb far too soon. It is almost painful for me to watch someone else care for her. I want her in my arms all the time.

I am lucky. I have a wonderful spouse and co-parent. But he works sixteen-hour days, so I'm alone with our colicky newborn from sun-up to sundown. I am one of the first of my close friends to have a child, so I have hardly anyone to ask if my feelings of fear and isolation are normal. My own family live hundreds of miles away, too far away to help care for the baby or alleviate this state of frenzy I continuously inhabit. To make matters worse, soon after she is born, we are plunged into the thick of winter, a night that steals bright sunny hours from the day, a cold that seeps in between the window panes.

This territory of motherhood is unrecognizable to me. It's as if I have parachuted into another country where I don't speak the language. When a friend or relative calls to ask how I'm doing, words fail me. Do they really want the truth? *I slept two hours last night and the baby won't stop crying.*

Who am I? Where am I? I don't know. Everything I once knew about myself as a human being, everything I understood to be a part of my identity, endured a seismic shift the moment I gave birth. I am now awash in something that defies categories or descriptors. I linger in the in-between, the otherworldly. And in this space I don't feel safe or secure anymore.

In 2001 I was not yet an avid user of the Internet beyond email, but I eventually stumbled into the BabyCenter community. I had first created an account with the website during my pregnancy but didn't bother using it. Now I eagerly perused the various topics of their message boards. Breast-feeding. Working outside the home while parenting. Co-sleeping. These simple categories organized motherhood for me in a way that I never thought possible. What's more, I met other mothers as clueless as I was, with children the exact same age, asking (and receiving answers to) many of the same questions I had.

The knowledge that thousands of mothers existed inside my computer brought me great comfort. Later I discovered blogs where parents (but mostly mothers) delved far deeper into the trials and tribulations of raising children. Their honesty shored up my confidence and quieted my anxiety. I felt seen and heard. We first-time mothers were no longer adrift alone on a raft at sea. Our solidarity and camaraderie would keep us all afloat.

In the early 2000s I didn't fully grasp how revolutionary it was for parents to tell their own stories about raising children in real time. I was sleep deprived, drowning in laundry, and trying to figure out how to balance work and raising a toddler. But these online forums, whether blogs or message boards, embodied their own vital social movement. They created safe spaces to tell parenting stories, to confess our greatest fears, and speak our truths. Parenthood was hard. It was devalued, especially when carried out by women, femmes, and nonbinary folks, especially when these women, femmes, and nonbinary folks were Indigenous, Black, or of color. In these sacred spaces, we reminded one another about our inherent worth.

The connections I formed became vital to me. My own voice slowly emerged from the fog. I started writing my own blog about parenting. I compiled my thoughts into short articles and humor pieces that I sold to regional parenting magazines. I blogged for Mothers & More, a national organization, and DotMoms, a group parenting blog, and wrote a column for Mamazine, an online literary journal.

It's not as if one day my fears about parenting evaporated. In the years following 9/11, my children and I were frequently targeted with racism and xenophobia while traveling. My second child had a nearly fatal allergic reaction to medicine when she was two years old. I had multiple miscarriages. But I no longer endured these fears and anxieties alone. The support I received gave me the strength and perspective I needed to push past them. And I now had a new tool, writing, to process my emotions about parenting.

There was a downside, however. Online parenting caused me to overanalyze and critique my parenting to a dizzying degree. I was never *not* conscious of how I was performing as a caregiver. Blogs and message boards could be raw, honest, and self-deprecating, yet at the same time performative and carefully curated. Siblings never seemed to fight, or if they did, these fights inspired mostly irreverent and humorous narratives. Co-parenting relationships didn't strain or suffer with the addition of children, but then suddenly a couple would separate. Even messy online writing about parenthood had a gleaming, ethereal facade with a redemptive arc.

In the early 2000s the online parenting communities with the largest readerships were monolithic. They were primarily white, U.S.-based, cisgender, abled, and straight. They rarely considered the fact that their rigid parental rules and worship of the American Pediatric Association contradicted traditional cultural practices across the world. Other white parents co-opted and colonized parenting practices in other countries and held themselves out as experts on child rearing in Asia, South America, or Africa. This particularly grated on me.

After six years I started to realize that it was time for me to move on from the online parenting universe. The online parents, for the most part, had done a very good job of raising me. They helped me to remove my training wheels, grasped the back of my bike seat, and gave me that first gentle shove. But I had now outgrown them. And once I figured out how to pedal, I could reclaim all the other parts of my identity that had nurtured and fulfilled me before I became a mother.

As my pregnancy progressed for my third and last child, I slowly untangled myself from online parenting. I disengaged from the blogs and the message boards. I unsubscribed from all of the parenting newsletters. In December 2007 I wrote my final post for DotMoms. A few months later, after my third daughter was born, I shut down my old parenting blog and started a new one that focused on books, writing, and politics—subjects that had more space to occupy my mind now that I wasn't spending so much time thinking about *how* I was parenting.

The world, of course, has continued to be a scary place for our children. Climate change, white supremacy, gun violence, poverty, and a global pandemic warn of what seems to be a very bleak future. These fears are real, and finding a community that allows parents to acknowledge and disclose them is vital. Thankfully, twenty years after I first became a parent, there are far more parenting voices participating in these online forums, and these voices, which now hail from all over the world, are more representative of the realities of raising a child at a time when the future feels so uncertain.

The lesson from online parenting forums that I still hold closest to my heart is this one: our truths about the hardest parts of raising children deserve a platform, and sharing our fears with one another can ground us and hold us steady. We may never be able to vanquish the black cloud, but once we find one another, we can walk together toward the light.

Reflecting Jasmine

The first time I saw a picture of an Indian on the cover of a novel was in the fall of 1995. I was a twenty-two-year-old law student browsing the literature section at an independent bookstore in Clayton, Missouri. As I scanned the shelves, a small photograph of a dark-skinned woman on the spine of a paperback caught my eye. The book was *Jasmine*, by Bharati Mukherjee, and the same photo was magnified on the cover: a woman standing in the opening of a window, her full lips slightly parted. What struck me most was her very brown skin. I took the book to the register and purchased it.

A Bengali Hindu, Mukherjee was born in 1940 in Calcutta (now Kolkata) and was educated in England and Switzerland before emigrating to the United States in 1961 to study at the Iowa Writer's Workshop. She was a pioneer.[1] At the time of her arrival, only some twelve thousand Indian Americans were living in the United States. This was four years before the institution of the Immigration and Naturalization Act of 1965, also known as the Hart-Celler Act, which abolished discriminatory quotas, eliminating race, ancestry, and national origin as barriers to entry and enabling the resettlement of thousands of immigrants from the subcontinent.[2]

Though I didn't discover Mukherjee's work until I was twenty-two, her prolific career began in 1972, the year before I was born. Her debut novel, *The Tiger's Daughter*, tells the story of a woman named Tara who returns to Calcutta after establishing herself in the United States, only to feel unsettled by how much her hometown has changed in her absence. In 1975 Mukherjee published her second novel, *Wife*, and a decade later the short-story collection *Darkness*, followed in 1988 by *The Middleman and Other Stories*, which won the National Book Critics Circle Award in fiction. *Jasmine* hit the shelves in 1989, at about the middle of Mukherjee's long literary career. Several novels, including *Holder of the World* in 1993 and the trilogy *Desirable Daughters, Tree Bride*, and *Miss New India*, followed.

In a small village called Hasanpur in Punjab, Jasmine, born Jyoti, is the fifth daughter of a grain tiller and the seventh of nine children. Her Hindu family had lived for generations in Lahore, but after the partition, when Lahore became part of the new Muslim country Pakistan, they were forced to flee to India. When she is seven years old, an astrologer declares Jyoti's fate—she will be widowed very young and exiled. She marries Prakash Vijh, who renames her Jasmine, when she's still a young teenager. When Prakash is killed, Jasmine is shunned by a community that believes her misfortune to be contagious. She escapes to the United States, where she first embarks on a new life in New York City. She's called Jazzy by friends, Jase by employers, and eventually she lands in Iowa, where her new husband calls her Jane.

Each new identity presents Jasmine with the opportunity of an anonymous fresh start (or so she believes) and the possibility of a better, more fruitful, more authentic life. And yet she still desires more. At the end of the novel, Jasmine is faced with a new opportunity on the West Coast, a relocation that will upend not only her life but the lives of those she loves. This thirst to escape, to chart her own path, to take control of her own destiny, overcomes her. "Adventure, risk transformation: the frontier is pushing indoors through uncaulked windows," she says. "Watch me reposition the stars, I whisper to the astrologer who floats cross-legged above my kitchen stove."[3]

In *Jasmine*, as well as in her other books, Mukherjee avoids rosy or romantic narratives about immigration. The American Dream, she makes painfully clear, is a lie that has inspired disenfranchisement, manipulation, violence, and abuse. In an interview published in the

Iowa Review in 1990, Mukherjee discusses her own experience with racism in the 1970s in Toronto.[4] Canada had just permitted the entry of five thousand Ugandan Asians following their expulsion by Idi Amin. Mukherjee found herself being treated as a "smelly, dark, alien other" and lamented, "You never got the benefit of the doubt, if you were a Canadian citizen of Indian or South Asian origin."

When I finished reading *Jasmine*, I was overcome by an unfamiliar literary fervor born of self-recognition. Jasmine's quest to both seize and reinvent her identity resonated with me. After polishing off the book in a day (it's a short 214 pages), I wondered which parts of my identity were a product of how others saw me or what others called me. How much had the white gaze and, in particular, whiteness in literature permeated and shaped how I saw myself in the world?

Over the years there have been several different covers for Mukherjee's *Jasmine*. On the cover of the 1999 edition, Jasmine maintains her dark skin, though half of her face is hidden by a shadow. On the hardback cover, a shattered ceramic pot is centered on a blue background. Within each shard is a painted profile of Jasmine, her skin a red-brown glow. On yet another, Jasmine's skin is more yellow than brown. Only the 1999 edition portrays Jasmine as dark-skinned as she is on the edition I own.

I've owned my copy of *Jasmine* for more than twenty years, and though I'm an avid reader, I still rarely come across covers featuring dark-skinned characters. When it comes to characters of color on book covers, the publishing industry has a problem. Even before the young-adult author Justine Larbalestier published her novel *Liar* in 2009, controversy around the book was brewing. Though the protagonist, Micah, was Black, the cover on the review copies sent to critics ahead of the publication date included an image of a white girl with long hair. Larbalestier, a white Australian author, made her disappointment about the cover apparent in a blog post that eventually went viral.[5] Young-adult authors and readers, galvanized by the post, protested on social media. Bloomsbury, the publisher, then replaced the old cover with a new one, which features a Black girl who stares directly at the reader.

In 2017 award-winning writer Nnedi Okorafor encountered similar issues with her publisher. In a series of tweets, she showed how the advance reading copies of her science fiction novel *The Shadow Speaker* were packaged with a cover featuring a white woman, despite the fact that its main character is Black.[6] Like Larbalestier, Okorafor was able to persuade her publisher to create a cover that more accurately represented the novel.

The history of publishing has always been steeped in whitewashing, and not even bestselling authors like Octavia Butler or Ursula K. Le Guin—who wrote extensively about her experience of whitewashing[7]—could avoid it. The absence of Black and brown characters in books and on covers achieves the same end: erasure.

I always wondered whether Mukherjee, who passed away in January 2017 at the age of seventy-six, had any input on the covers of *Jasmine*. A few months before she died, I contacted her to see if she was interested in being interviewed about her long and illustrious literary career; I planned to ask her about that. She responded with immediate enthusiasm and told me she'd reach out in a few weeks, after she returned from her travels. Sadly, owing to her declining health, I never heard from her again.

Not long ago I got in touch with her husband, the writer Clark Blaise. About the cover of *Jasmine*, he wrote in an email, "She had no say in it except to approve it." He added, "The cover on her first book, *The Tiger's Daughter*, featured all the usual tourist dreck, even had a Taj Mahal. So she was always sensitive to exoticism and fought it whenever given the chance." More than forty years ago, Mukherjee was challenging the stereotypes that Indian American authors continue to face today.

My copy of *Jasmine* is a bit worn and creased, but I preserve it the best I can, wedged between hardback copies of *Desirable Daughters* and *The Tree Bride*. Mukherjee's fruitful career as a writer demonstrates how she unapologetically wove Indian American immigrants and their stories into the greater narrative of America, how she demanded that characters who looked like her engage with and take ownership of the United States, and how a book cover, like the one on my beloved copy of *Jasmine*, offers Indian American readers the ability to reckon with the ways that they are both seen and unseen as they move through the lands they call home.

II Inheritance

You are not Atlas carrying the world on your shoulder.
It is good to remember that the planet is carrying you.

—VANDANA SHIVA

Recipe for a Person

My mother's pregnancy with me began with a negotiation. My Hindu Indian immigrant father would allow my half Puerto Rican, half Austrian Catholic mother to baptize me if he could give me an Indian name. My mother agreed to this stipulation, and my father began coming up with possible names.

My mother's beloved maternal grandmother, my Austrian great-grandmother, was named Angela. My mother had hoped to pass on this name to her own daughter someday. After my birth, she considered a few options and settled on Anjali because it sounded most like Angela. In the early 1970s, Anjali was considered an old-fashioned Indian name—few parents chose it for their own daughters. But my mother thought it was beautiful and the perfect tribute to her Austrian grandmother.

My mother pronounces my name AHN-juh-lee, perhaps a slightly more obvious ode to Angela. My grandmother, aunts, and uncles called me Angie when I was growing up. My father pronounces my name UNH-juh-lee, the actual pronunciation. And like most Indians I had a nickname from his side of the family: Anju.

I have always loved my name, but I have never really settled on the way to pronounce it myself. Most days I am AHN-juh-lee, some days I'm UHN-juh-lee. It's not the technicalities of sound that stump me. It's that I want to simultaneously honor both sides of my family. I want to preserve the link to Angela, my Austrian great-grandmother, whom I had the pleasure of meeting only once as a teenager at her home in Linz. I also long to feel connected to my Indian father and his family, and the cousins, aunts, and uncles with whom I am still very close today.

The compromise my parents made when I was budding in my mother's womb set the stage for my life. It's an analogy for what it means to blend multiple heritages into one being.

International phone calls in the 1980s, especially those made to India, on the opposite side of the world, had a distinctive character to them. The chorus of rings was tinny and grating, like a drill at the dentist's office. The rings might end in a dial tone or a busy signal. Other times, a voice recording would explain that our call could not be completed as dialed. We'd need to hang up and enter the string of numbers again. The phone calls my mother made to our relatives in Austria had similar bumps in the road but to a much lesser degree.

When I was younger, I used to picture the cross-continental journey of communication in my mind—words emerging like pulses from my parents' mouths, making themselves narrow and long like vermicelli until they could slither through the tiny holes in the mouthpiece. Then, the rolling and dipping through the spiral cord, sliding down like I did on the twisty slides at the playground, into the wall of the house, where they'd meet wires, traverse above the roof, and cross the street. It would continue, lines connecting lines connecting lines across oceans (how *did* the words cross oceans?) until they greeted my grandparents' home in Hyderabad, slipped through *their* walls, into *their* spiral cord, and emerged, finally free.

Static and echoes plagued many of the successful phone calls, though, and the delay of sound travel composed a unique though frustrating melody. When we didn't hear a response to a question, we might repeat it, but this repetition would collide with their answers, producing sentences in myriad fragments. It reminded me of my one year as a Girl Scout, when we gathered to sing "Make New Friends" in the round, our choruses layering one on top of the other.

International phone calls used to be outrageously expensive. Conversations were stilted and rushed, the dialogue simple and taut. Conveying any sort of emotion—warmth, joy, grief, loneliness—was a challenge. There wasn't the bandwidth for it.

How are you?

Yes, the kids are fine.

Are you in good health?

Yes, the kids are keeping up with their studies.

Yes, we will come visit you soon. Yes, I . . . uh . . . Yes. Yes! Very Soon!

Promises. Many of our conversations with family abroad were about promises.

Aside from English, my parents speak three languages, German, Telegu, and Hindi. My mother and her three siblings picked up German from Gertrude, their Austrian mother (my Oma), and other maternal relatives in Linz when my maternal grandfather was stationed in nearby Germany. My mother still speaks German to her siblings and spoke it with Oma until she passed away a few years ago. My father speaks Telegu and Hindi fluently and can understand Tamil.

I took immense pride in my parents' ability to speak "foreign" languages. It was as if they had their own secret codes to their own secret lives. But my parents didn't teach them to me or my brother, nor did we possess the curiosity to learn them. This is one of my greatest regrets. Part of it had to do with my quest to seem as American as possible, but another part of me felt I simply didn't have the right to these languages. Claiming ownership to a language that felt far away both geographically and psychologically seemed disingenuous. My parents' languages didn't feel as if they ever belonged to me.

Mixed people are oftentimes not seen as wholes, as authentically belonging to any race, culture, religion, or ethnicity. We are aberrations or unicorns, rumors whispered among nosey neighbors. We are the sum of all of our fragmented and fractured parts, an imaginary number in high-order mathematics that can't easily be quantified or calculated. And when we attempt to describe our reality, we are either exoticized, ignored, or shouted over.

Certainly, there is beauty in combining races, ethnicities, cultures, and religions into one family, but there is loss, too. Our lives are like sieves. We valiantly attempt to hold on to the traditions, memories, and stories of our ancestors, yet like international phone calls in the 1980s, too many details and nuances slip through. The state of being mixed is one of making do with what we have, the best way we know how. It can also be a state of isolation and loneliness, of not being understood. And unfortunately, sometimes the communities that we identify with most strongly are not eager for us to join them.

Add to this the lost connections, the frayed and abrupted lines: the dead ends in family trees. I was six years old when John Camacho, my maternal grandfather, passed away at age fifty-two. He had been estranged from his family for decades. None of his relatives attended his funeral in 1980.

When he died, my sole connection to my Puerto Rican heritage ended. I hold in my mind a single fuzzy memory of John that I'm not even sure is my own. He is sitting on the banquette in my grandparents' kitchen in El Paso, elbows propped on the table, a cigarette dangling between his fingers, a square brown ashtray front and center. His thick, graying black hair has a wave to it. He is laughing—at what I do not know. My entire Puerto Rican identity is embodied in this one thin memory. And when those who still have clear memories and stories about John are gone, there will be nothing left for me to give to my own children.

My Austrian heritage is fading from my identity, too, since my grandmother Gertrude passed away. Oma was the only member of her family to have settled in the United States. Her siblings have also died. I've no contact with second or third cousins. I visited Linz just once, when I was sixteen years old. I remember my great-uncle Gerald driving us to Steyrling, a small mountain town where my great-grandmother Angela and her family were from. It's where Angela fled with Gerald during World War II when he was only five years old, leaving my grandmother Gertrude and great-uncle Franz back at their home in Linz.

I have always lived in a kind of denial. I believed my memories would never fail me, that my relatives would live forever, that their possessions would always stay in our family, that photographs would never be lost, that rifts would never separate our families permanently. Sometimes I can no longer remember what is real, what is family lore or a rumor. My mixed racial and ethnic identity feels as if it's slipping through my fingers, like sands through the hourglass.

Will I still be who I am if I lose all the connections to all of the parts of me? Would it change how I describe myself?

In this place and time, I gravitate to the words that help me to see myself better in the world. Mixed. Southern. Brown. A woman of color or a person of color. My roots extend to India and South Asia, a subcontinent made up of multiple countries, cultures, and regions, just like me. These terms are not perfect representations, but they afford me the opportunity to be comfortable in my own skin, with my own ambiguity, to remain a work in progress—a wedge of clay that is continually molded but never quite ready to be fired in the kiln.

An AHN-juh-lee *and* an UHN-juh-lee.

Over the decades I have come to realize that identity, especially mixed identity, is an evolution. It is a journey through the medium of language. And this narrative will likely continue to change and grow, as I do.

Alias

INTRODUCTION

In the months before I got married,
468 people asked me whether I was keeping my name.

Zero asked my fiancé.

I decided to
hy-phen-ate
because I wanted to
shut-everyone-up.

As a feminist,
my decision
should have been
cut-and-dry.

But I grew up in the
Deep South
where
husbands ingested their wives' names
like Pac Man after pellets.

I was torn.

HISTORY

My surname-before-marriage—
maiden name if you're retro—
is Enjeti,
an eponym for an ancient Indian town,
though my family's diaspora has extended
oceans beyond the motherland.

HOOKED ON PHONICS

I've e-nun-ci-a-ted my name my whole life.
Even a telephone introduction compels a mini-monologue:

"en-JET-ee.
E
n as in Nancy,
j
e
t as in Tom,
i."

PSYCHOLOGY

Nancy and Tom are neither childhood friends nor neighbors.
These linguistic choices
reflect
a deep-seated envy
of easy, pronounceable, white-sounding names,
a subliminal ethnic erasure.

Most days, though,
I adore my father's family name,
its rhythm, its musicality,
its phonemic rapport with Anjali.

In sum,
inquiries about whether my last name would secede
from its nuclear union
compounded my agony.

PHILOSOPHY

Surnames embody, simultaneously,
testimony and obliteration,
an unequivocal gain and loss,
a dichotomy of DNA.

My forfeiture would strip me
of culture and race,
just like when, in holy matrimony,
my Puerto Rican grandfather's name
redacted my Austrian grandmother's.

WISHFUL THINKING

Were I a poet,
I'd compose a sonnet,
and dedicate each of its fourteen lines
to each generation of abandoned matrilineal surnames
in my bloodline.

DECISION

At the eleventh hour,
I chose to expand rather than contract,
to intertwine our complicated histories, our baggage,
to dodge what I perceived as the merciless pruning
of our merging family trees.

And though,
at times,
hy-phen-a-tion
is cumbersome,

a name is merely a title—

a glimpse, a teaser, a savory appetizer
of what's to come.

It should never be
burdened or trusted
with telling
the whole, unabridged, multilayered
story.

In Memory of Vincent Chin

An Elegy in Nineteen Acts

ACT 1: Prologue

It is the early 1980s. A fundraising event in Southfield, Michigan, the city of my birth, a suburb just north of Detroit. For one dollar, participants get a turn at hitting a bright yellow 1978 Toyota Corolla with a sledgehammer.[1]

A man in an unbuttoned blazer, a wide mustache above his lip, takes aim at the hood.

Force equals mass times acceleration.

The hammer crashes down. Metal against metal. Another upswing high above his head. Another blow. Again and again. Easily several dollars' worth. The skeleton of the vehicle puckers and buckles and flattens. Cheers erupt. Another man in a white button-down shirt and a dark tie swings at the passenger side door. Others gleefully take turns pummeling the car. It's all in good fun, or at least that's what the news reporter claims.

But a rage is brewing across the nation, especially in the Midwest. It is directed at Japan, a country on the verge of opening its first automobile manufacturing plant on U.S. soil in Maryville, Ohio. It is directed at Japanese people, who American auto workers believe are stealing their jobs, their livelihood. This scene, the bludgeoning of a Japanese car, will repeat itself elsewhere.

This anti-Japanese sentiment sows the seed for a brutal killing.

The year is 1955. Vincent Jen Chin is born on May 18, in the Guangdong province of China bordering the South China Sea.[2] Six years later, Bing Hing "David" Chin and Lily Chin meet Vincent at an orphanage and decide to adopt him. The family of three travel together back to the United States to their home in Highland Park, just outside Detroit. They eventually move to Oak Park.[3]

The year is 1973. I am born in Southfield, three miles away from the Chins. Vincent is a new adult, age eighteen.

The year is 1946. Tule Lake Segregation Center shuts down. It is the last internment camp to close after World War II, and the largest. At one point it held more than 18,700 innocent detainees of Japanese descent who had been forcibly removed from their homes.[4]

The year is 1988. President Ronald Reagan offers surviving Japanese Americans who were interned $20,000 per person, tax free, in reparations. Some eighty thousand would be compensated before the program was ended in 1999.[5]

The year is 1967. An uprising erupts in the predominantly Black Virginia Park neighborhood of Detroit after police officers raid a bar. Forty-three people die, thousands are arrested, thousands are left homeless.[6]

The year is 1971. My father emigrates from Hyderabad, a large city in south central India, to El Paso, Texas, for his medical training. He meets my mother at what was then called R. E. Thomason General Hospital. They marry one year later.

The year is 1965. Formerly a Ferris wheel for New York's 1964 World Fair, the eighty-foot Uniroyal Tire is installed next to I-94 in Detroit.[7] Its great height casts a long shadow over Southeast Michigan, the bottom knuckle of Michigan's thumb.

The year is 1980. After a few years living elsewhere, my family returns to the mitten state, this time settling twenty-two miles northeast of the Uniroyal Tire.

The year is 1982. During a speech in Detroit, House Speaker Thomas "Tip" O'Neill says that if he were president, he'd halt the import of Japanese cars and "fix the Japanese like they've never been fixed before."[8]

The year is 1991. Two Black women, Sandra Smith and Nicole Childress, call the police to report their discovery of a naked, dazed, and bleeding fourteen-year-old Laotian American named Konerak Sinthasomphone. Serial killer Jeffrey Dahmer persuades police officers John A. Balcerzak and Joseph Gabrish to release the boy to him. Later that day, Dahmer kills and dismembers the child. Balcerzak and Galbrish are fired but later reinstated.[9] If they had checked, they could have learned Dahmer sexually assaulted Konerak's older brother three years earlier.[10]

The year is 2017. In a meeting with Japanese business executives, President Donald Trump states: "Try building your cars in the United States instead of shipping them over. That's not too much to ask. Is it rude to ask?"[11]

The year is 2016. President Barack Obama, son of a Kenyan immigrant, signs a bill, sponsored by Congresswoman Grace Meng (D-NY), that removes the term "oriental" from Title 42 of the U.S. Code.[12]

The year is 1968. Yuji Ichioka, incarcerated as a child with his family at the Topaz War Relocation Center during World War II, coins the term "Asian American" to join Asian Americans into a single sociopolitical coalition.[13]

The year is 1882. Congress passes the Chinese Exclusion Act, which prevents Chinese laborers from immigrating to the United States. Subsequent immigration acts of 1917 and 1924 expand this to bar immigrants from nearly all Asian countries.[14]

The year is 1988. Sixteen-year-old Mark Wahlberg pummels Vietnamese American Thanh Lam with a stick and punches Johnny Hoa Trinh in the face. Two years earlier, Wahlberg hurled rocks at Black children while shouting racial epithets.[15]

The year is 2017. Adam Purinton shoots two Indian men, Srinivas Kuchibhotla and Alok Madasani, in Olathe, Kansas, because he believes them to be Iranian. Kuchibhotla dies from his wounds.[16]

The year is 1904. Novelist Jack London, in an essay about Asians titled "The Yellow Peril," writes: "The Korean is the perfect type of inefficiency—of utter worthlessness. The Chinese is the perfect type of industry. For sheer work no worker in the world can compare to him. . . . The head men of Japan are dreaming ambitiously, and the people are dreaming blindly, a Napoleonic dream. And to this dream the Japanese clings and will cling with bull-dog tenacity."[17]

The year is 2016. The state of Michigan records one of the highest number of racial incidents following the presidential election.[18]

The year is 1991. Los Angeles police officers Timothy E. Wind and Laurence M. Powell strike Rodney King more than fifty times with batons, even while he is lying still on the ground, after King has already been tased.[19]

The year is 1981. Yale college senior Maya Lin's proposed design for the Vietnam Memorial wins a nationwide contest over some 1,420 other entries. When her identity as a Chinese American is revealed, she is met with racial slurs and threats of violence. Numerous benefactors, including H. Ross Perot, withdraw support for the construction of the memorial.[20]

The year is 1965. With the passage of the Immigration and Nationality Act, restrictive quotas that limit the number of Asians allowed to immigrate into the United States are lifted.[21]

The year is 2020. An Asian American teenage boy is attacked by bullies who accuse him of having the coronavirus.[22]

The year is 1989. Michael Moore releases his first feature-length documentary, *Roger & Me*, about General Motors' decision to move automobile plants out of his hometown, Flint, Michigan, and the evictions and poverty that follow.[23]

The year is 2019. Arthur Martunovich uses a hammer to bludgeon three Asian American men, Tsz Mat Pun, Fufai Pun, and Thang Kheong Ng, at a Brooklyn restaurant. All three victims eventually die of their injuries.[24]

ACT III: The Killing

On June 19, 1982, a twenty-seven-year-old Chinese-American draftsman named Vincent Chin celebrates his waning bachelorhood with friends in Highland Park, Michigan, eight days before his wedding to fiancé Vickie Wong. The young couple have been engaged for a year. Wong plans to wear two wedding gowns on June 27—a white American gown for the nuptials and a red Chinese dress at the reception. The honeymoon is to take place in Aruba, where they will also celebrate Wong's twenty-fourth birthday.[25]

At Fancy Pants strip club on a steamy Detroit night, two laid-off auto workers, Ronald Ebens and his stepson Michael Nitz, shout at Vincent and his friend Jimmy Choi: *Chink, Jap,* and *Nip. It's because of you little motherfuckers we're out of work.* It is a fit of misdirected racial rage against Japanese Americans, whom they blame for Detroit autoworkers' layoffs. After an altercation, Vincent and his buddies abandon the strip club. Ebens and Nitz soon follow. They grab a Louisville Slugger baseball bat from the trunk of Nitz's car and hunt them down. Ebens and Nitz find them in a McDonald's parking lot. Ebens swings the bat at Vincent full force. Vincent manages to briefly escape but collapses to the ground. While Nitz pins him down, Ebens swings at Vincent's head four times. Vincent dies four days later at Henry Ford Hospital. Some four hundred wedding guests attend his funeral instead.[26]

ACT IV: Hampton Road

I live with my family twelve miles away in a small white colonial home in a blue-collar neighborhood. I am eight years old.

The patriarch of the family across the street, Mr. C, is a union man, an employee of Uniroyal. The matriarch, Mrs. C, has the most beautiful golden hair I've ever seen, the warmest smile in the world, and the very best laugh. I can't help giggling when I hear it. We break bread with them, join them for mass at St. Joan of Arc Catholic Church. Their children are like older cousins. We have no extended family living in Michigan, or in the Midwest, for that matter. This family becomes our surrogate family.

In the recliner in their blue-carpeted room, I eat handfuls of popcorn, watch football. Mrs. C makes her family's famous sticky buns, and sometimes I help. I coat my hands in flour and dredge the rolling pin. She calls her own mother Mimi, and I call her that, too.

Mrs. C stays up all night with my mother, sewing a tutu I need at the last minute for a school performance. It is magical, that tutu, white tulle with orange specks. Mrs. C creates a glittery silver star for the center of my leotard, and a ribbon of tinsel for my arms. I don't remember a thing about the performance. I only remember the love I felt from her while wearing that costume.

When I think of Detroit, and autoworkers, the first thing that comes to mind is this family who loved my family as their own.

ACT V: Cognition

Our living room's dark brown carpet serves as the perfect canvas for my Legos, bold bricks of red and green and yellow and blue. The television blares. Here, after the killing of Vincent Chin, I hear the word *oriental* for the first time during news broadcasts. This is where, for the first time, I learn about injustice.

My thought process is this: Vincent Chin was Chinese. Chinese people are from the continent of Asia. Vincent made his life and died in the lower right-hand part of the Michigan mitten, where we also now live.

My thought process is this: My daddy emigrated from India, a country in Asia, in 1971. He did research at Harper University Hospital in downtown Detroit. The day Lily Chin decided to remove her only son from life support, Daddy was at work just a few miles away.

My thought process is this: If Ronald Ebens and his stepson Michael Nitz don't care that Vincent is not actually Japanese, they probably won't care that my Indian dad is not Japanese, either. They also won't care about me.

In my young mind I am negotiating racial proximity to whiteness, which means safety. I remember looking at the face and skin and eyes of my Asian friends at school and comparing them to my own. Who is safe? Who is not safe?

Five years later in 1987, the same year the documentary *Who Killed Vincent Chin?* debuts,[27] I receive an answer. A hate group known as Dotbusters aims to rid northern New Jersey of "Asian Indians." They pummel the skull of Dr. Kaushal Sharan with a baseball bat, causing him lasting brain injury. A few days later the Dotbusters bludgeon Navroze Mody with bricks in Jersey City, killing him.[28]

When classmates begin inquiring about whether I wear a "dot" (a bindi) on my forehead, I initially assume the questions are innocent, that they don't know about the crimes some eight hundred miles away in New Jersey. But then one boy tells me that he uses the dots for target practice.

Chinese are Japanese cars. Indians are targets. Their bodies echo the sounds of hammers and bricks and bats.

ACT VI: The Weapon

The same year Vincent is killed, I play my first and only season of recreational softball. We are the Lakeshore Optimists, our colors light blue and navy. My coach tells me I am the best shortstop on the team. At home plate, when my bat makes a hollow cracking sound against the ball, I know I'll make it to first base, maybe even second. My feet kick up dust as I sprint down the baseline.

There's something particularly grotesque and inhuman when one aims a bat, a hammer, a baton, or a stick at another human being. On contact, the act of violence vibrates up the weapon, tingles through the fingertips, the palm, the wrist, the arm. The pain feeds the rage, the rage fuels the pain. Another strike. The perpetrator extinguishes breath.

Two years after Vincent is killed, we move from Michigan to Tennessee. That October my favorite baseball team, the Detroit Tigers, wins the World Series. Mr. C, still living with his family on Hampton Road, sends me a commemorative wooden bat with the win engraved on the barrel. I sleep with it at night in my bed.

I dream of Hampton Road, the Lakeshore Optimists, and Vincent Chin.

ACT VII: Fault Lines

Ronald Ebens: "It was preordained to be, I guess. It just happened."[29]
  Ronald Ebens, thirty years later: "I'm as much to blame.[30] . . . I'm
75 years old, and I'm just tired of all that after 33 years."[31]

ACT VIII: Translation

*Vincent should take some responsibility. He practically handed me the bat,
for Chrissake, begged me to bash his skull in. I shouldn't have done it, but
he asked for it when he escalated things. He lost his cool. It was only a bat,
not a gun. Things had been tough for me. The layoffs had been tough for
my stepson. We were all scared. We have families to take care of. Vincent
should have left it alone. I'm the calmest person I know. I never lose my shit
like that.*
    I am also the victim.
    I am also the victim.
    I am also the victim.
    I am also the victim.
  Ronald Ebens is "tired." He is also in his eighties. He lives with
his family in Nevada. Michael Nitz's whereabouts are unknown.

ACT IX: In Memory of Lily Chin

Lily Chin, née Yee King Fong, has been described as warm, funny,
and sharp, with a mischievous smile. She never gave up. She was a
warrior, a fighter, a champion.[32]
  She was also very tired.
  Tired from working for more than three decades in a laundro-
mat. Tired with the grief from losing her husband, who died from
kidney disease six months before Vincent. Tired of never receiving justice for her son. Of growing old without Vincent. Of never
having grandchildren. Of the cancer eventually ravaging her body.
Of birthday after birthday after birthday without her son. Of the
anniversary of his death. Of knowing that if she and her husband

had never adopted Vincent from an orphanage in China, he might still be alive.[33]

With no justice for Vincent, it becomes too difficult for Lily to continue living in the United States. "He was my only child. Take him away and I am bare," she says in an interview. "I have nothing to call home."[34] She gives away most of Vincent's belongings aside from photographs and flies back across the Pacific Ocean to live in Guangzhou, China, with her mother.

As she ages, as her hair turns white, as her skin wrinkles, as her gait slows, as the light in her eyes dims, she must think about how her son Vincent never got the chance to grow old, to marry, to father children, to advance in his career, to celebrate each passing year with loved ones.

Lily dies in 2002 at age eighty-two. Her final resting place is alongside Vincent at Forest Lawn Cemetery in Detroit. She has outlived him by forty-five years.

ACT X: Parenting

I picture Vincent in a bathtub, Lily kneeling next to him on the floor, scrubbing his little shoulders with a washcloth, making sure she is wiping away every mark of dirt and grime. I see her wrapping him up in a fluffy towel, see Vincent squealing and falling into her chest. I see the two of them snuggling on the sofa, her son in the crook of her arm watching cartoons and falling asleep to the rise and fall of his mother's chest. I see her bringing a spoonful of soup to his lips, blowing on it so that it does not burn his tongue. I see her tucking him into his bed at night, and flicking off the switch.

When I try to picture a baseball bat smashing into one of my own children's heads, her beautiful face twisting in pain, then the stillness, my heart falls away from my body.

ACT XI: Activism

We must disaggregate data on Asian Americans. We must recognize that some Asian American groups are far more marginalized than others. But we must also form alliances under a larger umbrella to build coalitions and fight for justice for all oppressed communities.

We must reckon with our deep-seated anti-Blackness, and the ways we prop up white supremacy to align ourselves with whiteness. We must acknowledge that we live on land stolen from First Nations.

We must.

We must.

We must.

We must.

Our lives depend on it.

ACT XII: Judgment

In March 1983, Ronald Ebens and Michael Nitz plead to third-degree manslaughter. The prosecution fails to interview the police officers who witnessed Nitz and Ebens killing Vincent in the McDonald's parking lot. No Wayne County prosecutor is present at the sentencing to push for a harsher, more just punishment for Vincent's killers.[35]

The chief judge of the Wayne County Circuit Court, the Honorable Charles Kaufman, doesn't believe Ebens and Nitz are the type of people who should have to go to jail. He explains:

"We are talking here about a man who has held down a responsible job with the same company for 17 or 18 years, and his son who is employed and is a part-time student. These men are not going to go out and harm somebody else. I just didn't think that putting them in prison would do any good for them or for society. You don't make the punishment fit the crime; you make the punishment fit the criminal."[36]

Judge Kaufman orders only four years of probation, a $3,000 fine, and $780 in court costs.[37]

Ebens and Nitz are good people, after all.

Federal civil rights charges, the first ever brought on behalf of an Asian American, are filed. Vincent's killers are initially indicted but eventually acquitted on all counts.

In 1987 Ebens, Nitz, and Lily Chin enter into a civil settlement whereby Ebens will pay Lily $1.5 million, plus interest, for killing her son. Lily receives nothing. In 2017 the estate of Vincent Chin sues the Ebens family for eight million dollars, the original judgment plus the interest now owed.[38]

To this day, neither of Vincent's killers has spent a single day in jail or paid the Chins a dime.

ACT XIII: Memory

On the thirty-fifth anniversary of his death in 2017, a short film asks Asian American and Pacific Islanders if they know who Vincent Chin is.[39] Some do. Others have never heard of him.

The images of Vincent Chin's photo in 1982 that flashed across our television screen nightly for months flood my mind. I remember the fear that settled in the pit of my stomach. I remember wondering whether my family would be safe.

I decide to write this essay about him.

ACT XIV: Legacy

In the wake of Vincent's killing, Asian American activists mobilize in the Detroit metro area and across the country. They rally. They march. They organize. They call for justice. They demand tougher prosecution under federal hate crimes on behalf of Asian Americans.

For the community, Vincent's death is a wake-up call. It changes the course of jurisprudence in Michigan going forward. In 1985 the state passes the Crime Victim Rights Act requiring prosecutors to be present at sentence hearings so that the voices of the victims can be heard.[40]

So that justice can be served.

ACT XV: Migration

Import (noun). A piece of merchandise or commodity from a foreign country.
Immigrant (noun). A person who migrates to another country to take up
residence.

At age two, while Vincent is still toddling around in the orphanage in China, Japan exports two Toyopet Crown cars to Los
Angeles.[41] They are the first Japanese cars to touch U.S. soil.

Five months after his death, in November 1982, the very first
Honda manufactured in the United States rolls out of the brand-
new Maryville, Ohio, plant. In 1985, only three years after Vincent's
death, the United States lifts quota restrictions on Japanese cars im-
ported into the United States.[42]

In 1988, 900,000 Japanese automobiles are produced in the
United States. Subaru, Nissan, and Toyota plants spring up coast to
coast.[43] The reliability and price of Japanese cars seem to alleviate
some of the xenophobia toward Japanese and other Asian Americans.

Apparently, white Americans love a good deal.

ACT XVI: Desensitization

To Ebens, Chin is a piece of metal. An unwanted, unyielding material that threatens his autonomy and agency, a Japanese car that
deserves scrapping. Perhaps Ebens and Nitz have watched the news
of disgruntled auto workers bashing cars with sledgehammers and
thought, *Now, wouldn't that be fun to do to a Japanese person?*

When does Vincent Chin cease existing as a human being in their
eyes? Is it when they first spot him with his friends at the Fancy Pants
club? Is it the moment Chin first defends himself against their slurs?
Is it when Nitz reaches into the trunk of his car and pulls out a baseball bat, when Nitz pins Vincent down, when Ebens first holds the
bat up in the air, high above his head?

Do they register even a millisecond of regret? Do they close their
eyes when the bat makes contact with Vincent's skull? Do they find
any part of their own brutality difficult to witness?

I guess we'll never know.

ACT XVII: Last Words

If Lily Chin had known Vincent was going with his friends to Highland Park, she would have persuaded him to stay home.[44] Those would have been her last words.

Before her son loses consciousness on the pavement of the McDonald's parking lot, he mutters his last words: "It's not fair."[45]

ACT XVIII: Gravestone

Forever in Our Hearts
Beloved Son Vincent J. Chin
May 18, 1955–June 23, 1982[46]

Forever, indeed. Rest in Power, Vincent Chin.
He would have been sixty-five years old today.

ACT XIX: Afterlife

Aruba is hot, the sun bright and high in a clear blue sky. Vincent and Vicky hold hands as the ocean laps at their feet. He breaks away, goes deeper, plunges his hands in the brisk salty water and splashes his new wife. She whips around, feigns anger, as a newly married wife does, and kicks water back at him. He dives in, she takes off after him. When he resurfaces, she jumps on his back, wraps her legs around his waist, her arms around his chest. She whispers something in his ear, kisses his cheek. They continue walking like that along the shore, the horizon charting their new path together.

An elderly woman who passes them smiles. *Newlyweds.*

At dinner, by candlelight, Vincent and Vicky talk about where they see themselves in five years, in ten years. They want to stay in Michigan to be near family, near Vincent's mother Lily, where their children will have grandparents and aunts and uncles and cousins.

They clasp hands across the table.

Vincent looks into his wife's eyes and in them sees their entire, beautiful future.

Treatment

In 1980, sixteen years after the passage of the Civil Right Acts, on Ninth Street (now MLK Boulevard) in downtown Chattanooga, three Ku Klux Klansman shoot five Black women, Viola Ellison, Lela Mae Evans, Katherine O. Johnson, Opal Lee Jackson, and Mary Tyson.[1] Miraculously, all five women survive. Though their assailants are acquitted of the crime, the women win a federal lawsuit against them to the tune of half a million dollars.[2]

The following year, in June 1981, the Centers for Disease Control publishes a report about five young gay men diagnosed with *Pneumocystis carinii* pneumonia in Los Angeles. One month later, the *New York Times* publishes its first article about a rare cancer that seems to afflict gay men. In September 1982, for the very first time, the CDC calls this disease Acquired Immune Deficiency Syndrome (AIDS). In 1983, Human Immunodeficiency Virus (HIV) is identified as the virus that causes AIDS. In my hometown of Chattanooga, some 350 are infected with HIV or AIDS from the early 1980s to the early 1990s. Approximately 90 percent of them are men, and 77 percent are white. They range from ages twenty-five to fifty.[3]

We move from suburban Detroit to Chattanooga in March 1984, one month before researchers discover that HIV *is the cause* of AIDS.[4] In the years before the 1995 invention of the "cocktail"—a highly active antiretroviral therapy (HAART) that decreases viral loads–a diagnosis of HIV or AIDS is a death sentence. Few treatments alleviate patients' suffering.

My father, a pulmonologist, critical care specialist, and academic who has devoted his entire career thus far to research, is offered a position in a medical practice at a hospital in Chattanooga. My parents are eager to escape Michigan winters and look forward to living near my mother's sister and her family. They hope this will be our last move.

We leave Michigan in the midst of a recession and the collapse of the automobile industry. The first home we have owned, a three-bedroom colonial in Southeast Michigan, sits empty and idle on the market. So we move into the lower level of my aunt's rented split level. My brother and I are thrilled to be living with our cousins—all of us are around the same age. A creek runs alongside the house, and we spend hours barefoot, building dams with rocks, and constructing huts with small twigs. Melting popsicles drip down our forearms. We catch roly-polies on the pavement and watch them curl up into balls on our palms.

That first summer in Tennessee, before school starts, is one of the best in my life.

Thirty-six years later, my father and I are seated in my office in Georgia. My parents have recently moved from Chattanooga to my suburb of Atlanta, and we now see each other more than we have since I left for college. My father's elbow is propped on an armrest, and the chair squeaks with the slightest movement. The door is closed to block out kid and dog noise. I'm directly opposite him, hunched forward, an incongruent reflection, my laptop a barrier between us. I'm hoping the lack of distractions, and the formal nature of this interview, will compel my father to be more open with me about things I've been trying to talk to him about for years.

Our similar personalities can make it difficult for us to agree. When it comes to the past, we seem to be equally unreliable narrators, spinning memories into lines that rarely intersect. For years I've been trying to talk to my father about the racism our family endured in the 1980s and 1990s in Chattanooga. He's the only one of my two parents who experienced it—my mother is white passing. But whenever I bring it up, he downplays it. I get frustrated. The cycle repeats itself.

Here in my office, while our conversation is being recorded, I press him to be more forthcoming. I learn for the first time that soon after we moved to Chattanooga in 1984, another Indian physician warned my father that his new hospital "ran off foreigners." Just prior to our arrival, doctors had driven away another Indian physician. The man warning him was also being driven away. He was heading to Huntsville, Alabama, another small city, for a crack at a different job in the Deep South.

"Watch it," he told my dad before he left. "They will never let another Indian succeed."

One of the residents issued another kind of warning. He told my father not to assume goodwill in people who are nice to his face, because they hate his guts behind his back. White colleagues were oftentimes condescending to him. One white doctor told my father that he'd never be able to get away with anything because of who he was. Others accused him of having a conflict of interest with respect to business decisions or refused to give him funds he needed to treat patients. My father knew this was because of his race.

After a few months living with my aunt, my family finds an apartment in North Chattanooga. After three months at a nearly all-white public elementary school, I begin sixth grade at a private school where I am the only brown child in the entire grade (there is one Black child). Just as at my last elementary school, I am the first brown person some of my classmates have ever seen.

During the first few weeks, three white boys, apparently bewildered by my looks (their whispers and pointed fingers tell me so), demand that I "go with" them. They corner me in the classroom and encircle me at recess like vultures. When I keep saying no, they laugh among themselves about my refusals. I sweat bullets every time I have to rise from my desk and go to the supply cabinet to get another sheet of construction paper or a new pencil because I know they will be watching me.

I wonder why flattery feels so much like bullying.

One day one of the boys with freckles says I *have* to go with him. I say yes even though I don't like him, even though I am repulsed by him. But I'm exhausted. The white boys have worn me down. All I want is to stop being the center of their attention, their prize, their first sighting of a brown girl.

Soon after this experience, my father tells me what happened when he entered one very sick patient's room. The patient held up a cross to him, as if warding off a vampire, and told him he is going to hell because he is a Hindu. "They're just naïve," my father says, laughing.

I feel the rage swell inside me. My daddy has been compared to a bloodsucking creature with fangs. *Why is he laughing?* I want to smash all the dishes in our kitchen. I want to crawl into a hole and never emerge again.

My confusion over this story, over his jovial delivery, replicates in other family conversations about other people's ignorance or jealousy. We never use the word *racism* in our home to describe our own experiences, and so I find myself wondering whether *anything* qualifies as racism. Perhaps it exists only in my own mind. I am lost in all of these silences, this terrible treatment of me, my father, and my brother that seems invisible to everyone except me.

In the 1980s, public use of the N-word is considered uncouth, vulgar, and uncivilized. But the words *f*g* or *f*ggot* roll easily off people's tongues. Even though the slurs are not directed at me, my stomach lurches at the familiar harsher, lower pitch of its middle consonants. Those two g's. They ring in my ears, days, even weeks after I hear the words.

Is this by design? Are bigots emboldened by gutturals?

Mitzi Ward's beloved older brother Nick Brock was "the funniest person anyone knew, a real 'Mr. Personality' who had it all." Born in the small town of Englewood sixty-five miles northeast of Chattanooga, he relocated to the city for college in 1985. Nick played piano, was involved with local theater, had a large but close-knit group of friends, and loved to hang out at local clubs. He wasn't just the life of the party—he *was* the party.

In January 1994, during a time when the South had the highest proportion of reported AIDS cases in the United States,[5] Nick was diagnosed with what was then known as "full-blown" AIDS. He was only thirty years old.

"It was the nineties," said Mitzi. "People were dropping like flies." A diagnosis carried such shame, she said. "It was meant to make someone feel dirty."

Nick shut himself off from almost everyone. Aside from Mitzi and their mother, he told no one of his diagnosis, not even his closest friends. Mitzi respected her brother's right to privacy. Even though they had always been close, he'd never come out to her. So aside from telling her husband about Nick's diagnosis, Mitzi kept his identity (gay or bisexual, she didn't know) a secret.

Nick's health declined rapidly. Mitzi and their mother, his sole caregivers, decided to move him to a townhouse where they could better care for his needs. When Mitzi entered his old apartment to retrieve his belongings, she discovered dozens of bottles of vitamins, supplements, and skin creams. She wondered how long he had known he was sick, and why he didn't tell her.

One of the biggest silences, Mitzi found, resided in the nave of the Christian church. When Nick contracted a dangerous staph infection, Mitzi reached out multiple times to a Presbyterian pastor recommended by her cousin to ask him to visit and comfort Nick. For some time the pastor refused to return her messages. When he finally did pay a visit, he sat in the far corner of Nick's room, away from the bed. He wouldn't hold Nick's hand or even touch him.

In October the year of his diagnosis, Nick was admitted to the hospital for the last time. He never told his friends of his diagnosis and did not want any of them to see him sick. As much as it pained them, Mitzi and her mother obeyed Nick's wishes and turned his friends away when they came to visit him at the hospital.

Steadfastly loyal to her brother and his memory, Mitzi has maintained her silence about the cause of Nick's death until now.

Maintaining her silence has been very painful and isolating for her. "I physically hurt," she says. "It was nauseating. It was an emptiness—a loneliness—I can't describe."

She regrets preventing Nick's friends from seeing him in his final days. "They didn't love him any less. They didn't care how he got the virus. They loved him and they wanted to be there for him. And we didn't let them. They didn't get to say their goodbyes."

A stereotypical immigrant, my father worked like a dog. He was away from the house fourteen hours a day, twelve days out of every fourteen, and off only every other weekend until I was at least thirty years old. For decades his alarm was never set later than 4:30 or 5 a.m., even on weekends.

When I did see him, he was seated in his recliner, his reheated dinner plate on this lap, excitedly asking my brother and me about school and friends. But by this late hour, we'd already given our mother the full rundown of our days and no longer had the patience to regurgitate it. Besides, I had homework to do, music to listen to, friends to call.

AIDS and HIV patients did not make up the bulk of my father's patients. He mostly treated asthma, emphysema, and non-AIDS-related pneumonia—a good number of his patients were smokers. But before the AIDS cocktail arrived in the mid-1990s, he estimates he saw somewhere between forty and eighty infected patients. He was a fierce advocate for their treatment and was able to save some of them. We'd sometimes run into his patients while out as a family. They'd lavish praise on him and tell my brother and me how grateful they were to have our father as their physician.

In my office, I ask him whether seeing people so sick, knowing there was not a whole lot he could do to ease their suffering, affected him. He shrugs. "It was fine."

"Fine" was and continues to be his standard response. He was fine all those nights he stumbled through the door, his face strained and worn. Fine when I found him snoring in the recliner, arm flung over his eyes, a blanket of new medical journals on his torso, fountain pen ink underlining passages recounting the latest treatment options for his sickest patients.

"Fine" is not my father being callous. It is him minimizing the sacrifices he made to his own mental and physical health to save his patients' lives. It is him burying the fact that we lost so much time together as a family because he had to work himself to the bone to save lives and be taken seriously as an Indian doctor. It is him glossing over all the sacrifices he made to ensure his patients received the best treatment.

In 1985 the musicians of USA for Africa, headed up by Michael Jackson, Stevie Wonder, Lionel Richie, and Harry Belafonte, joined forces to record the bestselling song "We Are the World" to raise money for Africans suffering from famine. The 1980s was also the age of the melting pot, when white people were "color-blind" and brown and Black people were expected to dissolve quietly into whiteness in perfect harmony.

AIDS started killing gay men, and then it started killing everyone. The Reagan administration treated the epidemic as if it was some kind of a joke.[6] President Reagan may not have been as openly cruel and crass as President Trump has been about those diagnosed with Covid-19 in 2020, but make no mistake, he was equally heartless. And like Covid-19, from the beginning AIDS disproportionately impacted Black and Latinx people. In the first five years after its identification, 25 percent of AIDS patients were Black and 14 percent Hispanic, at a time when these groups represented only 12 percent and 6 percent of the population, respectively.[7]

Chattanooga in the 1980s was the buckle of the Bible Belt, the epicenter of evangelical Christianity and conservatism. Being gay was a lifestyle "choice," and this supposed choice wrought dire consequences and damnation. The "Bible thumpers," as we used to call them, wore their prejudice on their sleeves. On Sunday mornings, when Christian preachers took over the airwaves for their hours-long fire-and-brimstone sermons, they likened HIV and AIDS to a God-ordained genocide.

"Progressive" Christians assumed what they deemed a more loving but equally violent stance. They hated the sin (which they described as gay sex) but loved the sinner (a gay person). They wallowed in their altruism, encouraged conversion therapy, and used their "forgiveness" of gay people to cement their status as compassionate Christians.

Another force was at play here, too. The South distrusted the East and West Coasts and those immoral drug-using, loose, gritty urbanites from San Francisco and Los Angeles, New York City and Washington, D.C. That HIV and AIDS first embedded themselves in large cities seemed like a testament to the ways of the small-town South, to its more moral, traditional, and faith-based sensibilities, which insulated it from the wrath of Satan.

In his memoir *My Own Country*, infectious disease physician and author Abraham Verghese, an Indian American immigrant like my father, confirms this same attitude in his early years of treating HIV and AIDS patients in northeast Tennessee, only three hours from where our family lived. "This was a small town in the country, a town of clean-living, good country people. AIDS was clearly a big city problem. It was something that happened in other kinds of lives."[8]

Good, upstanding southerners do not get HIV or AIDS.

William Adams is from Delano, Tennessee, a rural town of 1,500 some sixty miles northeast of Chattanooga. He is the fifth of six boys. His voice and mannerisms, his appearance, and especially his penchant for neatness, cause him to realize he is different from his brothers. One night in the late 1980s, he and one of his brothers are listening to the radio. The topic is AIDS.

"I remember lying in bed and internalizing that [AIDS] was going to happen to me. I knew that night I would eventually be infected even though I hadn't had sex yet. I knew that it was my destiny—that God was going to punish me for being homosexual."

During a sermon at his family's Southern Baptist church, the minister condemns gay people to death. "He was running around, shouting, praising God for this thing that was going to wipe the planet of homosexuality," William says. "This thing that would kill them all. And he praised God for it."

William knows he is one of the damned. He has no choice. He must remain silent. He must never discuss his true identity with anyone.

My father was bewildered by those prejudiced against gay people or people infected by the virus. He says he found most of the hospital staff he worked with to be compassionate toward the patients. At the same time, he knew of at least a few dentists and physicians who would refuse to treat HIV or AIDS patients.

One patient in his mid-thirties who was close to death begged my father to make sure that another physician, who had treated him badly, was kept away from him. "He told me that even if he was dying a miserable death, he did not want this other doctor near him." My father was shocked that this other doctor, a very religious Christian respected by the community, could harbor such bigotry.

My father also found hospital rules around sterility to be overblown, contributing to ignorance and unreasonable fear. Those first years, any hospital staff entering an AIDS or HIV patient's room had to wear masks, gloves, and gowns. The bronchoscopy labs would be covered in sheets that would be thrown out at the end of the day. "All of this was because of the lack of understanding of how the virus was transmitted," he said.

These extra protective measures also increased the sense of isolation and shame patients felt. One of the images that sticks out most in Mitzi's mind is the giant label on the outside of her brother Nick's medical records. "All of his charts were stamped really big with HIV and AIDS." And because the charts were kept on the outside of his door, the entire floor of the hospital could see it. It was the first thing anyone who walked in the door knew about Nick. It saddened Mitzi that her brother and his illness were so stigmatized in this way, that his medical chart functioned like a skull and crossbones.

One thing was certain. My father's gay patients, even those born and bred in Chattanooga, always treated him with utmost respect.

I imagine they must have known how hard it was for an Indian immigrant doctor to work in the Deep South. Just as my father knew how hard it must have been to be a gay person with HIV or AIDS.

In 1992, after I outgrow my pediatric dentist, my mom sets up an appointment for me with her adult dentist, Dr. K. I am no longer living at home full time, but I figure visiting her dentist during college breaks is easier than searching for a new dentist in North Carolina, where I don't have a car.

My new dentist's office is a tiny brick section of a one-story strip mall. The door is narrow, and the small windows let in little light. The office itself has a small front desk and a low ceiling. A few plain chairs dot the waiting area. There is no giant aquarium, no large fancy television, no dramatic artwork covering the walls. I wonder how Dr. K can manage to stay competitive in a market that seems saturated with dentists whose offices resemble modern museums.

I adore Dr. K from the get-go. He has a wide, bright smile and sparkling eyes. His beard is always perfectly trimmed. His wire-framed glasses suggest he is serious, but he is anything but. He cracks jokes while drilling my cavities. We spend several minutes of each visit talking like old friends. He calls out my accomplishments to his hygienists elsewhere in the office. "Did you hear that, Mary, Anjali is majoring in psychology. Isn't that great?" He is thrilled when I decide to apply to law school. "Won't Anjali make a great lawyer, Janet?" At each visit, Dr. K makes me feel like a celebrity.

During the years I am his patient, I go through one big transition after another. At eighteen, I begin college in North Carolina. Soon after graduating, I enroll in law school in St. Louis. That fall, I get engaged to my college sweetheart and am planning our wedding long distance. A year before graduating from law school, I get married. I then move to Philadelphia to complete law school while my husband starts medical school.

My life is moving at such a dizzying pace, I hardly have the time to process it. The few times I do are while sitting in Dr. K's chair, my mouth wide open, his tools pushing and probing at my teeth. When he asks about me, I don't hesitate to be honest with him. It's as if

I'm sitting in a confessional. "I can't seem to catch my breath," I tell him once, when wedding planning, the Socratic Method, frigid St. Louis winters, and a long-distance relationship with my fiancé are on the verge of breaking me. I don't remember what he said. But I remember what he did. He set his tools down, placed a hand on my shoulder, tapped it twice, and then went back to work.

I know Dr. K is gay, and has a long-term partner. Though people seem to like him as much as I do, this is the 1990s in Chattanooga. It is a hostile environment for any member of the LGBTQIA+ community. (At the time, in Chattanooga, and elsewhere, the commonly used terms, regardless of accuracy, are *gay* and *lesbian*.)

Especially before the cocktail, fear of catching HIV reaches fever pitch. In 1991, a year before my first visit with Dr. K, a twenty-three-year-old AIDS activist named Kimberly Bergalis, who contracted HIV from her dentist during a 1987 molar extraction, dies.[9] Hygiene practices change radically in the last years of Bergalis's life. Dentists begin regularly wearing gloves, goggles, and masks. The public gains a better understanding of how the virus spreads. But in our fire-and-brimstone city (anywhere, actually), homosexuality, as it is called then, can't be easy for Dr. K, especially in the years immediately after Bergalis's death. I worry about how others treat him, but I do so silently.

Dr. K never comes out to me. I ask him about his daughters but stop short of asking about his partner. I don't know if Dr. K knows that I know he is gay. While lying back in his chair, I often wish I could signal to him that I'd be interested (if he cared to tell me) to learn his partner's name, what he's like, what the two of them enjoy doing on the weekends. Here I am, going on and on about my great fiancé. Dr. K might want to share about the love of his life, too.

I stop seeing Dr. K in 1998, soon after I get married and move to Philadelphia, some seven hundred miles from Chattanooga. With work and school, it seems I'll never make it back to my hometown for routine dental work. For a few years I neglect my teeth completely. I then decide I'd much rather go back to Dr. K, even if it means I only get my teeth cleaned every year or two. Besides, I have just given birth to my first baby. I have so many things I want to tell Dr. K about her. And I want his advice on how to raise a daughter. Maybe I'll bring her along to my next visit so he can meet her.

In the summer of 2002, my mother phones. I am at home with my infant hoisted on my hip while cradling the phone on my right shoulder. She tells me Dr. K has died by suicide. He was only forty-seven years old.

The news knocks the wind out of me. Over the next few weeks, I feel like I am living in a fog. I replay our last conversations over and over. I can't remember whether we ever hugged.

Dr. K lived in a terrifying era—AIDS when there was no viable treatment for it; being gay when many people, especially the white evangelical Christian southerners who made up our community, openly declared that gay people deserved to be abused, fired from jobs, excommunicated from the church, and cut off from their families.

In 2002, the year of Dr. K's death, most Americans still believed gay marriage should be illegal. But their numbers were rapidly shrinking. By 2010, gay marriage opponents were substantially in the minority.[10] Despite the fact that the LGBTQIA+ community still continues to face violence and abuse at an astounding rate (especially Indigenous, Black, and other people of color), Americans in the new millennium were starting to become more visible and more vocal in their support of LGBTQIA+ rights. We were beginning to turn a corner, even though we still had (and still have) many miles to go.

What continues to haunt me is the feeling that I could have been a better friend to Dr. K. I could have let him know more explicitly, especially during the time before the cocktail, when antigay bigotry was at its worst, that his identity didn't change how I viewed him as a dentist or as a person. I wish I had asked about his partner when the two of us were alone in the treatment room. I wish I had let him know that I knew him, and saw him, and loved him all the same.

I had made it clear during our visits that I adored him, that I valued his opinion each and every time he offered it. But about his identity, I remained silent. To this day I deeply regret it. Isn't this what we all want in life—for those we love to see and acknowledge our truths?

All of our silences reproduce like spores, inhaled and exhaled into the ether, their growth exponential. In the safety of my circle of friends in the eighties and early nineties, among a range of identities, we openly condemned those who preached that gay people were going to hell, that AIDS was God's punishment. We extrapolated the hypocrisy of *love the sinner, hate the sin*. But we did this only in safe spaces, among like-minded people.

Our condemnations did not involve discomfort, risk, or confrontation. We ran the same mental calculation many do, and ultimately decided to prioritize our own personal safety over the safety of those who needed it most. Our silence won out.

William is living in Chattanooga with his partner when, in the summer of 1991, he comes down with what he thinks is flu. His fever spikes to 104°F. After his test results come back, a doctor reveals his diagnosis. William is HIV positive. He bawls at hearing the news, and is terrified for his partner, who he knows must have HIV, too. He doesn't tell his parents about his diagnosis.

When William recovers from the fever, he mentally prepares to die. "That's what most people with an HIV or AIDS diagnosis did." Six of his friends have died of AIDS, countless others are infected with HIV. He thinks he'll just enjoy life the best he can.

He picks up smoking—a habit he would have never developed if he'd known he was going to live for so long. "For me, it was the mental part of the diagnosis that was so hard—being diagnosed with a fatal disease in my twenties, not knowing whether I'd make it to the next month." In 1993, after losing a dear friend to AIDS, he finally reveals to his parents that he is gay. They respond lovingly that they've always known.

William's treatment is abysmal. Two dentists outright refuse to see him because of his diagnosis. When his landlord, a police officer, realizes he and his partner are gay, she throws them out of their rented home. "I want your f*ggot asses out of my house," she tells his partner. The landlord phones William's mother to tell her that her son is gay. His mother executes the ultimate southern clapback—she says she will pray for her.

In the early 2000s, a police officer patrolling Alan Golds, a local gay club in Chattanooga, accuses William of purposely bumping into him. He throws William to the ground and handcuffs him. A dozen or so officers soon show up. "They beat the hell out of me," William says. A lawyer advises him to take a plea, because no judge will believe him over a cop.

In 1998 William returns for his first doctor's appointment in seven years. He doesn't think there's any point, because he's going to die anyway—still, having survived this long, he is curious about how much time he has left to live. That's when the doctor informs him that there are new drugs available. During the first round of meds, William is violently ill. Other drugs are approved, and he tries again. Eventually William finds a regimen that suits him.

But it's not until 2003 or 2004 that William stops sensing death outside his door. What finally does it? When he searches the obituaries for people he knows are infected with the virus—a practice dating back years—he no longer sees anyone he knows.

Wow, he thinks, *I'm probably going to live!*

Today William works at an Italian restaurant in town. He is in great health. He and his partner have been together for twenty years.

Ninety minutes into my conversation with my father, I relay a list of the kinds of racism I experience today. And then I tell him that the refusal to see and acknowledge racism is harmful to others. The refusal to see or acknowledge any kind of bigotry in its myriad forms is harmful.

"We have to see it, in order to fight it," I tell him.

He takes this in slowly, looks at me with his dark, gentle eyes. "Maybe I wasn't sensitive about what you kids went through back then," he says.

It is only a partial affirmation, but one coming from a sincere and genuine place. A sense of closure washes over me. I feel seen and heard, and because of this I am able to extend an olive branch, too.

"I think you were trying to protect us," I say. "I think you thought that if you avoided calling what we went through *racism*, it wouldn't hurt us as much."

My father nods, though I'm not sure how he feels about my pronouncement. He is simply spent, which is okay. Today is not a day of resolutions. It's a day to open a door, leave it ajar, and see what might find its way through in the future. We have talked more about our personal experiences with racism in these ninety minutes than we have in more than forty years together. Today we have cracked the silence.

Here's what also comes out of our conversation. I come to realize that my activism today originated in my father's compassionate treatment of his HIV and AIDS patients. He was the one who showed me as a child, time and again, what it looks like to champion those who endure rampant discrimination. He would never call himself an activist. But activism takes many forms, and this is how he unknowingly modeled activism to me. And I am and have always been my father's daughter.

I hug my father tightly. He rises from the seat, slightly stiff. A few minutes later, he and my mother put on their shoes, and from the window I watch as they enter their car and head back home.

Borderline

The Pre-Op floor is quiet, anesthetized even, for a Monday morning. My gown cloaks me three times over, yet fails to keep out the chill. The stiff sheet encasing my torso is dotted with the stains of dried tears.

Almost fourteen weeks pregnant, I await a D&C, a Dilation and Curettage.

Three days earlier, I celebrate the retreat of morning sickness with cheery greetings to my husband and children. The buttons on my pants refuse to come together, like two stubborn toddlers. I glance underneath my bed to the maternity clothes I've been storing for two years and remind myself to toss them into the washing machine.

Later today, I think, I will tell the world about my pregnancy.

In my loosest clothing (the last outfit I will wear with a smile for a long time) I pose in front of the full-length mirror in my bedroom. My posture exaggerates an early second-trimester pregnancy. I massage my third child, eager for the day when it kicks back, eager to introduce our baby to my two older daughters. In March 2007 we will be a family of five.

That afternoon, at a routine checkup with my doctor, the all-knowing Doppler skates back and forth across my slick belly. Loud echoes pulse off the walls in the exam room. I await her chipper voice assuring me that everything looks great, her instructions for me to take care until my next visit. But she continues drawing figure eights, in smaller circumferences, outlining every organ.

Finally, she breaks the pattern.

"I don't hear anything that sounds like a heartbeat," she says.

An ultrasound later confirms that something went terribly wrong. The fetus floats around in my fluid, lifeless, a buoy in the ocean. From a supine position, my stares command the heart on the screen to flicker. But my plea fails—my meek attempt at prenatal discipline goes unanswered.

This horror is compounded by timing. Because it is too late on Friday afternoon to schedule the surgery, my baby and I must remain joined until Monday.

At home I feel lost, defeated, enraged. Crying jags punctuate ordinary conversation. I now detest my swollen body, and in an attempt to punish it for its physical deception, I stuff it into skinny jeans. The seams crack into my skin.

Despite my depleted state, I drive my daughters to an orchard for pony rides and face paintings. As we run though the corn mazes, stopping and starting at false openings, trapped among the stalks that rise above our faces, I hide my tears in a sweatshirt sleeve while clutching my belly.

Three days later, in Pre-Op, scrub-wearing workers stream in and out, poking and prodding without consolation. The nurse monitoring my blood pressure never looks up from my trembling arm.

As I'm being wheeled into surgery, my grandmother, my Oma, is seven hundred miles away in Tennessee, cramped and kneeling in the pews of her church, praying for a procedure without complications.

When I return home afterward, as soon as my husband opens the door to the house, the phone rings. It is my Oma, Gertrude. Underneath her thick Austrian accent and muffled sobs, she offers a sentiment I will hear over and over again from many others.

But she is the one who says it first.

"Anjali," she whispers, "I am so, so sorry."

On March 13, 1938, Gertrude, age twelve, glances out her living room window. Adolf Hitler's booming voice reverberates through the streets of Linz, Austria. He embraces cheering salutes of *Heil Hilter* from every angle.

Gertrude feels sick to her stomach.

Within hours, the familiar doorways of her childhood, the store where her mother buys each day's groceries, the bank, and her neighbors' homes, are draped with images of swastikas. Her father shakes his head in disgust and increases the volume on Radio Free Europe. A neighbor turns him in for betraying the Third Reich. He is dragged away from his family by ss soldiers.

Four years later, Gertrude is a sixteen-year-old living at home alone with her twelve-year-old brother. Her mom has fled to her own mother in Steyrling, a small town in the Austrian Alps, to give birth to her third child far away from the German occupation of Linz. Gertrude's father, captured by the Allies, is a prisoner of war in Russia. In her parents' absence, Gertrude is the head of the household, attending school, working, and taking care of her little brother.

One gray afternoon, while she is making dinner, sirens cut through the air, followed immediately by the crescendo humming of an air raid. Gertrude and her brother tear down the stairs to the basement. Within seconds, a hard thud jolts the ground below them, knocking them against the rear wall.

After, when Gertrude and her brother force open the door to the daylight, they discover the remnants of a bomb splattered in the backyard garden. Shards of glass and wood from their home's blown-out windows and collapsed roof coat the dismembered furniture.

Across the street, corpses are stacked like piles of firewood.

In the days that follow, Gertrude and her brother pick through the wreckage, rescuing family artifacts. They sleep on the kitchen floor, the only safe space, until their mother returns from the mountains.

The following year, just after Gertrude completes her schooling, the Reich sends her to a Nazi work camp, *Arbeitsdienst*, in Czechoslovakia. She rises at 3 a.m. and dresses in a red and blue Nazi-regulated uniform to march and sing German nationalist songs. The overseers, called *Führer*, then transport Gertrude and the other female workers to a farm to chop down trees that tower over them, shave off the leaves, and then split the logs into quarters.

Outside during the winter, Gertrude sees her breath from morning until night. Her uniform fails to shield her from frigid temperatures. She has no gloves to protect her cracked and callused hands, and most days she can't feel her feet. An angry red rash erupts on her legs from the regulation wool tights.

She sleeps on a straw mattress in a Nazi barrack with eleven other girls. They take turns staying up all night, stoking the fire and adding coals to keep the *Führer* warm. In the morning, icicles surround them while they bathe in the washroom. The water freezes upon exiting the showerhead, hitting the tile like hail.

Gertrude's stomach aches from raw hunger, her daily nutrition a small bowl of pudding-flavored water and a slice of black bread. At night, she listens to the whispers throughout the barracks of sore, exhausted, and frozen bodies. One girl speaks of a camp just down the Danube River from Linz.

"They herd all the people through the doors," she says. "They never come out again."

Late in the night, after everyone else is asleep, Gertrude wonders about this camp that no one leaves, not far from her family home.

On a hot, humid day in the spring of 1995, I drive up from college to attend the Rally for Women's Lives in Washington, D.C., with three other women's studies students who are proud to call themselves feminists.

After a four-hour drive, we emerge to signs that read KEEP ABORTION LEGAL, CHOICE NOW and salute one another on the Metro and in line for the Porta Potties. On a small patch of grass on the Mall, we position ourselves among our comrades, shouting chants, singing songs of solidarity, and listening, mesmerized, to the activists advancing our cause.

To protesting pro-lifers lining the Mall, I shout, "An acorn is not a tree," confident that a metaphor about botany confers a medical understanding of the difference between an embryo or fetus and a living, breathing newborn.

Though I have never had an abortion myself, my feminist consciousness and curriculum have transformed me from a silent bystander to an activist, leading me to believe I know what it might be like to terminate a pregnancy.

In early 2001, seven years after I marched on Washington, I am pregnant for the very first time. At the six-week ultrasound, I discover evidence of life, pre-birth life. It moves and wiggles, as if signaling to me. The technician points to a beating heart.

In the few moments it takes to view a pulsing embryo in a darkened room, my whole pro-choice world is blurred. I find it impossible to deny the existence of what I can see with my own eyes. The question of viability, a term I once considered crucial in a conversation about abortion rights, seems irrelevant in light of my impending motherhood. Because when I show my friends and family members pictures from the ultrasound, I do not call it "my embryo" or "my pregnancy," I call it what I believe it truly is—my baby.

Five years later, in the summer of 2006, I am a mother to two children and expecting my third. During the pregnancy, two ultrasounds at six and nine weeks reveal a growing, thriving baby. At nine weeks, when we identify its limb buds, I imagine myself kissing hands with tiny dimples, rocking a baby to sleep in my arms, and the sensation of a newborn face pressed up against my cheek. I consider the holiday card we will send out to our family, featuring an infant sandwiched between two adoring big sisters.

Because my pregnancy is progressing well, I cavalierly dismiss my doctor's suggestion to schedule an eleven-week diagnostic ultrasound.

Because, I naively explain, we will have this baby no matter what.

After the war, at an American GI social, Gertrude is drawn to a man with dark, slicked-back hair, captivating eyes, and deeply bronzed skin. The soldier notices her, too, puts out his cigarette, and saunters over.

Gertrude learns that John is a Puerto Rican serving in the U.S. Army. They dance and laugh late into the night. He doesn't care that she can barely speak English, and she doesn't mind that falling in love with an American might mean a permanent departure from her homeland.

They marry in 1947, and in 1948 my future Oma and Opa cross the ocean by naval transport to New York City, to settle in the Puerto Rican section of the Bronx. Gertrude picks up English while ushering for movies in Times Square.

In late 1949, Gertrude becomes pregnant. Nausea wakes her at dawn and persists until late afternoon. She pats cold compresses on her forehead with one hand and, with the other, clings to the four-page letters her mother sends her every week from Austria. She boils pots of water for *Kamillentee*—chamomile tea, her mother's antidote for all stomach ailments.

In 1950, days after the beginning of the Korean War, Gertrude gives birth to a son. The U.S. Army transfers John, a brand-new father, away from his family to Trieste, Italy.

Gertrude is alone in New York with a newborn baby, her only relative a mother-in-law who detests her for her "Anglo" blood, her German tongue. During her sleepless nights, the nausea that only recently abated returns with a vengeance. She is pregnant again. Over the next few months, alone in her drafty apartment, Gertrude stumbles in the dark to fix her son a bottle before running to the bathroom to throw up.

After a few months she is reunited with John in Trieste, where she gives birth to her daughter in July 1951.

In 1952 the U.S. Army stations John in Massachusetts. Gertrude must stay behind with her infants at a hotel near a port on the Italian Riviera. She does not have her own bathroom or kitchen, and in the middle of the night she creeps down to the building's kitchen to warm milk for her two babies. Several months pass before she boards a ship back to the States with her swaddled newborn and toddler son.

Two years later, while living in Massachusetts, she gives birth to their third child.

Gertrude is worn out from being woken up two or three times a night by children's nightmares, cries for a bottle. She worries about her husband's safety in far-off lands. She is frustrated by a language where her "that" always sounds like "dat," eliciting cruel snickers from shop clerks and neighbors. She misses her family, her girlfriends from school, the taste of schnitzel and *Knödel*, and the texture of European black bread.

She is determined that this third child will be her last.

From 1954 to 1958 the family moves from Massachusetts to Alaska, to Washington State, to Texas, and then to Germany, where an old girlfriend tells Gertrude about a pill that prevents babies.

Oma wants this pill. Every month she stares into the toilet bowl in a state of panic anytime her period is late. Her younger daughter has serious vision problems; she is nearly blind in both eyes. Oma cannot imagine changing diapers and cleaning bottles again while taking care of a child with severely impaired vision.

A few weeks after she begins taking the pill, Gertrude experiences extreme dizziness and nausea. Lying on the floor, she watches the ceiling mercilessly spin above her. She can barely walk across a room without stopping for a break.

Gertrude flushes the remaining pills down the toilet, begs John to help her prevent another pregnancy. He refuses. He is a proud Puerto Rican Catholic man and sees no need to deny his seed its rightful territory.

In 1962, Gertrude's period is late. She frantically checks her underwear before each bath. Her stomach bloats, her breasts return to their familiar ache. She curses at John and throws shoes at the wall in their tiny flat. She muffles her cries in the wool coat that hangs in their closet.

She grows round with another pregnancy, gives birth to her fourth child, her third daughter, and then the following year she, John, and their four children sail back across the ocean, heading this time to El Paso, Texas.

With a family of six, the refrigerator sits nearly empty. John's military salary barely meets their household expenses. Gertrude must get a job. She turns over much of the baby's caretaking to her eldest daughter, who is now twelve.

While her four children are still sleeping, Gertrude rises at 4 a.m. and drives in the dark to the local bakery to knead bread dough, mix batter, and squirt icing on cookies for eight hours. She returns just as her children arrive home, where she begins an afternoon and evening of cooking, cleaning, and mending. She collapses into bed late at night, with only a few hours of sleep before her alarm goes off again.

Shortly before her fortieth birthday, the nausea returns. Her breasts burn. Her underwear remains unstained. She is pregnant, again.

This time she is resolute. She tells John, point-blank, that she is getting rid of it. John knows his wife; he knows she means what she says. He does not want her to do it alone.

One evening just before sunset, Gertrude and John leave their four children at home and drive to downtown El Paso. They park their car near the foot of the Sante Fe Bridge and walk over the slow trickle of dingy water known as the Rio Grande into Juárez, Mexico. She smooths the skirt of her black dress and keeps her eyes forward. He pretends to enjoy the landscape—slum houses of corrugated metal, mud, and cardboard.

When they reach the Mexican side, they hail a cab to a hospital. An army buddy has told John, "The taxi driver will know exactly where to take you."

Soon after entering the hospital, Oma is surrounded by Spanish voices used to caring for American women. They gown her quickly and lay her down. Oma concentrates on her children at home to calm her nerves while the staff begins administering the anesthesia.

After the surgery, my grandparents retrace their steps over the bridge. This time Gertrude shuffles slowly across the border while holding on to John's arm. He resignedly pats her hand and helps her into the car. They arrive home by midnight.

When John is stationed in Germany again, Gertrude becomes pregnant two more times. Her second abortion occurs while on "vacation" in Austria, where a midwife, a friend of the family, will "take care of it" in Gertrude's mother's home.

Oma lies on her back, without anesthesia, while the midwife inserts a catheter to open her uterus. After the midwife leaves, the cramping and bleeding begin. Gertrude miscarries the following day. The entire family returns to Germany a few days later.

The following year, she boards the train from Germany to Austria, again under the guise of a vacation. This time, hours after the procedure, buckets of blood drench her dress. Her mother paces back and forth, examining the rags and the debris in the toilet, searching for an expelled lump.

There is nothing but blood.

The next morning, Gertrude is rushed to the hospital in Linz. On the way, Gertrude's mother mutters prayers of the rosary under her breath. Angela fears they are too late when she sees the blood soaking the towels that she placed under Gertrude in the car.

The doctor who will perform the D&C flips impatiently through the patient chart, shakes his head at Gertrude's stained and gowned body—this botched, illegal abortion. He asks her, since she is married, why would she end her pregnancy?

On the verge of losing consciousness, while the blood continues to flow onto the hospital floor, Gertrude recalls the *Arbeitsdienst*, the American GI social where she met her husband, suitcases in strange lands splayed open with clothes for four children, her two youngest children with severe vision impairment, the yeast-scented bakery before sunrise, morning sickness, the sleeplessness and stresses of new motherhood.

"Because," she replies in her native tongue, "I am tired. I do not want any more."

On a Tuesday one month after my D&C, the phone rings. I don't hesitate to pick it up—phone calls to my house have finally returned to the routine of annoying telemarketers and friends scheduling play dates, not offerings of apologies for my loss that cause me to sob into my tea.

My doctor's voice surprises me. "The baby was a boy," she says.

The genetic testing revealed a chromosomal abnormality. He would never have survived the pregnancy.

I concentrate on not dropping the phone, and after hanging up, I sob over the kitchen sink while dinner burns on the stove.

Later that night I pull out my ultrasound photos, scanning closely for evidence of a life gone awry. I see nothing but a sweet, perfect baby.

The following spring, the raw pain and grief of miscarriage subside. When a friend becomes pregnant, I insist that she show me her ultrasound picture.

She hesitates before pulling the thin paper out of her wallet. My hand is shaking when I grasp it. Numbers crowd out its top right corner, indicating she is eleven weeks along. I identify the baby's limbs, its curved torso, and a tiny, upturned nose.

I wonder who this child might be: An athlete or a thespian? A teacher or a scientist? An introvert, an extrovert? I remember what it's like to have hope, to conceive dreams for a baby who is mere months away from taking its first breath, to guess at personality traits, to create a vision for a family.

In that moment, while smoothing the creases of the waxy paper, I uncover an uncomfortable truth about my third pregnancy, my capabilities as a mother, and the limits of what I mistook for unconditional love: If I had shown up for my eleven-week diagnostic ultrasound and, instead of seeing a nonviable fetus, found a struggling, misshapen life—

I would have had an abortion.

Opa dies of a heart attack in 1980, when I am six years old, leaving Oma a widow at the age of fifty-three. Her three older children are grown, her youngest child, my aunt, a senior in high school.

She has been working for years in the shoe section of a large department store, fetching several sizes of the latest heels, wedging sneakers onto cranky toddlers, ringing up back-to-school loafers. At the end of each shift, her knees and ankles were sore from bending and prying. The arthritis flared up in her wrists from threading and lacing.

Her low wage, along with her husband's military pension, barely covers the living expenses for her and her youngest child. Had she not had the abortions, Opa's death would have left her a single mother to three more much younger children.

Oma has many regrets. She regrets the war that separated her from her family, the loss of her beloved homeland to the Nazi regime, the loneliness and isolation she experienced as a foreigner in foreign lands, the limited options for birth control in the 1960s, Opa's premature death, and the pregnancies she never wanted.

But she does not regret getting the abortions.

And while I, her first grandchild, will never fully understand what it might be like to have led such a life, or to terminate a pregnancy, I have evolved from the college student who feigned empathy for another person's dilemma on the Mall in Washington, D.C., the textbook feminist with the good fortune to view life in black and white, into a mother armed with hindsight and history—both mine and Oma's—who now knows what it might be like to regret conception, to confront despair, to grieve the lack of second chances, to become pregnant with a baby I would have loved but never would have birthed.

Because if I shed my politics and my preferences, and separate my love from my logic, I find myself telling a different kind of story about my pregnancy and loss: Only luck and a few weeks' time made the difference between what ended as my miscarriage and what could have been my abortion.

In the summer of 2007, after two more miscarriages, I am pregnant again. Though this pregnancy is free from complications, anxiety plagues and controls my day. I have panic attacks, frantically call family members when a few minutes pass without feeling the baby's movement. Nightmares, restlessness, and insomnia.

When I have an ultrasound, I refuse to look at the screen until the technician confirms a heartbeat.

Oma, now in her eighties, lives two hours north in a retirement home, enduring the same stresses about my baby's health. Although she is decades beyond her own pregnancies, she senses the urgency of my own. She has assumed an understanding of technology and terminology—crown-to-rump measurement and beta hCG level—that didn't exist when she was building her own family. She knows the day and time of each pregnancy appointment and distracts herself with soap operas and game shows until the phone rings with good news.

During our monthly visits, when we sit together on the couch, I lift her hand and place it on my belly. When we feel the baby's kicks, we breathe a sigh of relief.

Had she not gone blind after retiring from the shoe department, Oma would have packed up her belongings, sold her small ranch home, and made one final journey back across the ocean to the Austrian Alps, the Danube, and the geography of her childhood—minus the violence of war.

But instead she remains here, in her adopted country, awaiting the arrival of her newest great-grandchild.

A few days after I give birth to my third daughter, my mother brings Oma to the doorway of my home, where I greet her with a hug and guide her slowly by the elbow through the foyer, into the living room.

Oma leans over, feels for the edge of our leather sofa, and follows it around to the far armrest. I adjust the pillows behind her back and position my restless newborn along her forearm, in the crook of her elbow.

Her measured rocking quiets the baby immediately. It's as if my sweet daughter has been waiting all morning for the comfort of her great-grandmother.

I cross to the other side, lower myself slowly onto the adjacent sofa cushion. My head rests easily on Oma's shoulder, and the hypnotic rise and fall of her chest eases my eyes closed. As my shoulders release the stress and tension of the last nine months, and of the last couple of years of grief, I find, at my grandmother's side, a deep, restful sleep.

On the Unbearable Whiteness
of Southern Literature

The first white-authored southern novel I read when my family moved from Michigan to Tennessee was Olive Ann Burns's *Cold Sassy Tree*. It told the story of a preteen boy named Will Tweedy whose family is thrust into scandal when his grandfather, newly widowed, marries a much younger woman.[1] The story takes place in the early 1900s in northeast Georgia, but the book was published in 1984, the very same year I officially became a southerner. Small-town gossip was still very much a force eighty years later, and that novel helped me understand the ways it traveled and changed narratives, especially in the Deep South.

In the vast majority of white-authored southern novels I read, nostalgia served as a harbinger for racism, and southern pride was a stand-in for white fragility. These books were tethered and intoxicated by a romanticized, anti-Black, and whitewashed history of the South.

Enter Harper Lee's iconic *To Kill a Mockingbird*, first published in 1960.[2] To use a term made popular by Spike Lee and sociologist Matthew Hughey, "It is the time-honored Magical Negro narrative."[3]

Many of us who grew up in the South know this novel by heart. White attorney Atticus Finch of sleepy Maycomb, Alabama, represents Tom Robinson, a Black man who has been accused of rape by a white woman, Mayella Ewell. In the book we learn a good deal about Atticus, his quiet, moral manner, his tenderness with his children, his kindness toward their Black cook, Calpurnia, and the lengths to which he will go to seek justice.

He is our hero. He is our white savior.

We don't learn a whole lot about Tom. This is because Tom only functions as a device (a Magical Negro) to educate the white characters Jem, Scout, and Dill (as well as white readers) about injustice. We don't know much about Tom's family, his interests, his personality. All Lee needed from Tom was for him to be the victim, and for white characters to understand racism through his victimization. Hence Tom has no dimensionality or characterization.

To Kill a Mockingbird's descendent, John Grisham's 1989 book *A Time to Kill*,[4] fails in a similar fashion. Jake Brigance replaces Atticus Finch as the white savior to defend a Black man named Carl Lee Hailey who is on trial for killing the men who gang-raped his young daughter in Clanton, Mississippi.

Carl Lee has a slightly meatier role in *A Time To Kill* than *Mockingbird*'s Tom Robinson, but he is still a flat character whose primary function is to elevate the heroism of Jake Brigance and teach white characters about racism. Carl Lee's child has been terrorized and traumatized, but it's Jake who gets our attention. It's his fears and future that are centered in the story.

Both *To Kill a Mockingbird* and *A Time to Kill* fetishize Black pain to redeem white characters, and in doing so they also redeem the non-Black readers who can celebrate an ending where justice is (supposedly) done. These novels then feed into an equally racist metanarrative whereby the mere act of reading these books transforms white and non-Black readers of color into less racist people.

The consumption of these books is wholly performative. It affords readers the false sense that they've achieved a deep understanding about racist structures and racial distributions of power, so they can become the white savior in their *own* narrative about racism. *I'm not like them. I'm not racist! I'm a good person!* This frees them from more closely examining their own internalized racism and acknowledging their complicity in systemic racism.

I know this because I've heard non-Black readers say as much. In the 1980s and early 1990s, when I encountered these books for the first time, conversations with white southerners invoked a popular refrain. *We need to remember our pasts.* This ambiguous penance erased present-day racism and their own role in it. In the white imagination, the act of reading, followed by the act of *remembering*, served as the act of undoing racism.

This is the toxic life cycle that reading racist white southern literature continues to perpetuate.

Let me say here, briefly, that when I first encountered many of these texts as a teenager in the 1980s, I was incapable of parsing the white supremacy infused in their narratives. How could I? I was steeped in whiteness myself. Most of my cultural references were white. My seemingly evolved white teachers, whom I loved, praised these books. I read *To Kill a Mockingbird* for the first time at age twelve, and it remained my favorite book until my mid-twenties. I devoured Margaret Mitchell's *Gone with the Wind* at age thirteen, and if asked, I would have likely deemed it the quintessential southern novel. After all, this is what I had been told.

Decades before movements like #WeNeedDiverseBooks and #OwnVoices, I believed that white southern authors who told stories about Black pain were performing a valuable service to the non-Black community.

So why shouldn't their books be celebrated?

In the summer of 1999, I read Melinda Haynes's debut novel *Mother of Pearl*.[5] The book is set in the small town of Petal, Mississippi, in the 1950s. It tells the story of a friendship between a twenty-eight-year-old Black man named Even Grade and a fifteen-year-old white girl named Valuable Korner. The book has issues throughout, but the end in particular is wholly incognizant of the racist forces of the day. Spoiler alert: after Valuable dies giving birth to a son she names Pearl (whose father is no longer in her life), Even Grade decides to raise Valuable's white son as his own. Apparently the white baby's summer tan will cure anyone's suspicion about whether this white child belongs to a Black man. End of story.

Mother of Pearl was the first book that gave me pause about all of the white-authored southern novels I'd treasured before it.

When I learned that Oprah named *Mother of Pearl* as her next book club pick, I filled out an online form on her website to relay my sharp critique about the book. To my shock, a producer from the show called and wanted to hear more about what I thought. They were considering inviting me to be a guest on Oprah's book club show. A second producer called a few days later for a more extended interview.

I was no critic back then. I was twenty-five years old, one year out of law school, and a judicial clerk for two judges in Family Court in Delaware. I didn't possess the kind of language I have today to home in on exactly why I found the book to be problematic. I fumbled for words and repeated myself. The best I could do was describe the book as "unrealistic." But even that word seemed wholly inadequate for the issues I found in the book.

Unbelievably, the producers found my responses worthy. They flew me to Chicago to discuss *Mother of Pearl* with Oprah herself, Haynes, and a few other readers. The limousine ride from O'Hare to the hotel downtown was my first ever.

Oprah is as luminous in real life as she is on television. After we situated ourselves on sofas, she breezed into the studio, sat on a sofa next to Haynes, and proceeded to conduct the conversation with grace and wit. At one point I managed to express my disappointment with the end of the book in a way that was more gentle than in my interviews with producers—Haynes was sitting right there, after all—but before I could fully state my case, Oprah moved on to another part of the book. That short clip is pretty much my only contribution to what later aired of the book club show. The producers wanted an episode that praised Haynes and the book, and that's exactly what they got.

I flew back to Philadelphia wondering, for the first time ever, what it was that I loved so much about white southern literature.

Much has been said about Kathryn Stockett's 2009 debut novel *The Help*,[6] which has since sold more than ten million copies. The book tells the story of a white aspiring writer named Eugenia "Skeeter"

Phelan who attempts to improve the lives of Black maids in 1960s Mississippi, specifically those of Aibileen and Minny, by literally telling their stories in a book titled *Help* that Skeeter hopes to sell to a big New York publishing house.

In summary, a white author (Skeeter) mines the voices of Black maids (Aibileen, Minny, and several others) to sell her own book (*Help*), much as Stockett herself mined the voice of the Black maid who raised her (Demetrie) to sell her own debut book (*The Help*). By writing the book, Stockett herself becomes the white savior in her own real-life narrative where her debut novel rids the world of racism. And by embodying the voices of Black maids, she carries with pride the torch that Harper Lee and John Grisham have passed to her.

I'll defer to the wise critics—that is, the Black critics—who vigorously and justifiably skewered *The Help*. Roxane Gay's brilliant 2011 essay in *The Rumpus*, "The Solace of Preparing Fried Foods and other Quaint Remembrances" (which focused on the movie as opposed to the novel), challenged the absurd fascination with a story that tried, and failed, to narrate racism: "In *The Help*, there are not one but twelve or thirteen magical negroes who use their mystical negritude to make the world a better place by sharing their stories of servitude and helping Eugenia 'Skeeter' Phelan grow out of her awkwardness and insecurity into a confident, racially aware, independent career woman. It's an embarrassment of riches for fans of the magical negro trope."[7]

White critics, though, heaped praise. I will never be able to scrub my mind of the headline of one review in USA *Today*: "Good 'Help' Isn't Hard to Find, Thanks to Kathryn Stockett."[8] *The Help*'s white critical acclaim catapulted the book into the zeitgeist, spawning what I'll call *The Help* Effect. White readers, white critics, and white media anointed Stockett as *the* voice of the South. Her book gave the white savior / Magical Negro trope a shiny updated best-selling exterior.

Interviews with Stockett saturated the media. Many were nauseating. In the *Guardian*, Stockett described the Black maid who raised her. "Yes, she was called Demetrie. I started writing in her voice because it felt really soothing. It was like talking directly to her, showing her that I was trying to understand, even though I would never claim to know what that experience was like. It's impossible to know what she felt like, going home to her house, turning on her black-and-white TV. And I'm not saying I feel sorry for her, because she was a very proud woman."[9] The interview becomes more unbearable as it goes on. When asked whether President Obama's election is a sign that racism has decreased, Stockett turns to the theory of color-blindness. "I think if you're president, colour goes away completely: you're president and it doesn't matter if you're white, green or purple."[10]

This was not an isolated sentiment. It embodied a new, postracial South, one that white southern readers were more than ready to pounce on.

There is an enormous range and depth of Black southern authors, and it is these authors who deliver, time and again, authentic, riveting stories about the Deep South. When I read Alice Walker's *The Color Purple*, I recognized something in that book that I couldn't articulate as an eighth-grader—that unlike white-authored novels I'd read, this novel didn't exist to teach or show or prove anything to me. The same can be said about my first time reading Zora Neale Hurston's *Their Eyes Were Watching God*. Janie's fierce independence and her unwillingness to conform to societal norms went against every stereotype I held about women in the Deep South. And after I first discovered Maya Angelou's *I Know Why the Caged Bird Sings*, I fell in love all over again with language. I carried that book around in my backpack for months.

What I didn't realize in childhood that I can see more clearly today is how southern literature has always been a genre of exclusion. Identity determines an author's southern-ness more than the setting itself.

According to the 2010 census, 55 percent of Black people live in the southeastern United States.[11] Yet there are not nearly as many Black southern authors as there should be, and white southern authors all too often pen southern stories that belong to Black people.

The Deep South first belonged to Indigenous people. Yet too few southern Indigenous books have been published. "It's important that people in the South realize that they are living on Native land," said Choctaw Nation author LeAnne Howe in an interview.[12] "By ignoring or not knowing or never having thought of Indians before, you've really cut yourself out of hundreds and hundreds of years of experiences of the people that came before."

I can only imagine the number of Black and Native writers querying agents and editors with their southern stories. Or, for that matter, the number of Cuban American writers in Mississippi. Or Cambodian writers in Louisiana. Or Venezuelan American writers in Tennessee. Or Iranian American writers in Texas. The South has always been far more racially diverse than southern literature has reflected.

For years I pitched a novel about an Indian immigrant family who ran a gas station in a small North Georgia town. The family's lives were tangled in secrets dating back to a tragic accident a decade earlier. The book was about the bitterness that comes from unfulfilled dreams, the isolation one can feel when living far from a major urban center, and the toxic small-town gossip that can shape a family's narrative. The novel was as southern as a southern novel can get.

I submitted the book for many years. Several agents said they weren't sure how to sell it or didn't know who the intended audience was. I had grown up surrounded by southern books. This was an authentic southern story. I myself was southern. Why couldn't they sell it as such?

A few years later, a white southern author published a novel that featured white characters and wove in elements of Hindu mythology. The book embodied the perfect formula for the white gaze, southern sensibility, and a dash of Indian garnish to deem it both marketable to white readers *and* exotic. Here I was, an Indian southerner trying to sell a southern story about Indian southerners at a time when no other Indian southern author was publishing novels about the South. And a white southern author beat me to it.

In 2019 my reckoning took the form of another novel by another

Indian American author from the South, Devi S. Laskar's poetic debut *The Atlas of Reds and Blues*.[13] Though she now makes her home on the West Coast, Laskar grew up in North Carolina and spent several years in Georgia working and raising her children. The book tells the story of an Indian immigrant known only as Mother who is shot by law enforcement and bleeding in her driveway in a suburb of Atlanta. As Mother's life slowly drains from her body, scenes flash before her shaped by the region where she and her family have made their home, a region that has never welcomed them, where they are seen as foreign, where they are watched and surveilled. "From the periphery of her eye she makes out the women, white on white and peroxide blond glistening in the Monday sun, aviators reflecting as they stand guard over the clipped grass and pressure-washed concrete, chess pieces waiting for the next move."[14]

Atlas is a reminder that there are many stories about the South that have yet to be told, and that the South is far more racially and ethnically diverse than the publishing industry has ever perceived it. It is a region rich in history, in people, and in the stories Indigenous, Black, and other writers of color are feverishly writing every day, waiting, hoping, that they will someday see the light.

III Social Change

We ourselves must begin practicing in the social realm
the capacity to care for each other.

—GRACE LEE BOGGS

Gun Show

The air is warm. A thin sliver of sunshine peeks out from behind the clouds.

I am at the dining room table facing the window, my right palm flat across the grains, my body a lump of coal. I have stayed up way too late again, scrolling through the news on my laptop, trying to make sense of this country, and of how to raise children in it.

Two days earlier, on Valentine's Day, shortly after my cheery youngest child had left for school with a backpack stuffed full of valentines for her beloved classmates, a gunman entered Marjory Stoneman Douglas High School in Parkland, Florida, and murdered fourteen students and three faculty.

A dancer. A best friend. A coach. A soccer player.

Gone.

Another community destroyed by gun violence.

My heart, my mind, is with Parkland.

Six years earlier.

A gunman enters Sandy Hook Elementary School and shoots twenty first-graders and six staff members.

That year, all three of my children are in elementary school. My hands tremble until I hear the final school bell ring from my front porch, until I see my babies bound off the yellow school bus and feel them in my arms.

They don't yet know the horrors of that day, that we parents have been holding our breaths until the moment we can squeeze their little bodies against our chests, run our fingers through their hair, gaze once more upon their fleeting innocence. For them, school still means beloved teachers and fuzzy rugs with patchwork designs, "line leaders," squeaky sneakers on gym floors, and hula hoops at recess.

I keep the shooting from my kids for as long as I can. They are years away from owning phones, from being on social media. The immediacy of the news is the one thing I can still control about the big, terrifying world around them. But within a few days, first my fifth-grader knows, and then my third grader. My baby, a four-year-old in prekindergarten, is the only one blissfully unaware of the tragedy that day.

The cocoon we form around our children is porous. Eventually everything finds its way in.

The years dissolve. As I sit at the dining room table, reading about funeral arrangements for community members of Parkland, my children are older, stretched across three different schools—one in high school, one in middle school, one in elementary school.

A morbid thought enters my mind. I bristle at its truth. *At least if there's a school shooting, only one of them might die. I wouldn't lose all three at once.*

A few hours later, when I'm deep into work and have forgotten, for just a few minutes, about Parkland, I receive a text from my high school sophomore. "Mom, the fire alarm went off. We never have fire drills during lunch period." I reread my daughter's message a few times before I can fully grasp the meaning behind it, before the weight of it brings my knees to the floor. Our children have attended schools in this same district for twelve years. Scheduled fire drills never occur during lunch periods. Students are in class-rooms, in the gym, the media center, or at recess—never in the cafeteria.

When I am finally able to exhale, I respond: "Keep your wits about you and if anything happens run as fast and as far away as you can." It's an absurd reply. If this is an actual active shooter situa-tion, my daughter would be prevented from leaving school. Instead, in accordance to our district's lockdown protocol, teachers would huddle students into darkened rooms. They'd congregate under desks or in closets to silently wait out their fates. Even though there's virtually no evidence to support this procedure, students would be prohibited from leaving campus.[1] They would be forced to suppress any flight instinct they might have.

When we moved to this Atlanta suburb, one of the most appealing aspects of our new neighborhood was its proximity to the schools—the elementary and middle schools are walking distance, and the high school is a few miles down the road. If my children got sick, I could pick them up quickly and bring them home.

My thoughts about our home's short distance to the kids' schools has shifted dramatically over the years. *If there's a shooting, maybe I can reach the school quickly enough to stop it myself.*

Soon after Sandy Hook, lockdown drills commenced. Our school district eliminated the former "open door policy" the following year, and anyone entering the building had to be buzzed in by the receptionist at the front desk. Parents were screened and certified before volunteering at their own children's schools. Our tight-knit, neighborly community was imbued with suspicion. Our children were traumatized with reminders that at any moment a person could enter their classrooms and shoot them.

At every annual "well" visit, our pediatrician asks me whether we have guns in our home, and if we do, whether we keep them locked safely away. She never asks whether the epidemic of mass shootings has taken a toll on my daughters, whether lockdown drills at their schools cause them distress, whether they have nightmares of hiding behind their backpacks in dark corners as a gunman blasts through the doors of their classrooms.

For several minutes, my sophomore's reply remains a blinking text bubble that refuses to produce language. It then disappears completely. A lifeline abrupted.

I send more texts.

"Are you okay?"

"Please, tell me what's happening."

"Honey, I'm worried about you."

I instantly regret it. If my daughter takes the time to text back, she will jeopardize her own safety. I debate whether I should drive to the school or stay off the road so that the police can reach there more rapidly. I consider calling the front desk, but worry about occupying the school's main phone line. My mind races with images of students huddling under desks, kids we've known since they were all babies together in kindergarten, my daughter among them, as a school shooter stalks the hallways.

My phone vibrates with the panic of other parents—each ping a piercing foghorn. My husband calls from work and tries to reassure me that everything is fine, but I can sense the uncertainty behind his words. My neighbor is so shaken she jumps into a friend's car and races to the school. Somehow my own feet remain rooted to the floor of the living room.

I am frantic, on call after call with other parents, when a text from my daughter finally appears. She is safe. She and her schoolmates are all safe. They were never in any real danger.

Later we piece together the narrative.

Two days after Parkland, a SnapChat post originally published in 2017 resurfaced.[2] A white male is showing off what looks like a military-grade rifle in his right hand, its barrel pointed to the ceiling. The caption reads "Don't come to school tomorrow @Northview." Northview, our school, is also the name of a high school in Dothan, Alabama, the intended target. And what appears to be a weapon is actually a paintball gun.

The post had begun making the rounds among the students at my daughter's high school. A student who saw it pulled the fire alarm. The building went into lockdown.

I remember watching news reports after the shootings at Columbine, Sandy Hook, Virginia Tech, Marysville Pilchuck High School, and Umpqua Community College. Video footage scanned gently sloping lawns, brick buildings, sidewalks shaded by trees, benches, tall windows sparkling in the sunshine, level parking lots filled with police cars. I remember searching for telltale signs of vulnerability in the landscape that might foreshadow the danger that awaited those campuses, but finding none.

Two days after Parkland, the media sets up shop at our own school, which nearly every child we know between the age of fourteen and eighteen attends. Reporters flank the brown brittle grasses near the bus lane with their microphones, their steely eyes, their tight jawlines. They speak directly to the cameras about "the incident."

The beige-and-brown brick building sits proudly in the background. A long green awning juts out to the sidewalk. Thick pillars stand like soldiers on either side of the front entrance pathway. The place where my child spends eight hours a day appears as ordered and unassuming as any other campus in the United States that has experienced bloodshed.

My daughter's school could have easily been a mass shooter's next target.

The principal assures us in an email that our children are safe but are allowed to go home for the day if they so wish.

My daughter decides to attend the rest of her classes. When she returns home that afternoon, I try to hold myself back to give her some time and space to breathe, to process. I have many questions about what happened, and I know she'll eventually answer them. But in that moment, after she kicks off her shoes and settles at the kitchen counter, I ask her just one: "Why did you stay at school?"

Her response continues to haunt me.

"I might as well get used to this."

These are the days of our lives, two days after Parkland.

Two days after Parkland.

Truthfully, I do not know whether it is two days after Parkland. Perhaps it is twenty minutes or three or four days after Parkland. Perhaps it is three weeks after Parkland. But it is surely no more than that.

Lucia "Lucy" McBath, a spokesperson for Moms Demand Action for Gun Sense for America, who has begun campaigning for a seat in the Georgia State House, changes her mind.[3] She decides to run for Congress in the Sixth Congressional District, my home district, instead.[4]

On November 23, 2012, only nine months after George Zimmerman killed seventeen-year-old Trayvon Martin in Sanford, Florida, Michael Dunn gunned down McBath's seventeen-year-old son Jordan Davis in Jacksonville, Florida. Though a jury determined Zimmerman's shooting was self defense, under Florida's Stand-your-ground law, Davis's killer, Michael Dunn, was convicted of murder.

In her book *Standing Our Ground: The Truth and Triumph of Faith over Gun Violence*, McBath writes of her son's killing as the beginning of her journey to bring gun sense to the United States: "I was too lost in grief and anguish to realize that through Jordan, I was already being guided to a purpose greater than any I could have dreamed for myself. It was a call to action that I would come to understand had been mine all along."[5]

Early in the Democratic primary race, I meet McBath at an event on the second floor of a coffee shop in Chamblee, Georgia. She sits in the middle of a line of small square tables that have been pushed together. My friend and I are late, but we somehow manage to find seats right next to her. At the beginning of this intimate gathering, I am uncertain who I will vote for. But McBath is soft-spoken, warm, and personable. She listens intently to voters' concerns. She talks about gun violence, but also the health-care crisis in the United States, and the state of public schools. By the end of the morning, I've made up my mind. She will have my vote.

Still, I have doubts. Not about whether she's capable of doing the job, but about whether voters in this district will give her the opportunity. I worked myself to the bone as a volunteer for Jon Ossoff's campaign for the same seat in 2017. We came so close but lost.

Could a gun-sense candidate like McBath win a historically Republican district in a gun-loving, voter-suppressing state like Georgia?

Two months after Parkland, April 2018.

A man is sitting slightly slouched in a black leather chair. He's wearing a light blue button-down shirt. His legs, in blue jeans, are splayed open. He is polishing a rifle.

The text along the bottom of the screen reads *Brian Kemp Conservative Businessman*, though it omits a crucial detail. Kemp is currently serving as Georgia's secretary of state, the office that oversees elections, while also running to be the Republican nominee for governor.

This is a political ad, this mini gun show.[6] It is propaganda that plays up the mythology that people, specifically white people, are under attack. That they must arm themselves.

The rifle is pointed loosely in the direction of Jake, a young white man seated to Kemp's left who avowedly wants to date one of Kemp's young daughters. Kemp is threatening to kill Jake if he's not respectful. Of course he doesn't use those exact words, but the messaging is crystal clear. The ad concludes after Jake parrots Kemp's platform and hails the Second Amendment.

Two months after Parkland, Secretary of State Brian Kemp threatens a young man with gun violence in an ad. It is a grotesque flexing of the deep-seated tradition of white male entitlement to terrorism and vigilantism. It's emblematic of the state's militarization and policing of its own people.[7]

But the ad holds a deeper significance, too. In the context of an election year, with crucial contests on the ballot (including his own), it is a veiled threat to voters, specifically the likely Democratic Black voters whose voting rights have historically been suppressed by the State of Georgia, specifically by Brian Kemp himself.

The outrage over the ad comes swiftly, but it doesn't derail his campaign. He beats Lieutenant Governor Casey Cagle in the Republican primary election in July, and that November, Brian Kemp becomes the eighty-third governor of Georgia.

Also two months after Parkland.

It is early on a Saturday morning. Thirty-six-year-old Shukri Ali Said is hearing voices in Johns Creek, Georgia, only four miles away from my home. Her sister, Aisha, is not able to calm her. Shukri leaves the house she shares with Aisha's family and begins walking through their neighborhood.

Aisha wants help to transport Shukri, who has bipolar disorder and schizophrenia, to the hospital. She calls 911, explains that her sister is in the midst of a mental health episode, and says that she is walking through their neighborhood with a knife.[8] Shukri, like the rest of her family, is a Somali American and a Muslim. She is wearing a hijab and an abaya. After the call, Aisha awaits word that her sister has been found safe and sound.

That is not what happens.

Four Johns Creek police officers, Derrick Wilson, Ken Kennebrew, Phil Nguyen, and Richard Gray, accost Shukri just outside her neighborhood, right across the street from my daughter's high school. A dash cam recording shows the events leading up to Shukri's death. The Georgia Bureau of Investigation has allowed only Shukri's family (not even their attorneys) to view it.[9] This is the family's account of the last few minutes of Shukri's life:

After the officers confront her, Shukri walks away from them. She clutches her passport, repeats she wants to "go home." Within a minute or two after the officers approach Shukri, they tase her and shoot her with a bean bag.

"You shot me," Shukri says.

Two officers then shoot her with real guns. After the first round, she collapses to the ground, face down. She gets up while clutching her chest, and walks away from them. She is shot again, for a total of five times, and falls.

While Shukri is lying at their feet, the officers contemplate her background. One wonders whether she's Pakistani. Another muses she is Black. One of the officers says something along the lines of, *There are Black people here?*

The officers laugh.[10]

EMTs at the scene rush her to the hospital, where she is pronounced dead. From time stamps on the neighborhood security camera footage and the dash cam footage, it appears that the entire encounter with the police lasts no longer than three minutes.

I did not know Shukri or her family at the time of Shukri's death, but I reach out to Aisha to see if I can help in any way. We scout out a place for her sister's memorial service and order balloons. On a bright sunny afternoon at a local park, friends, family, and community members gather to share their love for Shukri. At its conclusion, we release the balloons into the sky.

That summer, the officers are reinstated to full duty. Because they have refused to cooperate with the Fulton County District Attorney's Office, no criminal charges have ever been brought against them.

Two years after her death, the police shooting of Shukri Ali Said has faded from the minds of local residents.[11] In June 2020, at a march in Johns Creek following the police killings of George Floyd in Minneapolis and Rayshard Brooks in Atlanta, my daughter holds a sign that reads *Justice for Shukri Ali Said*. Several people who live only a few miles from where she died ask us who she is. They have never heard about her or her violent death.

The appalling reality is that because the world could not witness Shukri's death, too few people will ever know about her life. For any Black person to have a chance at justice in a police or vigilante killing, there must be a video. There must be a gun show. For their lives to have mattered, they must meet the highest possible evidentiary bar—a viral video and a social media hashtag that will bring worldwide condemnation.

Two years after Parkland.

Twenty-five-year-old Ahmaud Arbery, a former high school football player and avid runner, goes for a jog in Brunswick, Georgia, on February 23, 2020. Three men in two vehicles soon follow—a father and son, Gregory and Travis McMichael, and their neighbor, William "Roddie" Bryan Jr. The McMichaels, armed with a handgun and shotguns, believe (wrongly) that Arbery is a burglar. They place two 911 calls during their pursuit. In the first call, Travis reports that Arbery is walking through a house under construction. Even the 911 dispatcher sounds bewildered as to the nature of the call: "I just need to know what he was doing wrong."[12]

After Arbery leaves, the McMichaels chase him down in their pickup truck. They find him running in the middle of the road. Bryan, still behind the McMichaels in his truck, records what he sees with his phone.

Arbery tries to avoid a confrontation, but the McMichaels and Bryan work together to block him. At one point Bryan hits Arbery with the side of his own truck. While Gregory remains in the McMichaels' truck's bed, Travis steps out of the driver's side and shoots Arbery, first in the hand,[13] and then twice more in the chest at close range.[14] Meanwhile Bryan records the entire slaying silently with a hand as steady as a rock. He doesn't plead with the McMichaels to stop. He doesn't call for help. He doesn't make a sound.

Bryan turns in his video footage of Arbery's death to law enforcement immediately. Two different district attorneys view it. The first, Jackie Johnson, recuses herself quickly. The second, George E. Barnhill, eventually recuses himself as well, after reaching the bizarre conclusion that there was no probable cause to arrest the McMichaels: "It appears their intent was to stop and hold this criminal suspect until law enforcement arrived. Under Georgia Law this is perfectly legal."[15]

Even with a recording, the injustice of Arbery's killing doesn't register in the white imagination. It isn't until two months later, when an attorney named Alan Tucker releases Bryan's video to the public, that nationwide outrage pressures the Georgia Bureau of Investigation to arrest the McMichaels and charge them with murder and aggravated assault, and later charge Bryan with felony murder.[16] Tucker, like the others, seems to have believed the video actually exonerated the McMichaels and Bryan.

At least three white people versed in the law watched the vigilante slaying of Ahmaud Arbery and concluded that his white killers were innocent.

How many people have to see an unjustified killing of a Black person to determine guilt? And how many non-Black people walk free because there never was a video to begin with?

Those of us fortunate enough to live in safe family environments, in neighborhoods not over-policed, where we will *not* be shot on sight by law enforcement because of our race, ethnicity, religion, nationality, gender identity, sexual identity, ability, or class—we live in a bubble, one shaped by privilege. After motor vehicle accidents, the second highest cause of death for children is gun violence, and this violence does not primarily occur at schools.[17] It happens everywhere—in homes and in the streets.

A fear centered only on school shootings, festival shootings, or movie theater shootings is a fear rooted in privilege. And this privilege erases the fear and risk of death that other, far more marginalized people experience every day. Mikki Kendall addresses this in her book *Hood Feminism*: "If you look outside the bubble that privilege has created where you don't have to worry about gun violence on a regular basis, you'll see it's a public epidemic that we ignore. Every state, every city, and every income level has been impacted by gun violence.[18] Any strategy to combat the gun violence epidemic in the United States falls short unless it addresses the disproportionate impact on Indigenous, Black, and other people of color who routinely encounter gun violence and experience trauma from it. We have no pathway forward in this movement unless or until we address this.

Gun-sense activists, including Moms Demand Action, have had hundreds of victories in their fight against the National Rifle Association and pro-gun elected officials.[19] Since it formed in 2012, Moms Demand has pressured businesses including Walmart, Kroger, and Aldi to prohibit "open carry" at stores. Louisiana Moms Demand members have prevented the state from expanding stand-your-ground at faith-based institutions.[20] Nevada members have succeeded in pressuring lawmakers to pass legislation mandating extensive background checks for guns bought in the state.[21]

None of these gun-sense victories happened in Georgia, where I live, except one.

McBath, who had lost her only child to gun violence, entered the brutal arena of politics, ran for Congress in Georgia's Sixth

Congressional District, the district of former House Speaker Newt Gingrich and former secretary of health and human services Tom Price—and won. She won in a state where guns are allowed in bars and on college campuses, where a person can carry a semiautomatic rifle just like the AR-15 used in Parkland.[22]

In 2019, Congresswoman Lucy McBath led efforts to secure $25 million in an appropriations bill for gun violence research.[23] For the first time since 1996, the Centers for Disease Control and the National Institutes of Health will have the means to study gun violence.[24] The mother of Jordan Davis has achieved one of the first significant federal legislative victories for gun sense in years.

Twenty-one months after Parkland.

The air is warm.

My eldest daughter is now a senior. She is swimming in all of the "lasts" that all children should get to celebrate when they are in the homestretch of high school.

A text from her appears on my phone.

There was another shooting at a high school outside of LA.
We broadcast it in the back of the journalism room during class.
Everyone was in tears

I rush to my laptop.

At Saugus High School in Santa Clarita, California, forty miles north of Los Angeles, a student had entered the school and begun shooting. He killed two students and shot himself in the head.[25] A dozen more students were injured.

"I'm so sorry, honey," I text. I don't know how else to respond. In the United States we talk and talk and talk about gun violence. We console one another with words that feel increasingly shallow. We know exactly how to make our country safer, but too many Republican legislators offer only "thoughts and prayers" instead of supporting meaningful legislation. Three years after Parkland, the shootings persist. And we parents continue to raise a generation of children who fear and become victims of gun violence.

To the Extreme

In 2013 I drive to a northern Atlanta suburb to report on a women's book club for a local arts publication. The book club has an intriguing hook—its half dozen or so members first meet up at a shooting range for target practice, and then they follow one another back to the bookstore to discuss the month's selection. I have never shot a gun before, never even held a gun, have been terrified of them, so I am surprised to find that I not only enjoy firing off a round but am fairly competent at it. Despite my nerves, I have a good time.

Back at the bookstore, the five members, white women over the age of forty, are kind, intelligent, and worldly. A few have spouses or children serving in the military. "That's why I love this bookstore, because it supports the military," one of the members tell me. This comment, in isolation, didn't unsettle me. But then another member brings up her deceased husband. "He believed in a strict reading of the Constitution." The owner of the bookstore adds, "He was one of the early members of the Tea Party movement." A few others nod their heads in support.

With that, a sliver of a radical right-wing movement has made its subtle but assured appearance at a book club. I'd not expected to find evidence of it so close to left-leaning Atlanta, in this fairly diverse suburb. I could have never predicted that less than three years later, Donald Trump, as the Republican nominee for president, would make open and hostile bigotry a tenet of American patriotism. That he would be the Tea Party movement's biggest, most successful legacy.

Besides, these book club women are as warm and welcoming as they can be.

The Tennessee where I grew up in the 1980s and early 1990s lies squarely in Middle America. God-fearing white evangelical Christians from "good families" populated our small city. They were *saved*, and they blessed your heart, and they named their places of worship when they introduced themselves. They were also some of the kindest people I'd ever met, excelled in school, were popular, and had impeccable manners. Truthfully, I oftentimes modeled myself after them.

I came of age in southeastern Tennessee at the time when, after decades of flirting and courtship, evangelical Christians cemented their relationship with the Grand Old Party.[1] In the 1980s, Southern Baptist minister and televangelist Jerry Falwell began planting his sermons at the intersection of the New Testament and constitutional law. He declared that prayer in schools should become not only a viable plank in the Republican Party platform but also a constitutional amendment. Falwell's Moral Majority, a movement he christened in 1979, gained steam with a series of national rallies. Members enthusiastically rejected the separation of church and state.[2]

Jim and Tammy Faye Bakker cohosted the Praise the Lord (PTL) Club and opened Heritage USA, a heaven-inspired amusement park. (The couple's marriage would not survive the numerous sexual and financial scandals that followed.)

On Sundays mornings at my home, it was hard to avoid the circus. Nearly every major television station blared hours of pastors tearfully lamenting damnation but promising the hope of being saved to all of Jesus's humble followers, with a plea to call in their credit card offerings to the 1-800 number at the bottom of the screen.

A fair number of the children and adults I knew subscribed to this ideology. Their faith was their life, as was their desire to ensure that others were saved as they had already been. *Did you hear the news? Elizabeth got saved on Sunday. Isn't that great?*

As a child, I wasn't bothered. Most evangelicals were friendly, they hadn't been openly racist toward me, and these were the low standards by which my preteen and teen self judged others. I silently dismissed their points of view and hoped they'd see the light soon enough.

In the weeks leading up to the 2016 presidential election, a dark cloud descended over me. I paced my home as every major network broadcast Trump's admission of sexual assault and his insults toward Mexicans and disabled people. When FBI director James Comey opened another investigation into Hillary Clinton's emails a few days before the 2016 election, halving Clinton's lead, I found myself unable to move from my couch in our living room.[3] This was where I once tearfully watched, hands clasped to my chest, as Barack Hussein Obama solemnly swore that he would faithfully execute the office of the president. This was where I had envisioned a different future for our country, where I still believed in the United States of America, however problematic it currently was.

After Trump's victory, pundits and politicians blamed Clinton's supposed refusal to engage with Middle America voters for her loss. An absurd parade of apology followed, shaming progressive voters, volunteers, and organizers for ignoring the needs of rural Midwest white cishet able Christian males. The overriding theme of this election autopsy, which played in an endless loop, was built upon one underlying assumption—Indigenous, Black, and other people of color do not reside in Middle America and therefore couldn't possibly understand the economic issues faced by working-class folks in flyover country.[4]

A few days after the election, an exceptionally bright and talented evangelical Christian from my graduating class admits in a long Facebook post that she voted for Trump. Several of our evangelical schoolmates rally around her to praise her for her "brave" post. This doesn't come as a surprise to me, and yet I spend the rest of the day feeling as if someone has kicked me in the gut. After I unfriend her, she writes me a private message about how she has always respected my point of view, and I should therefore respect hers, as if a violent ideology is a point of view worthy of equal consideration.

Her post, and the message that followed, was a bitter reminder that some of the people I had grown up with were bigots who had successfully cloaked their educated and sophisticated hatred of others in what they deemed faith and patriotism. And by doing so, they could pretend they were more civilized than the raging Trumpers with their red MAGA hats, Duck Dynasty camouflage, and tiki torches. Hannah Arendt put it best in *The Origins of Totalitarianism*: "The temporary alliance between the elite and the mob rested largely on this genuine delight with which the former watched the latter destroy respectability."[5]

Their poised, well-mannered expression of elite hatred seemed downright genteel compared to MAGAS. Which is what made them far more dangerous.

During World War II, British Royal Marine Arthur Thompson was on a mission in the Netherlands when he came across an abandoned camera that belonged to a Nazi.[6] When he later developed the film, it revealed Germans in uniform at play. They are frolicking in the outdoors, sunning, and gathering for lighthearted conversation. Their role in the massacre of millions of Jews lies just beyond the frame, but the story these photographs tell is an important one. The peaceful routines of the wealthy ruling class can go a long way to obscuring rampant violence.

This is the dominant theme in Éric Vuillard's *The Order of the Day*, which recounts the ostensibly mundane events that led to the Third Reich's annexation of Austria.[7] The novel opens on February 20, 1933, at a meeting of twenty-four wealthy Austrian industrialists, wheelers and dealers whose shortsighted goals for their profit margins prevent them from reckoning with the long-term devastation of violence and fascism. Here are "venerable patricians" in overcoats and felt hats entering through the double doors of a salon where they will agree to transfer money and power to Adolf Hitler. "The day passed, quiet and normal," writes Vuillard.[8] The irony of this sentence is what makes it so haunting.

For we know that what is to come is anything but normal, and we are powerless to stop it.

The transition from cordiality and civility to menace involves no more than pen and paper, nods of understanding, and firm handshakes—the exact kind of civility reflected in the photographs Thompson discovered during World War II. Take this meeting that Vuillard dramatizes between Hitler and Chancellor Kurt von Schuschnigg: "At that instant, Hitler might have smiled. When gangsters or lunatics smile, they are hard to resist; best to get it over with quickly and restore peace. And besides, between two bouts of emotional torture, a smile no doubt possesses a special charm, like a clearing sky."[9]

Which is to say that extremism launches with a whisper. It ignites in the ordinary, routine, everyday acts of people. When I look back over the decades and think about those who surrounded me, either by choice or by circumstance, I see the faint lines of extremism embedded in the heart of their beliefs. I see the hugs, and the handshakes, and the "take cares."

As our country embraces authoritarianism and fascism, it is vital to acknowledge the myriad ways we contributed to it. For too long, too many of us assisted supposedly good, decent people at bake sales to raise money for the preschool and cheered alongside them on soccer fields and carpooled with them to work, all the while looking the other way from the toxic ideals they harbored and proliferated. It was too uncomfortable for many of us, myself included, to call out their beliefs at a neighborhood party or unfriend them on Facebook. We found ways to justify our own inaction. *They're old. They'll die off soon anyway.* Or, *They're entitled to their own opinion.*

We failed to take a more aggressive stance to confront the malicious forces in our midst because confronting it oftentimes means confronting our own complicity in it. And complicity is like the sun. No one can stare at it for too long.

The Tea Party movement began in early 2009 with a rant that went viral. From the floor of the Chicago Mercantile Exchange, exasperated CNBC reporter Rick Santelli tore into President Obama's plan to relieve homeowners drowning in their underwater mortgages whose home values had plummeted to a net worth far less than their debt.[10] Instead of blaming big banks for creating predatory lending devices like credit default swaps, conservatives leapt at the chance to take to the streets against individuals who'd been lured with promises of a good investment at a time when property values were skyrocketing. The blaming and demonization of mortgage lendees echoed the hate unfurled at recipients of what was then known as Aid to Families with Dependent Children, or welfare in the 1990s.

Santelli's singular rant set ablaze the rapid mobilization of conservatives. By early 2010, some 650 local Tea Party groups spanned the country.[11] In addition to demanding drastic spending and tax cuts, a repeal of the Affordable Care Act (Obamacare), and unconditional protection of their Second Amendment right to bear arms, they directed their ire at women who wanted autonomy over their own bodies and immigrants who wanted to build a life in the United States.

It should come as no surprise that 2008 vice presidential candidate Sarah Palin and former congresswoman Michele Bachmann would be two of the movement's biggest and most visible champions (though they were often at odds with each other).[12] And it was the Tea Party movement that spawned the rebirth, at least since 9/11, of the grotesque, openly flaunted Islamophobia and xenophobia that pervade the United States today.

The movement was extremely well funded by the Koch brothers and other corporate titans, and the money they funneled to Tea Party groups paid off quickly enough.[13] The Democratic majority in the House took a beating in 2010, only three years after the movement's inception. Democrats lost more than fifty seats, and the Senate barely clung to its majority.

I have been fascinated by the Tea Party movement since its inception, not because I'm impressed with their degree of success (corporate money can and always did buy significant political power in this country) but with how they branded themselves. This form of modern-day extremism assumed a name that seamlessly blended the image of cozy gatherings graced by fine china with the bloodthirsty quest for freedom of colonial Boston's Tea Party. It was a brilliant marketing strategy that evoked both intimacy and revolution.

Who *wouldn't* want in?

Like extreme right-wing movements before it, the Tea Party succeeded in making its blatant bigotry more palatable to the masses. Its hate was draped in doilies. But prim and proper people who show up at your home with pound cake, instead of burning effigies or spray-painting swastikas on synagogues, are still extremists. They are surprisingly successful at marketing and mobilizing their hate. And instead of questioning where the pound cake came from or what their motivations are for bringing it, we thank them and take a bite.

After Jon Ossoff lost Georgia's Sixth Congressional District special election in June 2017, resistance energy in my neck of the woods seemed to deflate like a balloon. When officials working under Brian Kemp, then secretary of state, wiped the election server a few days after a lawsuit was filed challenging the result,[14] we only became more despondent. This election had been the first major act of resistance under Trump for many local Asian Americans and Pacific Islanders, and we had lost. I was beyond exhausted. I didn't leave my bed for several days afterward.

I officially jumped back on the train that was Democratic political organizing in a red state sometime in early 2018. Georgia Democrats had two women running for governor, both of whom had served in the Georgia legislature—Representative Stacey Evans and Minority Leader Stacey Abrams. Abrams handily defeated Evans in the primary.

I hoped members of the Asian American and Pacific Islander community, who seemed to have fallen by the wayside after 2017, would be ready to reengage. We had an outstanding candidate for governor in a state that was gradually turning blue. But even as we stared down the midterm election at Secretary of State Brian Kemp, who had built his career on the suppression of minority voters and refused to resign as the overseer of elections while running as the Republican candidate for Georgia governor, the AAPI community still seemed stagnant.

I had been hosting events at my home and elsewhere for local state-level candidates. Turnout had been disappointingly low. Some of the most enthusiastic supporters, the most vocal resisters who had once changed plans at the drop of a hat to attend rallies and events for Ossoff, had disappeared into the ether. My texts, phone calls, and emails pleading for their help to get involved, to flip our state senate and house districts, went largely unanswered. Or if they did respond, it was to tell me that their lives were too busy this time around.

It's hard to pinpoint the reason why the AAPI community was slower to mobilize in 2018. It could have been anti-Black racism, and the belief that a Black woman would not be able to win a governor's race in a state like Georgia. But our leaders in the AAPI community came out early and strong for Abrams (and her candidacy would eventually triple the AAPI turnout for the general election).

Eventually I met up with two fellow activists to mull over ways to get more AAPIs engaged. An idea began to take shape. I imagined what early meetings of the Tea Party movement might have looked like, with supporters sipping tea in neighbors' homes, sharing snacks, musing about kids' playdates and jobs. I thought about tea itself, and how it seemed to find a way to both soothe and open up people to tough but critical conversations.

Chai & Chaat was soon born.

We organized a panel discussion at my home featuring AAPI staffers working for the Abrams campaign or other state Democratic campaigns. A friend made fresh chai (I would spare my guests my own awful chai) and we served it along with Indian snacks. Some thirty to forty people showed up, one of the largest groups of AAPIs we'd managed to gather in a while. The panelists answered questions about early voting, voting absentee, and the candidates' positions on the issues. It was a hit. The second event, scheduled two weeks later at a friend's house, brought more than twice as many attendees. This was now *our* tea party movement, our resistance against extremism. And we were doing it with our own tea, one bag at a time.

It's easy to wring hands over the frequent use of the term *extremism*. In the United States, many still tend to avoid language that accurately describes oppression. After Trump's inauguration, too many Americans, even so-called progressives, refused to call Republicans racist. I still hear these sentiments regularly: *They're not racist, they just want lower taxes. They're not racist, they're just hurting. They're not racist, they're just tired of big government.*

After four years of Trump's presidency, even some Democrats still bristle at suggestions that the Trump administration was a fascist and authoritarian regime. They have come to reserve the language of extremism for circumstances so particularly gruesome, and have set such a high bar for its identification, that they have placed themselves in a state of denial regarding its more elusive but equally poisonous forms.

Too many people remain in a collective denial. It might seem more reassuring to believe that extremism lives only in Trump's outrageous tweets, white nationalist marches, and MAGA paraphernalia, but this is hardly the case. The most dangerous form of extremism is like a train approaching in a thick fog. You can't see it until it's about to run you over.

"Armchair" Activism in the Real World

In June 2007 my Australian cousin eleven years my junior coaxed me into joining Facebook. I hemmed and hawed, but the truth of the matter was that I had been terrible at responding to emails from my relatives who live abroad and saw Facebook's shiny new "platform" as a means to improve upon my dismal communication. I had also recently moved away from southeastern Pennsylvania, missed my friends terribly, and hoped to reconnect with them on Facebook. Within those first few months, I'd found them all, as well as high school and even elementary school friends.

Social media, as far as I was concerned, was a revelation.

For my first few years on Facebook, I shared links to a new blog where I wrote about books and politics. My presence was otherwise minimal. I posted, commented, "liked," and left. I didn't endlessly scroll, or debate people under their own posts.

My activism largely continued offline. When I joined a coalition of neighbors trying to stop the construction of a cell phone tower across the street from our local elementary school, I attended meetings and spoke at city council hearings. But it didn't occur to me to mention this activity on Facebook.

My engagement with social media began to shift in February 2012, after George Zimmerman's slaying of Trayvon Martin in Sanford, Florida, followed by the December shooting of twenty first-graders and six staff members at Sandy Hook Elementary School in Connecticut. During that year, I began to understand the value of social media as a political tool, and as a place to engage in critical conversations about tough issues. But I also quickly realized something else. *I* needed to grow more as a human being, to evolve, and to find more ways to contribute to causes and uplift marginalized communities. And I could do some of this work on social media. Little did I know what a driving force in activism social media would become.

The first decision I made after the 2016 presidential election was to cancel my trip to the Association of Writers and Writing Programs (AWP) conference in Washington, D.C. It was scheduled to take place in February 2017, a few weeks after Donald Trump swore an oath to serve the United States of America as its forty-fifth president. The thought of attending the largest annual writers conference in the country a stone's throw from the White House sounded downright repulsive. All I wanted to do was curl up in a blanket on my sofa and hide until the nightmare of this presidency was over.

The summer before, my husband and I had taken our three daughters to Washington for the first time. I snapped a dozen photos of them standing together in front of the White House, their arms linked, their smiles wide. "This could be you someday," I called out. When I was growing up in the 1970s and 1980s, I could never have imagined a woman president. In mid-2016 it seemed like a real possibility.

This dream, of course, vanished in cruel fashion. And now a monster who threatened to dismantle democracy and transform it into some kind of white supremacist autocratic theocracy was going to assume the highest office in the United States.

During his first weeks in office, my greatest fears became reality. The new administration scrubbed references to climate change and the LGBTQIA+ community from the White House website.[1] Trump characterized his relationship with the media as a war.[2] He signed an executive order to build a wall along the U.S.-Mexico border. His second executive order served as the first iteration of the Muslim ban. Travelers were blocked at U.S. international airports. Republicans threatened to make repealing the Affordable Care Act a priority, and Vice President Pence announced that he would scrutinize voter rolls to avoid any future so-called voter fraud.[3]

By the end of the first week, Trump had set in motion the implosion of the United States. The high I felt while marching with tens of thousands of people at Atlanta's Women's March wore off quickly. I found myself sinking into an emotional abyss I wasn't sure I could crawl out of.

Literature has always been my lifeline, but after the election, it seemed like a bizarre luxury. Books, my most precious treasures, my greatest comforts, would not directly solve the nation's current turmoil. What good was my pursuit of a literary life if a man who admitted to sexually assaulting women and defended white nationalists was at the helm of my country? Where and how did books fit into my life now?

In the three months leading up to the Association of Writers and Writing Programs conference, writer-friends declared that it was more important than ever to read and appreciate good literature, to tell our stories, and amplify the voices of those who would be most affected by the current administration. In theory, I agreed. But reading wouldn't be enough. And the question remained— would I still attend the conference?

I had already purchased my nonrefundable plane ticket to D.C., booked a hotel room, and agreed to split the cost with two friends. So instead of backing out of the conference, I decided to make my trip count.

On Facebook we began to organize a meeting between Georgia writers attending AWP and our Republican U.S. senators, Johnny Isakson, who'd just been elected to a third term, and David Perdue, cousin of Sonny Perdue, a former Georgia governor and U.S. secretary of agriculture. We christened ourselves GA Writers Resist at AWP. I had not lobbied elected officials for more than twenty years and was certain I lacked any useful skills to lead this effort. But I then picked up the Indivisible Guide.[4] There it was. An action plan.

And even I could follow it.

I first sent several faxes and emails to our senators' offices to request a meeting with their Georgia constituents, and when I didn't hear back, I did what several members of Indivisible groups had recommended: I simply picked the day and time most of us could break away from the conference and notified each office when our group of twenty or so writers would descend upon them.

Dictating the terms of our visit worked. Soon thereafter, we received confirmation that a staff member from each office would greet us on Friday at 12:30 in Senator Isakson's conference room to hear all of our grievances at once. The writing conference soon morphed into a political convention, as writers from multiple states organized the same. In our Facebook groups, we shared tips and strategies and discussed the issues we should bring up with our respective politicians. It felt like a literary revolution.

Our mission didn't end there. We decided to bring our fellow Georgians to Washington with us. Over social media, we blasted news to our friends and followers about our letter-writing campaign. We organized the letters by subject (health care, LGBTQIA+ rights, Muslim ban, and so forth) in separate folders so we could make sure the legislative aides in charge of those specific issues would receive their own. Many of us held letter-writing events in our homes. At a friend's Super Bowl party, I proudly wore my Atlanta Falcons T-shirt while passing out letters for attendees to sign.

In Washington three weeks after Trump's inauguration, the Mall felt like a graveyard for democracy. I picked up a vicious virus upon arriving, and despite taking a hefty dose of cold medicine, I managed to sleep only two hours before making my way to Capitol Hill.

Our group of more than twenty writers hailing from the Atlanta metro area and Athens, tote bags and backpacks slung over our shoulders, filled the hallway on the first floor of Russell Senate Office. In our arms we carried some seven hundred letters from Georgians terrified by the prospect of losing their health care, by the administration's denial of climate change, by the treatment of undocumented immigrants, cuts to public education, and Steve Bannon's role as chief strategist, among other issues. We proudly paraded into the conference room when called, filled every seat, and lined the walls of the room. For the next hour and change, we took turns criticizing the administration and demanded that our senators condemn it. When they tried to toss us out of the conference room way before our time expired, writer Jessica Handler called their bluff and told them we were staying for our allotted time. We didn't expect much from two Republican staff members, but it felt good to be heard. To do *something*.

My relationship with Facebook over the years has been hot and cold. But we couldn't have organized this meeting without it.

A few days before early voting in Georgia began for the 2018 midterm election, I came across an article from a news publication I wasn't familiar with called *WhoWhatWhy*, by a reporter named Jordan Wilkie.

The findings in his piece, titled "High Rate of Absentee Ballot Rejection Reeks of Voter Suppression,"[5] were alarming. By October 11, 2018, Gwinnett County, the second most populous and racially diverse county in Georgia, had rejected 398 ballots, a figure that represented 40 percent of all rejected absentee ballots in the entire state.

There were glaring racial disparities. "Asian or Pacific Islander voters are rejected at four times the rate of white voters, while black voters are rejected at nearly three times the rate of white voters." It indeed reeked of voter suppression.

In 2018 I had canvassed the homes of at least a few hundred Asian American voters. Whenever I came across elderly or limited-English-proficiency voters, I encouraged them to vote via absentee ballot, so they could avoid the hassle of finding transportation to their polling places, and take the extra time they might need to read and understand the ballot (or have someone translate it for them) before casting their votes. This was the advice many of us canvassers gave to voters who might need additional assistance.

The fact that I had encouraged voters to vote absentee, and that these absentee votes might not be counted, made me feel sick.

At 7:32 p.m. the Friday before early voting began, I tweeted a link to Wilkie's article with this post: "#*GwinnettCounty*, one of the most racially diverse counties in #Georgia is rejecting 9% of absentee ballots with #AAPI ballots 4x more likely and Black ballots 3x more likely to be rejected than white ballots. More media report on this please! #gapol #gagov."[6] The tweet received 14 retweets and 13 likes. I tossed and turned all night long, fretting that the article, and the information in it, wouldn't get the attention that it deserved. The next afternoon I taught a writing class on the other side of town, and in the evening I headed to an Asian American political event at a friend's house. I brought up the article's findings to a few people. They were appalled. *Yes, yes,* they said. *This is ridiculous. We need to find out why this is happening.*

After a twelve-hour day, I arrived home and curled up in bed. I opened Twitter on my laptop. My next post with a link to the article at 9:27 p.m. was more desperate. "We need more media coverage on this please!!! *#GwinnettCounty* is a minority majority metro Atlanta county that's rejecting minority absentee ballots at alarming rates!"[7] This time the tweet took off, garnering more than 2,600 retweets. In the days that followed, national news outlets picked up Wilkie's findings and wrote articles of their own. Civil rights groups filed two lawsuits in federal court challenging the high rejection rate of minority absentee ballots.[8] Eventually the lawsuits were settled. The state had to notify voters immediately if their absentee ballots were rejected.

The bulk of the credit belongs to Wilkie, who first broke the story, as well as to the grassroots organizations that helped identify the affected voters, and to the civil rights groups that filed the lawsuits in federal court to end the disparate treatment of Georgia's absentee ballots cast by minority voters. But this is an example, one of many, of how a viral tweet can lead to a few crucial, tangible outcomes in something as important as voting rights.

Online activism *alone* is not the Holy Grail for social change. And let's face it, some of the most oppressed people do not have access to the Internet and therefore aren't able to organize online. But for those with Internet access, especially those who can't organize in person because of disability, caregiving responsibilities, work, or lack of transportation, it can be a powerful method of engagement and advocacy.

There are a few downsides to online activism. It may not deliver the same sense of camaraderie that in-person activism does. As much as I love my online activist friends, in-person relationships with activists have yielded deeper friendships. If I make errors as an organizer (and I have made many), they help me problem-solve and encourage me to grow into a better person. When we butt heads, we have a stronger foundation to move through our disagreements. It can be easier to see other activists as human beings dealing with myriad personal issues when you hear their voices, look them in the eyes, and know and understand the totality of their lives.

Online activism also runs the risk of impeding the work of on-the-ground activists who are more in tune with the communities that are most impacted by harmful laws and policies. When Georgia governor Brian Kemp signed the "heartbeat bill" in May 2019, which would prevent abortions at the six-week mark (which has been struck down as unconstitutional), celebrities who had barely set foot in the state called for a boycott of our thriving film industry. It was a bizarre action plan, given that members of the film industry largely support reproductive justice. On social media the voices of film executives, who could weather a boycott, drowned out the low-paid workers and local mom-and-pop shopkeepers who depended on the industry to sustain them. They also drowned out Black and brown abortion providers who had offered safe abortions to Georgians for years.[9]

This issue can be avoided if we think locally and research local organizations and groups who do the work we are interested in supporting. They are the experts who have been on the front lines for years, and they will be doing this work long after a viral hashtag fades from memory. Amplify their voices online by sharing their posts at least as often as you publish your own. If you are able, support their work by donating to their organizations or their crowdsourced funds. Regardless of whether our activism is online or in person, if we are seeking meaningful, long-term social change, we must uplift the coalition-building of local activists who will continue to do this work long after everyone else has gone home.

The same goes for local progressive candidates whose platforms you support. They will never get the attention that candidates do in national races, so boost them. Follow them online. Retweet and share their posts. And during the course of their campaigns, text, email, or tweet links to their donation pages to those in your community who can afford to give.

In early 2020 I was getting ready to dust off my canvassing shoes. Winter was showing signs of burning itself off. The days grew longer. I had been itching to knock on doors again, to pull up my list of voters on the Minivan app on my phone, to champion Democratic candidates, and assist voters with information about the upcoming elections. The March presidential preference primary in Georgia was just around the bend, as was the May state primary, where Georgia Democratic voters would be picking candidates for key offices, including two U.S. Senate seats, a highly flippable Seventh Congressional District seat, and other crucial state races. I had only been canvassing for three years, since early 2017, but I had grown to love connecting with voters in person and answering their questions about elections.

And then Covid-19 hit U.S. shores and spread like wildfire from sea to shining sea.

I had expected political campaigning in 2020 to be challenging. I had not anticipated the menace that is Covid-19, and that a virus that would disproportionately impact Black, Latinx, and Indigenous likely Democratic voters could pose as great a threat to voting as voter roll purges or our state's hackable electronic voting machines.

Campaigns and voting rights organizations shifted organizing entirely online. Candidates began holding forums and debates using Zoom. Meet-and-greets, which under normal circumstances took place in voters' living rooms, now took place across various social media platforms.

Volunteers have thus far dumped most in-person organizing for phones, postcards, and social media posts. Our "armchairs" have become the primary portals for our current sociopolitical movement. Our Democratic revolution will predominantly take place on screens across the country.

But we are prepared. We now know how to operate online. And given that this is all we have in this moment, it will have to be enough.

Unnewsworthy

We lived in a white-siding-and-brick colonial on Hampton Road in Grosse Pointe Woods, Michigan. Our block crawled with children from preschool to high school, and on long summer days we roamed the streets shoeless, our bare feet callused like tires. At age eight I'd walk with friends to the main drag, Mack Road, where we'd turn in the aluminum cans we'd collected for coins to purchase Whatchamacallit bars or Big League chewing gum.

News spread fast on the stoops and porches of our neighborhood. At twilight, before the dinner hour, one of the mothers would exit her home, the screen door smacking shut behind her, clutching either a bottle of beer or a mug of tea. The other mothers had antennas, or at least they seemed to. As soon as the first mother lowered herself to the step and dusted off her hands in her trousers, another would appear on her porch in the waning sun, stretch, eyes locking across the street on her companion. She'd wander down the sidewalk, hands in pockets, and join the first mother on the step. Another would emerge from her house fed up with children and chores, and another. They'd gather like ants around bread.

I would watch them in my peripheral vision while we played kick the can in the middle of the street, hopped chain-link fences that connected all of our yards, or drank from a garden hose in the driveway. The mothers, five or six of them now, would nod their heads in agreement, slap their thighs in fits of laughter, tilt their heads for more serious topics.

Later, when my own mother returned home, she'd relay an abridged version of the news of our neighborhood—who might lose their job, who wasn't getting along with their in-laws, whose kids were still wetting the bed. When I was a young child, this was what I understood to be our family's primary source of news. This was how I knew what was happening in the world.

Soon after President Trump was elected, a complex graphic that ranked publications on a spectrum of bias from "most extreme liberal" to "most extreme conservative," went viral on social media.[1] Most of my friends who shared it did so with instructions: "Show this to your relatives who voted for Trump" or "Check to see if you get news from any of the sources on either side of this spectrum! This will give you an idea of where to get your news."

The intention behind the sharing of the graphic was good. After all, we'd just elected to the highest office a monster obsessed with insulting every historically marginalized group, homing in, at least at that point, on women, undocumented people, Mexicans, Muslims, and the disabled.

During his campaign, we anti-Trumpers watched as television, radio, print, and online journalists raced one another to air or publish segments on his rancorous screeds. They unfurled their theories to explain his rise in popularity, commented incessantly on his hostile eruptions and his supporters' ever-raunchier displays of loyalty and adulation, and attempted, with panel discussions on split screens, to uncover reason and logic where there were none.

Trump cast a spell on the media—a ratings spell—and journalists fell under it. The relentless coverage saturated the airwaves. Michelle Wolf, who roasted not only Trump but the media during the April 2018 White House Correspondents' Dinner, stated it plainly. "You guys are obsessed with Trump. Did you used to date him? You act like you hate him, but I think you really love him. . . . You helped create this monster, and now you're profiting off of him."[2]

Back to the graphic. Post-inauguration, it seemed like the perfect solution, a check and balance, a useful tool to sort out the good media from the bad, to acknowledge and remind consumers that some sources, such as Fox News and Infowars, were in fact "fake news" and that others, such as the AP or USA Today or NPR were "neutral" with "minimal partisan bias or balancing of biases," that publications like the Daily Beast lay just inside the "hyper-partisan liberal" aisle, and that the Federalist rested firmly within "hyper-partisan conservative."

Anti-Trumpers were desperately searching for a media equivalent to the law's scales of justice. Too many had assumed, wrongly, that all of *their* friends and family members were astute and measured in their partaking of the media, that they read from a wide variety of evidence-based, fact-checked sources.

I take no issue with the graphic itself—no one publication was mischaracterized or mislabeled. It serves an important purpose (though I would argue that the people who most need to view it are the least likely to entertain the idea of it). When considering how we receive information and what kind of information we receive, we have to start somewhere.

My biggest issue lies with the premise that publications as a whole can or should be ranked on bias when even news outlets of record regularly publish extremely biased pieces. The graphic is too simplistic, an easy out, a thumb in a leak of a thousand-foot-wide dam that's coming apart at the seams.

Articles must be judged for bias on an individual basis. We, as readers and consumers of the news, can't assume any publication is "neutral." We must read or watch or listen in a constant state of alertness, and study the news as a scientist would, with a microscope. The graphic plays on one of the oldest myths of journalism—that it is or has ever been possible for journalism to be neutral. Neutrality is as mythical as a unicorn. It exists only in the imagination.

Our family's news diet in the 1970s and 1980s followed a strict regimen. On Sunday nights we gathered for *60 Minutes,* the weekly news hour with the ticking second hand. Monday through Friday, we watched a half hour of local evening news followed by a half hour of national news.

I was ten years old when Peter Jennings became the regular sole anchor on ABC's *World News Tonight,* and to this day when I think of the news, it's his voice I hear. In our household he became our saint of newsworthiness, and we were loyal and devoted disciples. In the evenings when I curled up with a book on the sofa, his calm reading of the news was my background noise. When the stories were particularly poignant or distressing, he would prop his head on his right hand, index finger running along his sideburn, his eyes focused and contemplative. I grew up trusting whiteness, and I trusted that ivory, angular face as that of a dear friend.

When the Berlin Wall fell in November 1989, I listened raptly to Jennings's assessment of the collapse of Communist East Germany. Thirteen years later, I sought out his somber assessment of 9/11.

When the world was bleak, Peter Jennings was my security blanket. There is great comfort and ease in believing in a singular source for truth, the idea that we might know where to find the truth, in trusting wholeheartedly those who deliver it.

But it's far more difficult to reckon with reality.

Prior to the early 1950s, most American households did not have television sets. Evening broadcasts on the only three news networks, ABC, NBC, and CBS, lasted only fifteen minutes. By the mid-sixties, they expanded to half an hour.[3]

Over the last two decades of the twentieth century, "the news" has spread like a virus. Television newsmagazines like 20/20 (which began in 1978) modeled themselves after 60 Minutes, fusing investigative pieces with criticism and commentary.[4] The series generated an array of spin-offs, from Primetime LIVE and Dateline NBC to 48 Hours. Every gruesome death and every food recall received its due with the advent of television newsmagazines.

In 1980, Cable News Network or CNN, the brainchild of Ted Turner, debuted the twenty-four-hour news cycle. With so much time on the air, features, commentary, and lengthy discussions filled the space between urgent, breaking news stories. Near constant coverage meant, too, that television journalists had the time and the bandwidth to let a little more of their personalities shine through.

Local stations doubled the amount of time they broadcast news. Traffic projections and up-to-date weather forecasts flashed across the screen well before sunrise. With endless news cycles devoted to producing the events of the day, no wonder it became hard for us to figure out what, exactly, was newsworthy.

The earliest "fake news" I remember, long before it was called fake news, resided in the racks at the checkout lines of grocery stores. Near the candy stood issues of the *National Enquirer*, that tabloid newspaper that bore the large faces of celebrities and British royals. It was here, as I helped my mother place groceries on the conveyer belt, that I read gripping headlines about the tension between Princess Diana and Prince Charles alongside a story about a woman who gave birth to an alien.

In the 1990s, fake news emerged as a grassroots sociopolitical engine for the far right. Fox News debuted in 1996.[5] When I first heard the mythology it so casually unspooled, I consoled myself by thinking, *Only the fringe believe that garbage.* I still naïvely believed in the binary—fundamentalists and extremists took in fake news, and responsible and reasonable individuals consumed real news.

The scales began to fall from my eyes after 9/11, when the notion of "trustworthy" news I'd previously clung to disintegrated completely. It happened while I was listening to the radio on the way to work one morning, my hands at ten and two on the steering wheel, my travel mug of hot tea wedged in the cup holder. A few weeks earlier, every Republican but one and more than half the Democrats in the Senate had voted to go to war against Iraq, despite U.S. intelligence that identified al-Qaeda as the terrorist group behind the attacks.[6] Now on the car radio I heard one of the commentators state, "Well, we can't speak against the war anymore, now that we're going to war. We've got to support our troops."

Coverage of the Middle East, from the time I could remember, had been racist. But this was the first time I realized, in real time, that this was the beginning of the shaping of a narrative congruent with President George W. Bush's knee-jerk reaction, his anti-Arab

ire inherited from his father, and what he believed to be the fulfill-
ment of a preordained Christian prophecy.

It would be a death sentence for Iraqi civilians, far exceeding
100,000 in the decade after the war began in March 2003. These
stats would be buried so deeply in U.S. newspapers, virtually no one
would see them.[7]

In an article for the *Columbia Journalism Review* titled "Re-thinking
Objectivity," journalist Brett Cunningham criticized how the press
covered the March 6, 2003, press conference where President
George W. Bush, in attempting to justify the upcoming war, men-
tioned the words *al-Qaeda* or *September 11* fourteen times in a span
of fifty-two minutes. Cunningham concluded that the notion of
objectivity requires us to be "passive recipients of news, rather than
aggressive analyzers and explainers of it," and that the hell-bent
pursuit of objectivity can interfere with our ability to parse the
truth.[8]

Thankfully, "objectivity" is losing its grip in the field of journalism ethics. "Objectivity—or even the idea that people can aspire
toward ascertaining the best available truth—" writes Michiko
Kakutani in *The Death of Truth*, "has been falling out of favor."[9]

Though it may seem like a recent trend for media organizations
to cover political propaganda with the same fervor as they do mass
shootings or wildfires, the line between propaganda and fact-based
reporting has always been an elusive one. Way back in 1936, two
broadcast networks, CBS and NBC, aired Nazi propaganda while
covering the Berlin Olympics.[10]

Which is to say that what we've come to think of as "the news" has
never been unbiased or objective. (Not even the news reported by
beloved Peter Jennings of my childhood could achieve this.) Every
piece of news comes with a framing, an angle, a thesis, or lede, and
the act of setting out to tell a specific narrative, of deciding which
story is important and why, is an inherently subjective and biased act.

Yet this doesn't mean that there isn't *truth*. Truth is separate from
objectivity. And our inability to separate truth from objectivity may
be one of the reasons we find ourselves in the current tyrannical
turmoil we're in.

For decades, radio and television broadcasters have had a legal duty to educate and inform the public about issues of importance. The Radio Act of 1927 (which superseded the Radio Act of 1912), required that stations serve the public interest and that political candidates receive equal airtime.[11] The newly-formed Federal Communications Commission (FCC), with the Communications Act of 1934, superseded the second iteration of the Radio Act.

A 1949 report clarified the definition of "public interest" to mean a "basic standard of fairness." This has come to be known as the Fairness Doctrine, and it was codified into an official regulation in 1959. It required that licensees make the public aware of any issues that affected them, from local wildfires to the construction of a chemical plant.[12]

Though the Fairness Doctrine was ruled constitutional by the U.S. Supreme Court in 1969 in *Red Lion Broadcasting Co., Inc. v. Federal Communications Commission,* the FCC still repealed it in 1987 for fear that it violated the First Amendment right to free speech.[13] Even as recently as a decade ago, members of Congress have considered reviving it.

This question of what "public interest" consists of is intriguing to me. Would the spate of right-wing fake news exist if the Fairness Doctrine had banned it? It's a free speech slippery slope, of course. But given the avalanche of disinformation subsuming the airwaves 24/7, one wonders whether the 2016 presidential election might have had a different outcome if the U.S. media had been more tightly regulated.

There is a line between what constitutes a news event and what does not. Every day editors and writers make careful and calculated decisions about what information sees the light of day (and, it should go without saying, what online stories they feel will get the most hits). We as writers, we as readers, we as members of a democratic society have failed, drastically so, to delineate this murky, enigmatic line.

Gatekeepers, the vast majority of them white and male, decide what is newsworthy.[14] They decide the angle of the piece, how much airtime it receives, how it should be covered, and who should cover it. Gatekeepers decide that endless interviews with pathological liars like Trump's former counselor Kellyanne Conway and Trump's former White House press secretary Sarah Huckabee Sanders are worthy of valuable airtime. Gatekeepers make the decision to treat as equally important Hillary Clinton's harmless emails and Donald Trump's admitted sexual predation of women.

Demographics plays an important role. A wealthy white cishet abled male editor is not the primary target of a demagogue's violent rhetoric, and he therefore has the luxury of covering white nationalism from a place of emotional distance, a place of relative safety. He won't necessarily understand how the harm of his reporting outweighs any possible value of the story.

Reporters (mostly white) continue to cover Trump's rallies even though their reports shed no new light on Trump and only serve to embolden his supporters and amplify their hate. This hate has led to white nationalist killing sprees across the world, including fifty-one Muslims in Christchurch, New Zealand, eleven Jews at Tree of Life Congregation in Pittsburgh, and the fatal shooting of Lori Gilbert-Kaye at Chabad of Poway synagogue in California. Not only are Trump's missives unnewsworthy, they have a body count and a ripple effect.[15]

First the obvious. Our newsrooms need more reporters and editors from marginalized groups. Reporters and editors should reflect the population they report on. (The U.S. population is more than half female and almost 40 percent people of color.)

In a 2017 study, the American Society of News Editors found that minority journalists made up only 16.3 percent of personnel in 598 print newspaper newsrooms. The figure was somewhat higher in the 63 online-only newsrooms surveyed, with 24.3 percent minority journalists. Women made up 38.9 percent of traditional newsrooms and 47.8 percent of online-only newsrooms. In only one-quarter of news organizations did editors of color hold at least one of three top editorial positions. For women of color the statistics were downright dismal: they represented only 7.9 percent of traditional print newsrooms, 6.2 percent of local radio staff, and 12.6 percent of local TV news staff.[16]

Who is in the newsroom affects what gets reported and how. In the months leading up to and following the election of President Trump, a veritable subgenre of reporting emerged—the humanization of white supremacists. Here they were, white, rural, neighborly midwestern or southern Trump voters doing nothing but minding their own business, tilling their land, paying their mortgages, and of course voting for a man who hurled racist and xenophobic vindictives. These blissful, peaceful portraits of hardworking, neighborly Middle Americans, like the Jackson brothers profiled on NPR in January 2017, exuded the normalcy of Norman Rockwell paintings. Here's what one of the brothers had to say: "I feel that if a Muslim woman wants to move into this country, she needs to leave her towel home. Because the reason this country is here and safe today is because of Jesus Christ. We were one nation under God. The Muslims are into Allah. They can't live there [in their home countries] anymore because of all the turmoil and unrest. Here we still have somewhat peace. So if you're going to come here to enjoy this peace, follow our rules and be one nation under God. Or stay home."[17]

What purpose does quoting such blatant, bold-faced Islamophobia serve in the news? Is it really newsworthy? Were Muslims involved in writing or editing this piece? If they had been, would the article have existed at all?

Then came a series of articles by reputable publications about how these charming white Trump-supporting voters experienced hardships under Trump, too, because undocumented members of their communities were suddenly vanishing! Here they were, enjoying food at some of their favorite restaurants, only to find out that the restaurant owner had been deported. How would they satisfy their palates now?

Take an article from the *Seattle Times* with a particularly egregious headline: "A Washington County That Went for Trump Is Shaken As Immigrant Neighbors Start Disappearing."[18] The article reports on ICE raids, but limits the space allocated to the people who have been deported and the families they left behind. It's a master class on centering white fragility and white tears to tell a story that should have centered the families who are being ripped apart by punishing immigration policies. Trump supporters' "grief" over causing tremendous suffering (due to their vote and/or their continued support of Trump) is a story with no new information, insight, or value. Virtually none of these Trump supporters express regret for holding their poisonous opinions. These articles create empathy for Trump supporters, not for the individuals ICE has detained and deported.

Undocumented residents in the United States rarely get such sympathetic portrayals. They are reduced to their economic value in a capitalistic society. *He employed other Americans! He donated to charity! He rebuilt pews for the church!* Few articles devote space to the hardships families face after detention and deportation.

In February 2019 *Esquire* published a cover story titled "The Life of an American Boy at 17." It centered around a white, conservative high school senior from Wisconsin named Ryan Morgan.[19] This extensive profile of a Trump-supporting white boy appeared, of all times, during Black History Month. Meanwhile the Black maternal mortality rate and mass incarceration of young Black men continued to soar, and little justice was received for the police killings of unarmed Black people.

I'm still not sure what this six-thousand-word profile was meant to do. We see Ryan hanging out with his girlfriend and friends. He seems happy or at the very least content. He has a decent family life. Raised in Republican households, he is surprised by the vitriol. "Everyone hates me because I support Trump?" he says. "I couldn't debate anyone without being shut down and called names. Like, what did I do wrong? . . . I don't think he is racist or sexist.[20]

If there is a point to this piece, I suppose it's that Trump-supporting seventeen-year-old white teenage boys are decent human beings who have feelings, too. It's a superfluous one, considering that this is one segment of the population that has never been deprived of this assumption. Meanwhile Black children are never granted the benefit of the doubt. They're never even seen as children.[21] That an editor approved of Morgan for such an extensive profile is bewildering.

Despite seeing the effects of these stories on democracy, in the years since Trump has been president, the press continues to treat white Trump supporters as if their point of view, and the lies they believe, are newsworthy. More recently, in the spring of 2020, Joey Camp, a Trump voter in Georgia, had become seriously ill with Covid-19, but recovered. Camp was profiled in an article for the *Los Angeles Times*, where he opined that the United States should not shut down and that people were blowing the coronavirus outbreak out of proportion.[22]

On one side are the scientists, on the other a disbeliever in science. *Camp verses the Scientists.* The mere narration of Camp makes it seem as if this is an equal match, one that readers should take notice of.

Another subgenre of the white-tears or sympathetic racist narrative has more recently emerged. Let's call it the Interview of a Famous Racist, in order to (allegedly) challenge the very truths (bold faced lies) that those racists assert. Here the (white) journalist engages in a rigorous interrogation to prove that a proven white supremacist is, in fact, a white supremacist.

What's the point of *these* pieces? To let these racists know that *we* know they're racist even if *they* don't think they're racist.

Follow?

It's a scaffolded *gotcha* especially satisfying to progressive white and non-Black readers of color who enjoy performing outrage about racism.

Case in point: a January 2019 article from the *Huffington Post* titled "You Should Care That Richard Spencer's Wife Says He Abused Her," with the tagline "Despite the so-called alt-right's attempt to be respectable, violence seems to follow it everywhere—even, allegedly, into Spencer's own home."[23]

This 3,500-word piece features Spencer's wife, Nina Kouprianova, and her chilling account of the abuse she endured at the hands of her husband, notorious white nationalist Richard Spencer. Spencer, at a Best Western in Whitefish, Montana, is also interviewed.

Domestic violence is certainly an important and newsworthy topic, no matter the character of the survivor. Let's not forget, though, that Kouprianova shared Spencer's views (or at least went along with them) on ethnic cleansing. She may be a survivor of domestic violence, but she is also a violent perpetrator herself.

But the biggest fallacy of this piece is its framing. The entire article is based on a lie perpetuated by white nationalists—that they *aren't* abusive. It asks us: "Why should anyone care that someone like Spencer is accused of beating his wife?"

And it answers: "They should care because the abuse Kouprianova has described and documented would, yet again, put the lie to the whole idea of nonviolent white nationalism. Because it would show us once again that violence that sips fine wine and dresses up is still violence. I don't know how often we have to learn this. After all, there is no more American story than taking a man at face value, giving him power, and only later seeing all the horror he has wrought."

Raise your hand if you have ever believed that people who routinely engage in violence against Black people, brown people, LGBTQIA+, Muslims, and Jews make respectful and tender partners. Raise your hand if you have ever taken what white nationalists who sip fine wine say at face value.

The premise of the article rests on a false assumption, not facts or evidence. The result? It empowers the lie by providing it a large platform, which white nationalists can use to recruit new members to their hate group. Marginalized folks ultimately pay the price for this kind of harmful reporting.

The same can be said about a recent interview in the *New Yorker* of author Bret Easton Ellis, about his first nonfiction book, *White*, a collection of essays where, among other things, he disparages liberals for getting upset about Trump.[24] The interviewer, Isaac Chotiner, who very elegantly eviscerates Ellis's racist and sexist viewpoints during the course of their discussion, was roundly praised on Twitter for his unwavering follow-up questions.

It must be said, Chotiner is a masterful interviewer. But why interview Ellis at all? Why not interview another far more worthy author? Public flogging of hateful people is entertaining, but only for people who are not the target of such hate. Shouldn't journalism weigh shaming someone for their monstrous views against how much reading about those views harms oppressed people targeted by those views? What insight does interviewing a known racist or misogynist add to our understanding of either them or the systems of oppression they uphold?

It's tricky to report on oppression, to ensure the angle is one that probes an issue more deeply rather than sensationalizing it. If we have learned anything from the election of Donald Trump, it is that profiling hatemongers, and giving them major platforms for their ideologies, further dismantles democracy. It neither enlightens nor educates. And almost always, marginalized people pay the price when valuable airtime and print space focuses on the point of view of bigots.

What does it mean when some of the most prestigious news organizations in the world make editorial decisions that further harm marginalized groups who are not equally represented in their newsrooms? It means that human beings, and especially journalists and editors, must constantly interrogate their own white supremacy, and the ways that this white supremacy manifests in their work. They must strive to be antiracist reporters and editors who center those communities that are harmed the most, and reject the white supremacist constructs of "both sides" or "objectivity."

A rigorous interrogation of newsworthiness is not an excuse to forgo paying for the news. For journalism to diversify its staff, to abandon its toxic binaries, its pernicious allegiance to "objectivity," and to reconsider what it means to report on oppression, it still needs funding. But we have every right to be mindful about who gets our dollars, and when.

Being active, engaged readers means we have a vital role to play in this process, too. We must continue to demand better decision-making and pressure the media to cover only that which is truly newsworthy.

One Nation

On Nationalism and Resistance

On September 22, 2019, some fifty thousand people, mostly Hindu Indian Americans, fill Houston's NRG Stadium for the "Howdy Modi" summit where India's prime minister Narendra Modi and U.S. president Donald Trump meet to celebrate their increasingly authoritarian regimes.[1]

The two countries have similar origins as former colonies of the British Empire that successfully broke ties and subsequently built new democratic and secular nations. Both countries have elected demagogues hell-bent on dismantling their democracies by, among other things, waging war on minorities who they believe threaten their nationalistic goals.

Modi revoked Article 370, stripping the Muslim-majority Jammu and Kashmir state of its special status and leading to a crackdown on its eight million residents. India then passed the Citizenship Amendment Act, which offers refugees from Pakistan, Afghanistan, or Bangladesh who are members of multiple minority religions (Christians, Hindus, Jains, Buddhists, Sikhs, Parsis) a pathway to Indian citizenship. The pointed exclusion of Muslims from this protected group catalyzed protests across India, where Muslims are the largest minority.[2]

On the other side of the globe, through executive order, Trump codified a Muslim ban (its final iteration upheld by the Supreme Court).[3] He blocked the southern border, preventing many migrants from entering the United States to seek asylum, separated immigrant children from their parents, and instituted widespread raids carried out by Immigration and Customs Enforcement.[4]

The world is imploding under a new nationalism, and the "Howdy Modi" event in Texas is emblematic of this frightening surge.

At its core, nationalism is the belief that a population of one uniform identity creates a self-sufficient, fair, and prosperous nation. It is a defensive posture against increasing racial and ethnic diversity, the perceived influx of immigrants, the expansion of civil and human rights, and the rising electoral power of minorities. Nativism, anti-intellectualism, disinformation, and bigotry lie at the heart of this mission.

John Judis in his book *The Nationalist Revival: Trade, Immigration, and the Revolt against Globalization* frames nationalism as a backlash to globalism. Home, religion, and family, as well as the shared, arduous journey from Europe to start a life in the New World, unified U.S. settlers during colonization. In some sense, Trump's infamous motto "Make America Great Again" is an attempt to reach back into this past to recapture the old, ingrained, settler state of mind that mythologizes the Founding Fathers we learned about in our youth. Judis submits that "national identity is not just a product of where a person is born or emigrated to, but of deeply held sentiments that are usually acquired during childhood. Nationalism is not simply a political ideology, or a set of ideas, but a *social psychology.*"[5] James Meek in *Dreams of Leaving and Remaining* parses this mentality further with respect to pro-Brexit "Leavers": "Listen to your inner authoritarian. Don't be bound by the prim norms of racial tolerance. All you need is hate."[6] These sentiments have fueled elections over the past several years in what can only be described as a dizzying nationalistic timeline.

First Narendra Modi, an ardent Hindu nationalist and candidate for the right-wing Bharatiya Janata Party, won the 2014 Indian election to become prime minister. Then in the summer of 2016, the United Kingdom voted to leave the European Union (Brexit). That same summer across the pond, a pompous reality-television star clinched the Republican nomination for president. The following January, Donald Trump became the forty-fifth president of the United States.

Trump's win cemented an undeniable and daunting pattern. "Patriotism is being replaced with nationalism, pluralism by tribalism, impersonal justice by the tyrannical whim of autocrats who think only to punish their enemies and reward their hitmen," writes Adam Gopnik in *A Thousand Small Sanities: The Moral Adventure of Liberalism.*[7]

There was a brief reprieve in this tsunami of nationalism in May 2017 when France decisively elected Emmanuel Macron as president over right-winger Marine Le Pen. But at the tail end of 2018, Brazil would elect its own version of Marine Le Pen as president, Jair Bolsonaro. "In his thirty years of public life," writes Vanessa Maria de Castro in *In Spite of You: Bolsonaro and the New Brazilian Resistance,* "Bolsonaro has consistently and openly promoted a racist, homophobic, misogynist discourse in which he has also argued in favor of torture and dictatorship and expressed a strong hostility to human rights."[8] And in its July 2019 election, the United Kingdom persisted in its nationalistic zeal as Conservative Boris Johnson, one of the primary architects of Brexit, became prime minister.

The chronology of events from 2014 to 2019 reads like something out of a horror show. But the story of nationalism isn't only one of extremist regimes and takeovers. It is a story of resistance, of those who fight hard to retain agency and autonomy and to break through the boundaries and the borders that oppressive governments erect to contain them. It is a theme that imbues several books that attempt to make sense of this nationalistic era we find ourselves in by drawing on both current events and our world's deeply rooted history of nationalism.

Carolina De Robertis's breathtaking novel *Cantoras* is set against Uruguay's twelve-year military rule from 1973 to 1985, when some 180 dissidents were killed and 200 who were imprisoned for suspected political activity were "disappeared."[9] Five queer women, Romina, Flaca, Paz, Malena, and Anita or "La Venus," are in search of a refuge from the bustling city of Montevideo, in a country that wishes to erase them because of their identity. They find it at the edge of the country, in a tiny beach town called Cabo Polonio.

Even without plumbing and electricity, their small cottage is a haven where they can exist without being monitored, where they can be women who love other women freely and can escape, at least temporarily, the hammer of authoritarianism and the disapproving eyes of their families. That they are five women, as opposed to four or three, is significant. In Uruguay in the 1970s, a gathering of five or more persons not of the same family is illegal.

They name their community, this "strange new labyrinth of women," *Cantoras*.[10] Here is where they are safe to imagine a new country, a new world, to exist as their genuine selves. "The dunes rippled out around them, a spare landscape, the landscape of another planet, as if in leaving Montevideo they'd also managed to leave Earth, like that rocket that some years ago had taken men to the moon, only they were not men and this was not the moon, it was something else, they were something else, uncharted by astronomers."[11]

Indeed, the women are in uncharted waters. They are pioneers striking out against a punishing regime, against nature's elements in an undeveloped part of their country, against sociocultural norms that demand they be demure, marry, and bear children. No one captures the frustration of having these expectations thrust upon them more plainly than Flaca, a butcher in her father's shop. "I'm dead here in the city. Everybody is, we're all walking corpses. I have to get out of here to find out whether I can still be alive. Montevideo is a fucking prison, a huge open-air prison."[12]

Though Flaca now loves Anita, Flaca and Romina as former lovers attempt to forge a new relationship as friends. Flaca keeps Romina's devastating secret—that two weeks before the group's first trip to Cabo Polonio, the authorities disappeared her. After three days of imprisonment, Romina reappeared half-clothed on the side of the road. Though she does her best to hide her trauma, Flaca can read the pain on her friend's face.

While Romina doesn't blame herself for her detention, she does regret her naiveté. Even after the 1973 coup, she denied her country's march toward authoritarianism. Uruguay was always a progressive country compared to its neighbors. It was among the first to abolish slavery, to allow women the right to vote, to separate Church and State. Romina could not have predicted the military dictatorship that would upend their lives, as "their country was supposed to be immune to such collapse. Uruguay was special. A tiny oasis of calm."[13]

Eventually Uruguay's military rule is a predator with limbs that stretch to the outermost regions of the country, including the tiny fishing village of Cabo Polonio. Faced with this reality, the women must figure out how to find self-sovereignty, a self-rule within the mind. "Girls like her had to be saved from themselves," Flaca thinks. "They had to be saved from the horrors of normalcy, the cage of not-being. Which was the cage of this whole country and all the more for people like them."[14]

In their small hut by the sea, the women are ultimately seeking the story of their own liberation, one that resists both heteronormativity and the violent regime that has engulfed their beloved country. On the beach at Cabo Polonio, under the wide expanse of the sky, they come as close as possible to writing it. "Was this circle of women, this fire sparking into the night, the only place in all of Uruguay where such a telling could be heard and understood?"[15]

Disappearances are a tool of nationalism. What more effective way is there to rid a country of its "unworthy" residents?

The United States' "zero tolerance" policy was announced in April 2018 and led to the revelation that there had been government-sanctioned disappearances of asylum-seeking children from their parents and guardians at the U.S.-Mexico border. Though an executive order was issued to terminate the separations two months later, immigration advocates contend that it never ended.[16] The mass disappearing has resulted in hundreds of Central American children being placed in foster homes while their parents and guardians languish in detention facilities or are deported back to their countries. It's likely many children will never see their parents or guardians again.

Disappearances are also at the heart of Valeria Luiselli's *Lost Children Archive*. In this electric novel an unnamed narrator embarks on a road trip with her husband, her young daughter, and her stepson from New York to Apacheria in Arizona, home of the Apaches. Her husband intends to film a documentary about Chief Cochise, Geronimo, and the Chiricahuas, the last free Native Americans on U.S. soil. The narrator will be creating a sound documentary of what she calls the lost children—unaccompanied minors who arrive at the U.S.-Mexico border seeking asylum. Both projects are an attempt to revive people the U.S. government has disappeared—the Apaches long ago, and child migrants in the present day.

The narrator hopes, too, to assist Manuela, a woman she's recently met, whose two young daughters crossed the border and are now incarcerated in Texas in a former Wal-Mart turned detention center. Before the girls left their hometown in Mexico to reunite with their mother in New York, their grandmother had sewn Mancula's phone number into their dresses so they could call her when they were picked up by the Border Patrol.

It is this detail that torments the narrator the most. "Sometimes, when I shut my eyes to sleep, there was a telephone number sewed on the collars of the dresses that Manuela's girls had worn on their journey north. And once I was asleep, there was a swarm of numbers, impossible to remember."[17] These disordered numbers signify the cruel disruption of the family, and the ease with which children can be taken from parents whose only crime was to give them a better life.

Another, more subtle separation is at stake—the increasing emotional distance between the narrator and her own husband. Though they are heading together toward the bright sunshine of the Southwest, with each passing mile it becomes increasingly clear that they inhabit different journeys, and that this one could be their last. It is a graceful narrative thread Luiselli makes equally as compelling as the primary one about the lost children. Here is a nuanced telling of a different kind of isolation, and of the uncertainty of reunion, found within the intimate structure of a marriage. "Generosity in marriage, real and sustained generosity, is hard. If it implies accepting that our partner needs to move one step farther away from us, and maybe even thousands of miles away, it's almost impossible."[18]

The novel is a natural outgrowth of Luiselli's stunning 2017 essay collection *Tell Me How It Ends: An Essay in Forty Questions*, where she recalls her experience as a New York immigration court volunteer interpreter for unaccompanied minors seeking asylum in the United States.[19] A few of the questions that Luiselli asks the children she interviewed for the collection—for example, "How did you enter the United States?"—appear throughout the novel. And the exasperation she describes in *Tell Me How It Ends* lingers in *Lost Children*. In both books, Luiselli searches for the answer to a singular question: How does one help children in such dire circumstances?

"I am still not sure how I'll do it," muses the narrator in *Lost Children*, "but the story I need to tell is the one of the children who are missing, those whose voices can no longer be heard because they are, possibly forever, lost.[20]

Disappearances frequent the unnamed island in Yoko Ogawa's breathtaking novel *The Memory Police*. For fifteen years, the Memory Police have been disappearing objects, places, spaces, and even people.

Hats have disappeared. Birds have disappeared. Green beans disappeared so long ago the unnamed narrator can't remember how they looked or tasted. Even maps have vanished into thin air. "And since there is no map of the island—maps themselves having long since been disappeared—no one knows its precise shape, or exactly what lies on the other side of the mountains."[21] Not that it matters—the ferry that once transported islanders elsewhere has also disappeared. Many of these objects, especially early on in this haunting book, are quite ordinary. This is Ogawa's salient point. Items that may not hold much value when they exist, a hair brush, for example, grow exponentially in value once they cannot be found.

What's particularly disturbing is that after the items have vanished, so do the islanders' memories of them. "If it goes on like this and we can't compensate for the things that get lost, the island will soon be nothing but absences and holes, and when it's completely hollowed out, we'll all disappear without a trace."[22] The novel is a fantastical tale about the permanent deletion of history accomplished at a painstakingly slow pace.

The narrator is a novelist, a peculiar profession given her present situation. As her memories disappear, so does the language she needs to tell stories. Her mind is endlessly searching for a word or an idea that never leaves the tip of her tongue. It's an ironic predicament—she is attempting to create something new, while the world around her continues to disappear. Hers is a race against time, one that she knows she will likely lose.

The Memory Police have a specific mission when it comes to their disappearing of people—they remove the islanders who possess the unusual ability to hold on to memories of objects and people after they have disappeared. As such, they are the only true witnesses to these acts of terrorism. Others like the narrator, who lack the ability to remember what is gone, live in a state of perpetual panic, not knowing what or who will disappear next.

This anticipation of erasure imbues the narrator with a sense of hopelessness. Without a past, the future can never be more than bleak. "A new hole has opened in my heart, and there's no way to fill it up again. That's how it is when something disappears."[23]

Colonization is an all too common expression of nationalism. It is not enough for a nation to oppress its own minorities; it must also conquer the people of other nations or territories. The United States, which built its own nationhood by breaking away from Britain and decimating First Nations, brutally continues this tradition of colonization today.

In 2016 Nick Estes, a citizen of the Lower Brule Sioux tribe, made his fourth trip to Oceti Sakowin Camp, the largest of the camps near Standing Rock Indian Reservation, to join the water protectors who were protesting the construction of the Dakota Access Pipeline. His thrilling book *Our History Is the Future: Standing Rock versus the Dakota Access Pipeline, and the Long Tradition of Indigenous*

Resistance tackles the United States' twin evils of colonialization and capitalism, and their rule over Indigenous lands.

The 2016 protest at Standing Rock, one short chapter in the several-hundred-year history of First Nations resistance, forms the basis for Estes's larger question, "How does settler colonialism, a key element of U.S. history, continue to inform our present?"[24]

Nationalism, and the type of Americans included in the country's racist and nationalist vision, lies at the crux of this pernicious narrative. The Army Corps of Engineeers took pains to safeguard the health and welfare of the majority white North Dakotans residing in Bismarck by proposing a route for the pipeline away from the city.[25] Little thought was given to the livelihood of the Indigenous people who lived on the reservation abutting the chosen route.

A similar kind of noxious neglect ensued the following year, in 2017, when Hurricane María slammed into Puerto Rico, killing some 4,600 people.[26] The federal government's relief efforts moved at a snail's pace, recalling its similarly disastrous response in 2005 to the Gulf Coast's devastation by Hurricane Katrina (which primarily affected another population excluded from the U.S. government's nationalist vision, low-income Black people). Despite the fact that Puerto Ricans are U.S. citizens, mainlanders lamented the arrival of the thirty to fifty thousand Puerto Ricans moving to Florida after their communities were destroyed.[27]

Meanwhile the United States continues to strip Puerto Rico of its resources and deprive it of the most sacred right of citizenship, the right to vote in U.S. elections. This is by design. When Puerto Rico came under U.S. control in 1898, according to Ed Morales's exceptional book *Fantasy Island: Colonialism, Exploitation, and the Betrayal of Puerto Rico*, the U.S. government had to find a way to profit from the occupation while limiting the rights of the nonwhite islanders— islanders who, according to the 1901 case *Downes v. Bidwell*, weren't worthy enough. "How could the United States solve the problem of suddenly absorbing a great mass of colonial subjects who were racially unfit for inclusion in the rights granted to American citizens?" writes Morales. "By creating a new identity, somehow."[28] And though Puerto Ricans have always retained a strong national identity of their own, U.S. policies and laws continue to control, constrain, and disempower the U.S. territory.

The title of the book is intended to be a misnomer. For Puerto Rico is no longer a fantasy, and Puerto Ricans are not, nor have they ever been, treated as anything but second-class citizens, Morales argues. This lower status dates back to the United States' acquisition of Puerto Rico, and it manifests today in the aftermath of a harrowing collision of several forces—the territory's $72 billion debt (largely caused by Wall Street), its lack of economic autonomy under the federally appointed Fiscal Oversight and Management Board (FOMB), the destructive path of Hurricane María, and the Trump administration's repugnant response and denial of the death toll.

The book is a meticulous account of the enormous price that Puerto Rico continues to pay for the sake of its colonizer, and a crisis that appears to have no end in sight. "How long will it take before it becomes obvious that the original dream of American emancipation from European colonial control is inevitably connected to the US subjugation of a multiracial, 'foreign' people?"[29]

This idea of a colony's identity within the larger context of a colonizing nation is at the heart of Patrice Nganang's eloquent novel *When the Plums Are Ripe*. The book, the second in a trilogy about Cameroon's struggle for independence, deftly tackles Cameroon's attempt to assert its own national identity in the early 1940s when its colonizer, France, falls to Nazi Germany. The Free French, under General Charles de Gaulle, try to convince the villagers of Edéa to join their fight for liberation from the Germans.

But the villagers' loyalties are split as they debate their fate. Some pull for Germany, in order to punish the French for its twenty-five-year colonial rule of Cameroon. Others back the French. Cameroon's precarious situation gives rise to an identity crisis. "On the one hand, a German version, on the other, I don't know, maybe French? Or English? Doesn't she represent what we ourselves are: on the one hand, a former German colony, and on the other, a joint French and English mandate? How many realities do we

Cameroonians add up to in the end? Just who are we *in reality?*"[30] The people of Cameroon are left with no choice but to enter the war on the orders of another nation.

Against this backdrop comes Pouka, an idealistic poet returning to Edéa to start a poetry circle. He hopes to lift the spirits of Cameroonians and to distract them from the hardships around them and their new colonizer. But he soon learns that his higher purpose is for naught. The people who gather around him can't read. Their rigorous instruction in a higher art will have to be delayed until he teaches them the basics of grammar.

Still, the pursuit of art under colonization is its own form of resistance. And at a time when Cameroon is under the nationalist impulse of another nation, poetry serves as the conduit through which the villagers of Edéa can rediscover and reassert their agency and autonomy. It is a way for them to employ their own language, to define, and once again name, their own people.

The conflict and tension inherent in the struggle between a colonizing nation and an indigenous people's quest for their own national identity is also reflected in Maaza Mengiste's sweeping novel *The Shadow King.* On October 3, 1935, Mussolini and his Italian army invade the orphan girl Hirut's country of Abyssinia, or Ethiopia. The news is grim. "Mussolini is declaring his right to colonize Ethiopia. The emperor's soldiers are simply farmers with old guns. Italy is better equipped. Italy has planes."[31]

The planes that invade the Ethiopian skies drop leaflets declaring that Emperor Haile Selassie, the Shadow King, is not a true emperor. As propaganda blankets the ground, a legion of *ferenjoch* (foreigners) cross the border assuming Ethiopia will be a quick surrender. But "one hundred thousand men, however ravenous they might be for this beautiful land, can never total the numbers of Ethiopians intent on keeping their country free, regardless of mathematics."[32]

Enter brave Hirut. She joins some fifty other women who train as soldiers to protect the honor and rule of her emperor. *The Shadow King* is a glorious story about the women-led resistance against Italy's occupation. It is also a story about women warriors who must convince the men in their communities that they too are strong, skilled fighters, that they can also honorably protect their homeland.

Indeed, the most valuable weapon the Ethiopian army has against the foreign invasion may be the women warrior's pride in their nation.

"The women whisper it amongst themselves: We're more than this, we're more than this. They touch their faces, beautiful and plain alike, they press their palms against their breasts and on their stomachs and several plant a palm between their legs and laugh. We're more than this."[33]

Optimism in these times is a scarce feeling, but there are occasional glimmers of hope. In Hong Kong's November 2019 elections, Democracy candidates rolled over Beijing-backed candidates, clinching 8y percent of the district council seats, up from one-third.[34] In the same month as Hong Kong's election, Gotabaya Rajapaksa, a former defense secretary facing war crimes charges for his actions against Tamils during the thirty-year civil war, became Sri Lanka's next prime minister.[35]

Perhaps, a few decades from now, the full depth of nationalism's consequences, and how we both reinforced and resisted it, will be revealed. But it will take time. "Being right means nothing, except in history's long view, as we all know," ponders Pouka in *When the Plums Are Ripe*. "And the history in question here was improbable, unbelievable, the most obvious of tricks."[36]

The Little Sanctuary in the Shadow of ICE

On a muggy Saturday in July 2018, Brandi Rolleigh and Brandi Walton sat talking on the sofa of El Refugio, a small yellow sanctuary one mile from Stewart Detention Center in Lumpkin, Georgia.[1] Rolleigh, a forty-two-year-old Alabaman with blond curls and turquoise sneakers, had just returned from visiting her fiancé, Elvio Lopez-Martinez, who's a detainee at Stewart. Walton, thirty-four, was resting from her five-hour drive from Charlotte, North Carolina. Her gray dress swelled around her middle; she was eight months pregnant with her first child, a girl. Her fiancé, Edwin Yanes, was in the detention center as well.

"This is a nightmare you don't wake up from," Walton says. "I never imagined giving birth by myself. He is going to miss our baby being born." They wanted to be married before the baby came, and had planned a small ceremony in two days at Stewart. Getting married at a detention center involves obtaining approvals from the detention center chaplain, the U.S. Immigration and Customs Enforcement (ICE), and finally the warden at Stewart. Walton completed the several-weeks-long process at the end of June and was now counting the days until the ceremony.

This plan was largely possible because of El Refugio. In 2010 a group of immigration activists from Atlanta, La Grange, and Columbus, Georgia, gathered together and decided to open the hospitality center for people visiting loved ones detained at Stewart. To this day it is the only refuge near Stewart—the closest hotel is in Richland, Georgia, nine miles away, while the closest large airport is Hartsfield-Jackson Atlanta International Airport 140 miles away. This is typical of ICE detention centers, which are located in isolated geographic locations by design so that family members, attorneys, and journalists have little access.

Led by Anton Flores-Maisonet, the head of an organization called Casa Alterna that supports Latin American immigrants, the activists rented a three-bedroom house on Main Street for $450 per month. It needed significant repairs and a fresh coat of paint, but they pooled their time and their labor and were able to open the house at the end of November that same year. On my first visit, the red-brown front door displayed a wreath made of Guatemalan worry dolls, which, according to Mayan legend, absorb worries while one sleeps. Framed photos of families El Refugio has hosted lined the narrow, dimly lit hallway. At the back of the house, appliances and nonperishable foods crammed the kitchen, and signs of appreciation covered the refrigerator. "Yo Amo A El Refugio," one read.

El Refugio has provided free lodging and food to hundreds of detainees' family members, like Walton and Rolleigh, as well as attorneys who drive down from Atlanta to visit their clients. In addition to providing visitors a place to stay, El Refugio organized more than six hundred visits with detainees in 2017.

Amilcar Valencia, a Salvadoran American who lives with his family in Atlanta, has been the executive director since 2015. Over the years, he's established a good rapport with employees of CoreCivic, the company that operates the Stewart facility.[2] "We work hard to build a friendly relationship with the warden and officers," said Valencia. "We relay what we hear from detainees about the conditions of the facility and medical care. But we're primarily here to support the families. El Refugio is a true refuge in an inhospitable place."

ICE was created in the wake of 9/11, but recently the agency has been empowered to do a lot more than it used to.[3] During the first week of his presidency, Donald Trump issued two executive orders that greatly expanded the pool of immigrants that ICE could target for detention and deportation. Since that time, ICE has arrested immigrants with decades-old crimes, even if they have already served their time; immigrants convicted of misdemeanors; and even immigrants whose charges have been dismissed.

Edwin Yanes is among them. According to Brandi Walton, Yanes and his family emigrated from Honduras in 1999 through the United States' Temporary Protected Status program, which granted them temporary legal residence after Hurricane Mitch struck Central America in 1998. Walton and Yanes met in 2017 in Charlotte through a mutual friend. In early June of 2018, Yanes was arrested for possession of drugs and paraphernalia in the parking lot of a hookah lounge. The contraband didn't belong to him, and just two weeks later the charges were dropped.

ICE has the authority to place two-day detainers, also known as "holds," on immigrants in the custody of local or state law enforcement, if there is probable cause for which they can be removed from the United States.[4] This is what happened to Yanes when he was on the verge of being released from Mecklenburg County Jail in Charlotte. At the end of the forty-eight hours, despite the fact that Walton was present at the jail with the money to bail him out, ICE issued a second detainer. On June 6, 2018, ICE took Yanes into custody.

The couple had hoped Yanes would be released from jail so they could marry and make their lives in Charlotte, but they came up with a backup plan: Brandi and her newborn daughter would move in with Yanes's parents, and she would start nursing school in the fall. She's terrified of what will happen to her fiancé if he's removed to a country where he has no family and no friends, and where his life is at risk. "He tells me that if he gets deported, in two months he'll die."

Marrying a U.S. citizen used to be a reliable way for immigrants to live in this country legally, but this is not necessarily the case anymore, and it's unclear whether Yanes's earlier misdemeanors from 2013 and 2015, for possession of marijuana, will prevent him from receiving a green card after he's married.[5]

Brandi Rolleigh's situation isn't that different. Her fiancé, Lopez-Martinez, came with his sister and cousin from Tuxtla Gutierrez, Mexico, when he was seventeen years old. He prefers not to discuss the circumstances of his departure. "It's too difficult for him to talk about," Rolleigh says. "We'll talk about everything except why he came over." He worked for the same company for more than twenty years, and met Rolleigh in Muscle Shoals. She was dating someone else at the time, so at first they just talked and texted. Lopez-Martinez asked Rolleigh whether she'd give him a chance if things didn't work out between her and her boyfriend, and six months later, she did. They've been together ever since.

In November 2017, Lopez-Martinez was initially arrested for aggravated assault and ultimately charged with criminal trespassing—but, as in Yanes's case, the charges were eventually dropped. ICE nevertheless placed a forty-eight-hour hold on him, and four hours into the detainer, agents took him directly to Stewart. That was in May. Since then, Rolleigh has been his only visitor. He's told her he won't allow his sisters to visit because he would not be able to handle their crying.

Rolleigh feels isolated, too. She has no friends or family members in a similar situation, and before Lopez-Martinez was detained, she didn't even know detention centers like Stewart existed. "Nobody talks about this," she says. "This administration is only concerned with deporting as many people as possible without thought to what is happening to the family members or loved ones they are leaving behind. It's inhumane."

She didn't know what to expect at Stewart until El Refugio volunteers explained the process. "They walked me through the steps. I was scared to death," she says. "Having them there and explaining everything and just being really compassionate about it—it took some stress off."

Rolleigh and her fiancé speak on the phone every day. That in itself is a challenge. The phone lines aren't always open, and detainees usually pay at least a few dollars for a fifteen-minute call. Under the circumstances, she says Lopez-Martinez is "super positive" and looks for the bright side in every situation. "Being where he is—getting mad does him no good."

For couples like Walton and Yanes, and Rolleigh and Lopez-Martinez, not knowing how long they'll be apart from each other or whether they'll be able to begin their lives as married couples in the United States is a tremendous stress they endure every day.

Stewart Detention Center looks like a Caribbean resort after the apocalypse: two rows of fence fifteen feet high, topped with another few feet of spiraled razor wire, surround the maroon-paneled main entrance, flanked by palm trees on either side.

Of course this is no resort: it is one of the largest ICE detention centers in the United States.[6] The all-male medium-security facility holds close to 2,000 detainees, and given the financial incentives the U.S. government provides to for-profit corporations like CoreCivic, the center is almost always at or near capacity. That means that on any given day, Stewart's detainee population exceeds the 1,100 residents of Lumpkin.

According to the 2018 data compiled by the nonprofit group Freedom for Immigrants, Georgia with its four ICE detention centers incarcerates an average of 3,717 detainees, the fifth largest number in the country after Texas (15,852), Louisiana (4,415), Arizona (4,405), and California (4,353).[7] It is one of the worst states in the country for an asylum-seeking immigrant. According to the Executive Office for Immigration Review, in the fiscal year ending 2016, immigration judges nationwide approved 43 percent of petitions for asylum. In Georgia immigration courts, this figure hovers somewhere between a dismal 2 and 10 percent.

Moreover, reports have found numerous human rights violations, including excessive and unjustified use of solitary confinement, as well as poor access to medical care at Stewart.[8] The center is also routinely short-staffed.[9] El Refugio's volunteers, and the people they assist, are up against a lot.

Before the two Brandis met at El Refugio, P. J. Edwards, one of the organization's board members, led a brief training session for volunteers who would be visiting detainees at Stewart. Edwards, who lives in Smyrna, Georgia, volunteers with his wife Amy at El Refugio about seven or eight times a year. At the training, he talked about the backgrounds of the detainees they typically see at Stewart—asylum seekers from Mexico and Central America who have no family members in the United States—and how the volunteers should interact with the detainees: ask how they are being treated at the facility, but don't bring up their legal case. "The idea is to spend the time to be a friend for one hour for this person who is in the midst of a crisis," he said. "Let them lead the conversation."

When they arrived at Stewart, volunteer-visitors signed in, handed over their IDs, and were given forms to fill out. If visitors are seeking any comfort for the heartache that derives from the extended separations from loved ones, they certainly won't find it in this waiting room. The carpet is gray, the walls cream. Two giant floor-to-ceiling flags, one the American flag and the other the flag of the state of Georgia, line the back wall. Cell phones aren't allowed in the waiting room, and no writing utensils or paper can be brought in, either, though visitors can request a slip of paper and a pencil from one of the guards. There is no television, no toys or books for children, no vending machines, no music flowing through speakers, no table, not even a box of tissues. To use the restroom, visitors must first go through the metal detector to the other side of the waiting room.

As the volunteers waited, nine visitors sat on black plastic chairs. Most of them were women, their hair pulled back, their eyes swollen from sleep deprivation, or crying, or both. A toddler wearing purple pants and bright pink sneakers walked around with her bottle; when her mother went to the other side of the room, she ran back and forth through the metal detector, smiling at the visitors, as if playing a game of peekaboo.

At around 11:30 a.m., "Ana" arrived with her children, two daughters aged 14 and 12 and her 10-year-old son. The family had driven nine hours from North Carolina to see their father and husband, who was undocumented. They did not have money for a hotel and didn't know they could stay the night at El Refugio at no cost.

"Is it safe for my kids?" Ana asked—the first of three times. She said she might come by later that day. She didn't.

Later that afternoon, the volunteer visitors trickled back to El Refugio for a debrief. Over lunches they'd brought from home, they talked about what they learned during their visits. A Punjabi

Sikh detainee from India was so desperate to flee persecution that he traveled to Central America first, then through Mexico, then crossed over to the United States near San Diego. He'd been at Stewart for ten months, and his lawyer recently told him he would be removed. A nineteen-year-old from Guatemala had a younger brother and sister living in Marietta, Georgia. He'd been living in Georgia for five years when he was picked up by ICE after driving without a license on his way to work at a restaurant. Despite his four-month stay at Stewart, he appeared to be in good spirits. Today's visit was his first.

There was also a man from Gambia who'd been at Stewart for two years, although he'd lost his asylum case last November and was supposed to have been sent back. He said he had a son and a daughter in Gambia, as well as numerous brothers and sisters, and he'd fled because he was being forced to marry. Like the Indian national, he'd also crossed over first to South America, traveled through Central America and Mexico, and then entered the United States. He'd never received legal representation.

"Systemically, the detainees are unrepresented," Edwards said at the end of the session. "Here in Georgia, there are not enough attorneys who want to represent cases they know they're not going to win."

By late afternoon the gray clouds lifted, opening up the sky and letting the sunshine in. A new group of visitors filled the dining room and spilled over into the kitchen. Brian Kilheffer, a deacon from the Americus Mennonite Fellowship, was here with his two daughters and his guitar. A minister and doctor from Columbus, Reverend Sandra McCann, worked on a poster next to Holly Patrick, chair of El Refugio's Communications Committee. About fifteen others from Atlanta, La Grange, and Americus greeted one another cheerily, despite the somber reason for their gathering.

That evening, El Refugio was hosting a vigil to honor the life of forty-year-old Efrain Romero de la Rosa, a Mexican national who died by suicide after twenty-one days in solitary confinement.[10] An investigation found that de la Rosa had been previously diagnosed with schizophrenia and bipolar disorder.[11] His death was the fourth at Stewart in fifteen months, and the second suicide. During the first two years of the Trump administration, more than twenty detainees died in ICE custody, and since 2004, over two hundred detainees have died in detention facilities across the United States.[12]

The vigil began outside in front of the house. Patrick welcomed the group and read from a Unitarian Universalist hymnbook. Then the group drove to a grassy area just outside Stewart. A Lumpkin County sheriff and four CoreCivic guards (who knew about the vigil ahead of time) observed nearby. Some attendees held signs; Jason Muhlenkamp of Glenmary Home Missioners in Blakely, Georgia, passed out yellow flowers. The sun was hot and bright, and there was little shade in which to seek shelter. Patrick read the hymn "This Is My Song," and Kilheffer strummed on his guitar. Together everyone sang "O Healing River."

> O healing river, send down your waters,
> send down your waters upon this land.

An obituary, written with the help of de la Rosa's family, was read first in Spanish and then translated into English. De la Rosa, known affectionately by his family as "Bin," was born in Puebla, Mexico. After moving to the United States in 2000, he lived mostly in Raleigh, North Carolina. He worked in sales, loved Mexican food, and enjoyed spending time with his three brothers, his parents, and his nephews.

"Efrain's life was of value," P. J. Edwards said. "We honor him today and stand steadfast in our commitment to fight for justice in his name. May Efrain rest in peace and power."

The vigil concluded after a few verses of "Amazing Grace." And the small crowd, many of them regulars at these Stewart vigils, made their way to their cars to drive back home.

Two weeks later, Brandi Rolleigh is back in Lumpkin, Georgia, at El Refugio, after another seven-hour drive to visit her fiancé, Elvio Lopez-Martinez, at Stewart. Over the past two weeks, Lopez-Martinez has had two unsuccessful hearings in court and, on the advice of his lawyer, decided on voluntary deportation to Mexico. "That's what it came down to," Rolleigh says. "There wasn't going to be any other option."

The judge gave him sixty days to leave the country.

The couple are busy filling out the necessary paperwork to marry at Stewart before he has to depart. After Lopez-Martinez returns to Mexico, Rolleigh says, they will begin the process of his legal immigration to the United States. There are no guarantees it will work.

I ask Rolleigh whether she would take leave from her job in Alabama to live with Lopez-Martinez in Mexico. She sighs heavily into the phone. "I don't know right now," she says. "I'm kind of like in a hard spot. I just don't know."

Brandi Walton, now Brandi Yanes, did marry Edwin Yanes on Monday, July 23, but the ceremony did not go as planned. CoreCivic officers first claimed she didn't have an appointment to get married and then claimed Edwin was unavailable. Neither turned out to be true. After a significant delay, they married, though they were not allowed to hold hands during the ceremony. "We got married looking at each other through glass," she says. "I didn't get to hug him or kiss him. I barely got to touch his finger to give him his ring."

Brandi Yanes didn't make it back to Charlotte that night. Later the same day, she was feeling unwell and was admitted to a hospital in Atlanta. Two days later she gave birth to Mia, a month ahead of schedule. It was bittersweet.

"I saw so many couples at the hospital celebrating together and taking family pictures, and I don't have that. Mia and I were cheated out of making those memories with Edwin. He has always wanted a daughter, and now he has one but isn't able to be a daddy, and it's not fair to him or us."

A few days later, she made the trip back down to Stewart to introduce Edwin to Mia. "The first time he saw his daughter should not have been through glass and we shouldn't have to sit here wondering when he gets to hold her for the first time."

Because of Yanes's recent marriage to Walton and the birth of their new baby, Yanes's attorney Carlos Martinez is optimistic about Yanes's chance of being released in the near future, despite his two prior misdemeanors. "The marriage certificate and the birth certificate present a material 'change in circumstances,'" said Martinez.

Brandi Yanes can't imagine what she would have done if it wasn't for El Refugio, and the volunteers who helped her find a place to stay near Atlanta and care for Mia. "I would've more than likely slept in my car and had very little to eat," she says. "Everyone there has been a blessing."

Reckoning with Georgia's Increasing Suppression of Asian American Voters

Early on November 6, 2018, Election Day, Kavi Vu noticed that some voters appeared distressed as they exited Lucky Shoals Park Recreation Center, one of five polling places in Gwinnett County, Georgia. A volunteer with the nonprofit, nonpartisan civil rights organization Asian Americans Advancing Justice—Atlanta ("Advancing Justice" for short), Vu had been standing outside to answer questions about voting and offer her services as a Vietnamese translator.

When she began asking the mostly African American, Asian American, and Latinx voters about their voting experiences, she learned that after two-and-a-half-hour wait times, many of them had voted via provisional ballots.

Why? As it turned out, Lucky Shoals was not their correct voting location. "A lot of people had lived in Gwinnett County their entire lives and voted at the same location, and all of a sudden they were switched up to a new location," Vu said.

So when poll workers offered voters the option of voting at Lucky Shoals with provisional ballots rather than driving elsewhere to wait in another line, the voters took them up on it. They left with *I'm a Georgia Voter* stickers and printed instructions for how to cure their ballots. But poll workers didn't verbally explain to the voters that they'd need to appear at the county registrar's office within three days to cure their ballots, nor did the poll workers make it clear that the votes would not count at all if the voters failed to do so. What's more, as the day wore on, poll workers ran out of the provisional ballot instructions altogether.

Vu was alarmed. In an attempt to reduce the number of voters using provisional ballots, she began offering to help voters locate their correct polling place using the Secretary of State website. That's when poll workers began repeatedly confronting her about her presence outside the polling place. "They told me to stop speaking with voters in line, even after I explained what I was doing."

By midafternoon Vu counted roughly a hundred voters who had wrongly reported to Lucky Shoals. When she finally left, eight hours after arriving, she was "heartbroken" over the dreadful conditions at the polling place and the number of votes by minority voters that would likely never be counted.

Elsewhere in Gwinnett County, Mohammed Shahid appeared at his usual polling place at noon only to be told that his name did not appear in the voter registration system. Shahid, who speaks fluent Bengali but only limited English, explained as best as he could that he had been casting ballots successfully at the same location for years, that he voted in-person for Clinton in 2016 and absentee in the primary election just a few months earlier. The poll worker told him there was nothing she could do. She turned him away and failed to offer him a provisional ballot, as is required.

Shahid felt that his hands were tied. "I left the voting place without voting," he told me over the phone. "I have a language issue. What else could I do?"

Peggy Xu and Arah Kang were both volunteers for Jon Ossoff's campaign for the Sixth District congressional seat last year and Stacey Abrams's campaign for Georgia governor this year. Xu began to panic when she didn't receive an absentee ballot by late October 2018. On the twenty-fourth she contacted the Fulton County Election Board and was emailed an affidavit cancelling the first absentee ballot. She then filled out and returned an application for a second absentee ballot. She was assured her second ballot would be mailed to her Washington, D.C., residence, where she was living temporarily, by October 29, one week prior to the November 6 election. It never arrived.

Kang, a college senior in New England, finally received her absentee ballot a few days before the election. She immediately filled it out and expedited it back to the Fulton County Elections office. According to the Secretary of State website, it was never received.

Both Xu and Kang had successfully voted via absentee ballot for the 2016 presidential election, and in person for the 2017 Sixth District special congressional election. When they posted about their frustrations on Facebook, they received a flood of messages from friends and friends of friends, mostly millennial minority voters in Fulton and Gwinnett Counties, who never received their absentee ballots. Within forty-eight hours they created a database of forty disenfranchised voters. Most of the voters had taken great pains to follow up with their election board offices multiple times in an attempt to track down their absentee ballots. None was able to vote.

"We compiled this data in only two days," said Xu. "If a list like this was compiled for the whole state, imagine how many people would be on it."

"Forty people is not a hiccup," said Kang. "It's a wake-up call."

On October 15, the first day of early voting, my phone started buzzing almost nonstop with messages from Asian American and Pacific Islander (AAPI) friends.

"The line is too long I have to go back to work."

"The voting place shut down because the computers aren't working."

"A friend told me the machine switched her vote from Abrams to Kemp—what if this happens to me?"

"They're telling me I'm at the wrong voting place."

I spent hours trying to help them sort out various issues online at the Secretary of State website and through the voter protection hotline.

For the past thirteen years I've lived and voted in Johns Creek, Georgia, a northern suburb of Atlanta with a 25 percent Asian American population. These voters reached out to me because I had spent most of 2018 volunteering for Democratic campaigns. I had knocked on their doors, texted them to remind them about the election, invited them to my home to meet candidates or discuss strategies for turnout.

But the number of issues they were having when trying to vote? I had never before seen anything like it.

AAPIs were the fastest-growing racial group in the South between 2000 and 2010, and in Georgia the AAPI population has exploded.[1] Since 2000 it has grown by 131 percent, to more than 480,000.[2] Historically, though, AAPI voters have had one of the lowest voter turnouts among racial minorities. For the 2016 presidential election, it was around 49 percent nationwide, below white and Black voters and only slightly ahead of Latinx voters. But in Georgia, AAPI voter turnout was 52 percent for that election.[3] Foreign-born Asian Americans tend to have a higher voter turnout than U.S.-born.

Of far greater importance are the reasons for lower turnout. They may include a general failure to mobilize AAPI voters, the minimal contact political candidates make with AAPI voters, or language barriers.[4] In Georgia, more than 40 percent of individuals with limited English proficiency speak an AAPI language. And because they speak dozens of languages, including Tagalog, Korean, Mandarin, and Vietnamese, advocacy groups must find a range of translators to assist them.[5]

Over the years, especially recently, Atlanta-area Asian American organizations have launched vigorous voter registration programs to increase turnout for elections. The result? Some 6,400 AAPI statewide registered in 2014, and another 6,500 registered in 2016.[6]

Despite these impressive gains in electoral power, the voting rights of all minority voters have been drastically impeded since the Supreme Court's 2013 decision in *Shelby County v. Holder* gutted the Voting Rights Act of 1965.[7] States like Georgia with a history of voter suppression no longer require "preclearance" from federal courts or the Department of Justice to alter voting procedures. *Shelby County v. Holder* allowed Brian Kemp—who became secretary of state in 2010 and was sworn in as Georgia's governor in January 2019—to ramp up his suppression of minority voters.

He first strengthened the "exact match" policy, which required that signatures on voter registrations mirror the signatures on identification from the Georgia Department of Driver Services or the Social Security Administration. Many times, the discrepancies between signatures are minor—a missing hyphen, transposed letters, the day's date instead of the birth date, or a nickname signed for a legal name.[8] But because Asian Americans' names when romanized don't always neatly conform to the Anglo pattern of one first, one middle, one last name—nor do compound Latinx names—the requirement of exact match has disparately impacted them.

Kemp's more egregious version of exact match resulted in the purge of some 35,000 voters between 2013 and 2015, more than 76 percent of whom were African American, Latinx, and Asian American voters.[9] African Americans were eight times more likely and Latinx and Asian American voters six times more likely to be kicked off the rolls than white voters.[10] Civil rights groups sued the state. In a settlement, Kemp froze the program, restoring all 35,000 to the voting rolls in September 2016.[11]

But Kemp didn't slow down. To the contrary, he accelerated his suppressive tactics, purging half a million voters from the rolls on a single day in July 2017, 107,000 purportedly because of Georgia's "use it or lose it policy," which disenfranchises voters for not voting in the past three years (though several voters have come forward to state that Kemp attempted to purge them even though they voted regularly).[12]

Another analysis found that Kemp purged some 300,000 voters for purportedly no longer living at the listed address—even though some of these voters never moved.[13] The vast majority of voters affected were minority voters. A month before November 6, Kemp froze 53,000 "pending" applications, alleging discrepancies under a new version of the "exact match" law.[14] Though most of the pending registrations could be cured easily with photo identification at polling places, 3,000 were held up over potential "citizenship issues."

One of them was an eighty-year-old Vietnamese woman whom Cam Ashling, founder of Georgia Advancing Progress PAC, attempted to take to vote during early voting. When Ashling tried to pull up the voter's information on the Secretary of State website, she learned the woman had been flagged because of exact match and that they had to drive to the other side of Gwinnett County to appear in person at the Voter Registration and Elections Office with her naturalization papers *before* she could cast a ballot. "This is a major burden on Asian American voters, especially when it's the state's fault," said Ashling. Local civil rights organizations sued the State of Georgia again—now one of multiple lawsuits over exact match in the past several years—and won, including an injunction that allowed those voters to vote with proof of citizenship.[15]

At about the same time, Gwinnett County, a majority minority county with 12 percent AAPI voters, began rejecting absentee ballots at a rate of 8.5 percent (by comparison, Fulton County, the largest in Georgia, had rejected only 1.7 percent of its absentee ballots).[16] African Americans' ballots were rejected four times more often than whites' ballots, and Asian Americans' ballots were rejected six times more than whites'.[17] According to Victoria Huynh of the Center for Pan Asian Community Services (CPACS), a nonprofit, nonpartisan organization, many AAPI voters were not notified that their ballots were rejected. "They were stunned," she said. "They had no idea there was an issue with their votes until our organization contacted them."

Kemp, the Republican gubernatorial candidate who oversaw his own race, finally resigned as secretary of state two days after Election Day.[18] Neither Stacey Abrams, down less than two percentage points, nor Carolyn Bordeaux, the Democratic candidate for the heavily Asian American Seventh Congressional District, overcame their opponents' leads.[19] Kemp's merciless purging and blocking of minority voters, coupled with Georgia's outdated, hackable voting machines, means Georgia voters will never know who veritably won the gubernatorial and Seventh Congressional District races. And voters like Xu, Kang, and Shahid are left wondering whether votes like theirs, had they been counted, would have changed the outcome of the election.

It may be easy to forget the victories alongside these tough losses, but the victories, especially against exact match, have been substantial. A few days before the December 4 runoff election, Advancing Justice challenged a Georgia law that required that translators assisting voters be close family members, caretakers, or voters registered in the same precinct. (Some half a million voters in Georgia have limited English proficiency, most of them Asian American or Latinx.) Acting Secretary of State Robyn Crittenden, appointed after Kemp's post–Election Day resignation, settled out of court. Voters will now be able to select any translator of their choosing to assist them at the polls.[20]

Still, the road to the 2020 election seems certain to be a brutal one. "We remain concerned of continuing efforts by our state to suppress the voices of immigrant communities—especially as they become more empowered to politically engage," said Phi Nguyen of Advancing Justice. "Our elected officials must step up and do more to protect the rights of all voters."

Georgia's AAPI voters are steadily turning bluer. According to exit polling conducted by the Asian American Legal Defense and Education Fund (AALDEF), 61 percent of Asian Americans in Georgia voted for Barack Obama's second term in 2012. And though a smaller number, 55 percent, supported Democrat Jason Carter for governor over Republican Nathan Deal in 2014, out of 560 respondents, a whopping 71 percent of AAPIs in Georgia voted for Hillary Clinton in 2016.[21]

If we break this down by ethnicity, Bangladeshi Americans and Pakistani Americans are the most reliable progressive voters in Georgia, with 97 percent and 96 percent casting their vote for Hillary Clinton. (Given that Bangladesh and Pakistan are Muslim-majority countries, and that Trump made xenophobia and Islamophobia central to his campaign, it's easy to guess why.) At the other end of the spectrum, Chinese and Vietnamese voters supported Clinton at 61 percent and 59 percent respectively.

The trend toward progressivism seems to have continued for the 2018 midterms, where 78 percent of Georgia's AAPIs voted for Abrams for governor. By comparison, the AAPI population in Georgia is more Democratic than the contingent in Texas, where 64 percent voted for Democrat Beto O'Rourke for U.S. Senate, or in Florida, where 71 percent voted for Democrat Andrew Gillum for governor, or in Nevada, where 68 percent voted for Democrat Jacky Rosen for U.S. Senate. The progressive AAPIs of Michigan were the only group that came out ahead, with 91 percent voting for Democrat Gretchen Whitmer for governor.[22]

Prior to the 2016 election, I had no idea that so many AAPIs in red Georgia were Democrats. Members of my community in Johns Creek rarely discussed elections. *We don't do politics* was a popular refrain. In the years before Trump, AAPI progressives largely kept their views to themselves.

This silence began to dissipate during the 2017 Sixth District special election when the AAPI community became more organized. During his first term in the statehouse, Representative Sam Park, the first Asian American Democrat and the first openly gay person elected to the Georgia legislature, headed the Asian American outreach effort for the Ossoff campaign. This was one of the first times, if not *the* first time, that a Democratic campaign in Georgia poured significant resources into engaging the AAPI constituency.

I worked with Representative Park as a community volunteer to help get Democratic AAPI voters to the polls. This is how I came to understand the untapped power of Georgia's progressive AAPIs electorate. A meet-and-greet at my house with Jon Ossoff brought 75 people, mostly Asian Americans. An outdoor event for AAPIs on Mother's Day at a local clubhouse brought more than 250. Gatherings at mosques, at temples, and at Asian restaurants garnered hundreds of AAPI Ossoff supporters.

Over four months of canvassing, I knocked on the doors of several hundred houses, most of them belonging to Asian Americans. At first, voters quickly closed the door after accepting Ossoff campaign literature. As the election approached, they lingered on their porches and asked me questions about voting, the election, the candidate. By the time early voting for the runoff election rolled around, three weeks before Election Day, they couldn't wait to get to the polls. Neighbors who told me they didn't see the point of voting voted. Friends who used to skip every election except presidential elections voted. Many of them voted for the first time. And getting them on board resulted in a chain reaction—they rounded up their own reluctant voter friends and got them to the polls. The evolution, and how quickly it happened, astounded me.

On the day of the election, I was stationed outside my polling place on a folding chair as a volunteer poll watcher. I had been up at 6 a.m. placing signs along the street leading up to the polling place. I hadn't slept much over the past few weeks.

A car pulled up to the curb in front of me. An elderly Pakistani American woman, an Ossoff supporter I'd met once before, jumped out of the driver's seat, ran to the other side, and guided a much older Pakistani woman out of the car. They moved slowly up the stairs, arm in arm, and entered the building.

Maybe I was just exhausted. But as soon as the door shut behind them I started crying.

Though progressive Asian Americans built a sturdy infrastructure for engagement leading up to Election Day, there is scant publicly released data that indicates the number of Asian Americans who voted for Ossoff versus the Republican candidate, Karen Handel.

Still, when 2018 rolled around, the Democratic AAPI model for the Sixth District special election could be dusted off and implemented at a statewide level. Grace Choi led this effort for the Democratic Party Coordinated Campaign, as the AAPI constituency director. Those of us who volunteered our hearts out for the Ossoff campaign began mobilizing again. We organized meet-and-greets with candidates, canvassing events, and rallies that centered the AAPI constituency.

For those of us working on the ground, the fact that the vast majority of Georgia's Asian Americans ended up voting for Abrams (more than the percentage that voted for Clinton two years earlier), coupled with the fact that Democrat Lucy McBath ousted

Handel from the Sixth District congressional seat only eighteen months after Ossoff's loss, wasn't entirely out of left field.

But it was immensely rewarding all the same.

Compared to progressive AAPI voters, conservative AAPIs seem far more secure and outspoken in their political beliefs. Not long ago two Chinese American voters told me that because Trump supporters "are very vocal" in the Chinese American community, they oftentimes felt as if they were the only Democrats in the room. A conversation I had with an Indian American neighbor a week later ran along similar lines. "What can you do?" he told me. "Indians are Republicans and you can't change their minds. Trust me, I've tried."

Despite recent Democratic victories in Georgia, the perception of Asian Americans as conservatives appears to be deeply entrenched—perhaps because, not too long ago, many Asian Americans *were* Republican. The shift of AAPI voters from Republican to Democrat didn't begin until after 1992, and it didn't gain significant traction until 2008, when the majority of every Asian ethnic group in the state voted for Obama.[23]

What's more, for a while, prominent AAPI elected officials dominating the media, like former Louisiana governor Bobby Jindal and former South Carolina governor and subsequently U.S. ambassador to the United Nations Nikki Haley, were Republican. And though several Democratic AAPI members of Congress are currently leading the resistance—including Representative Ted Lieu, Senator Tammy Duckworth, Senator Mazie Hirono, Senator Kamala Harris, and Representative Pramila Jayapal—the assumption that Asian Americans are Republicans persists in the AAPI community.

How do we counter this narrative, especially at the state level? We elect more AAPIs to office.

The political history of Asian Americans in Georgia, whether Democrats or Republicans, is a relatively short one. Judge Alvin Wong of the Dekalb County State Court holds the distinction of being the first Asian American elected to a judgeship in the entire

Southeast.[24] Republican Charlice Byrd served in the Georgia state-house for eight years beginning in 2005.[25] In 2008 Democrat Tony Patel, the former chair of the state Democratic Party's AAPI caucus, ran for (but lost) a statehouse seat. In 2010 Rashid Malik ran for state senate and lost. Republican B. J. Pak won his house seat in 2011, making him the first Korean American elected to the state legislature in either party, and served until 2017. In 2013, five Asian Americans ran for local offices and two won.[26] In 2015, six ran for local offices and another two won.[27]

Democratic representative Sam Park's historic November 2016 win was fueled, in part, by the two Asian American women who helped steer his campaign, field director Pallavi Purkayastha and campaign manager Bee Nguyen. Park's campaign left a vibrant legacy. In 2017 Nguyen won the house seat Abrams had vacated to run for governor, becoming the first Vietnamese person elected to the Georgia legislature. Purkayastha served as campaign manager for Nguyen's race, and would head Democrat Angelika Kausche's race for House District 50, flipping it blue for the first time.

In 2019 the state legislature saw three Asian Americans serving—the most in Georgia's history. All three are Democrats. Park is in his second term, Nguyen won reelection to a full term, and Sheikh Rahman began his first term in the Georgia Senate. Rahman is the first Muslim elected to the state senate, and the first Bangladeshi American elected to the state legislature; like Kausche, he is an immigrant.

Seeing is believing. To have more impact as a voting bloc going forward, progressive Asian Americans will not only need to participate more in politics and civic engagement, they'll need to recruit others in the community to do the same. "When we do not see ourselves reflected in the body elected to serve us, becoming politically engaged becomes more challenging," says Nguyen. Rahman hopes to begin an AAPI caucus in the legislature, though his focus will remain on voter turnout. "Our main challenge is still how we can increase our folks at the polls."

If Georgia's progressive Asian Americans want to increase their political capital, they'll need to continue to evolve as a forward-thinking, radically inclusive constituency, because Republican AAPIS are getting bolder, even downright aggressive, in their tactics. While the shift to more progressivism among Asian Americans in Georgia has been impressive, some AAPI voters still supported Kemp, with his shotgun and chainsaw and explosive political ads,[28] despite the fact that many of their countries of origin have among the lowest violent gun deaths in the world.[29] We have miles to go before we have the same kind of Democratic turnout success as Black women, 97 percent of whom voted for Abrams.[30]

Regardless of national origin or ethnicity, Republican AAPIS in Georgia hit the ground running for elections. They throw money at GOP candidates, host lavish fundraisers, and frequently post photos of themselves posing with Republican candidates on social media. Nonpartisan organizations ensure that GOP candidates attend (and oftentimes speak at) their cultural functions, even at the risk of jeopardizing their nonprofit status. In other words, conservative AAPIS are winning the publicity game and don't shy away from promoting their candidates or proclaiming their loyalty.

Progressive AAPIS are going to need to step up their game to stay ahead. What's more, they're going to need to align and uplift Indigenous, Black, and other people of color, reject the model minority myth, and adopt an unapologetic progressivism that condemns all forms of bigotry. They're going to need to come out for Black Lives Matter and asylum seekers, the low-income community, the LGBTQIA+ community, and the disabled.

And above all else, progressive AAPIS must interrogate their own bigotry. Too many are anti-Black, homophobic, transphobic, and xenophobic. Too many AAPI immigrants spout false Republican talking points about the "migrant caravan" and the need to come to the United States "the right way." They ignore police violence against unarmed Black Americans, and too few have voiced their objections to the antigay Religious Freedom Restoration Act, a bill vetoed by former governor Nathan Deal, but which Kemp has said he will sign into law as long as it reflects the 1993 federal law.[31]

This is no time to rest on our laurels.

In 2018 the Indian festival of lights, Diwali, fell a few days after the midterm election. In between texting hundreds of voters who might need to cure their provisional ballots, I picked up three boxes of cashew burfi and eighty pieces of naan at our local Indian restaurant for our neighborhood's celebration in Johns Creek. In the intervening days, though we grew less optimistic about Abrams's likelihood of becoming the next Georgia governor, we beamed about our historic wins. "We did it," people exclaimed to one another.

After Ossoff's loss in 2017, the same progressives at the Diwali party spooning paneer and biryani onto their plates grew even more determined. They donated to campaigns, canvassed, and mobilized their networks to vote for Democrats straight down the ticket. We were now reaping the fruits of our labor—a blue wave, the first ever, for Johns Creek. Democrats here flipped the state senate and house seats, and McBath, who had lost her seventeen-year-old son Jordan Davis to gun violence in Florida in 2012, bested Handel for the Sixth District congressional seat. The trifecta of wins felt miraculous.

But the progressive AAPI community must continue to be vigilant. In the December 4, 2018, runoff election for secretary of state, the office responsible for Georgia's myriad election issues, Republican Brad Raffensperger surpassed Democratic candidate John Barrow. Despite the dozen or so pending lawsuits against the state, Raffensperger is hell-bent on enforcing Kemp's policies. As a result, voting rights of minority voters are continuing to erode.

Still, one more city in Georgia is blue, and Asian Americans in Johns Creek played a significant role in making it happen. It's not necessarily a revolution, but it's a much needed spark.

Identity *as* Social Change

When my father immigrated to the United States from India in 1971, many of his relatives followed in his diasporic footsteps. By 2006, the year his mother, my Avva, passed away, our only family members left on the subcontinent were his sister, his eldest brother, and their spouses. Today only a single aunt and uncle of mine remain. All of my first cousins immigrated to either Australia, Singapore, Europe, or the United States. Even though I have never lived in India myself, with each relative's migration I felt more untethered to a country I had grown to love as much as my own.

After Avva passed away, no one had space in their flats for her sari chest, an imposing rosewood armoire more than six feet tall and three feet wide. None of our relatives abroad wanted to deal with the hassle or expense of importing it. When I learned the piece of furniture that once held Avva's neatly folded saris was up for grabs, I leapt at the chance to bring it back to Georgia. It arrived several months later, after a harrowing and outrageously expensive journey, in a state of utter disrepair. Part of the base had broken off, so it stood at a slant like the Leaning Tower of Pisa, threatening to topple over at any moment.

After its restoration, I discovered something on its floor I hadn't noticed before—a fading white six-pointed star. Simple, yet elegant. Perfectly centered. A square border surrounded it like a picture frame. It was a muggulu, a design Avva created out of flour.

She would never have called herself an artist, but Avva created this art in the mornings in the courtyard and in the pooja room at her home. I can still picture her squatting in her sari, a stream of powder flowing from between her index finger and thumb. She did this in long swift strokes like the conductor of an orchestra. Stars, swirls, dots, and flowers blanketed the ground.

After her death, the developers who purchased my grandparents' house converted it to condominiums. The canvas for her artwork became the foundation for a newer, more modern Hyderabad known as the Silicon Valley of India. The sari chest is all that remains of my grandparents' home, and my childhood memories of Avva's artwork.

Over the years, I've contemplated how to preserve the muggulu best. Should an artist friend restore it with a fresh supply of rice flour? Should my daughter trace it with white acrylic paint for a more permanent solution? How do I recreate something vital to my heritage, to my identity, so that it will always stay with me?

Who am I? I am a woman of color. I am brown. Mixed race. Indian, Austrian, Puerto Rican. I represent multiple souths—South Asia, southern India, and the Deep South in the United States. I am an immigrant's daughter. Claiming each of these identities has shaped and refined my perspective of the world. It has helped me to find and immerse myself in a community that nurtures all of these parts of me. And the act of claiming my identity has empowered me to engage on a sociopolitical level, to grow my empathy, to reflect on the ways I fall short in the liberation of others. And to learn how to rectify this.

The claiming of identity and the evolution of a point of view sow the seeds for social change. For if we are lucky, if we follow the idea of the self far enough, it can end at a community that prioritizes compassion and justice in order to build a kinder, more equitable, more humane world.

In the summer of 2019, two friends and I decided we needed to work harder to keep members of the South Asian American community in Georgia more politically engaged year-round. The problem, as we saw it, was that our South Asian friends tended to come together for various Democratic campaigns, but as soon as the election passed, we lost touch, dispersed, and disengaged with politics until the next election season ramped up.

The three of us decided to start the Georgia chapter of They See Blue, an organization for South Asian Democrats.

Like any movement, ours began small. In August 2019, about a dozen people showed up to our first meeting at an Indian restaurant. Six months later we packed 150 people into a room for a 2020 Election Kickoff event featuring Georgia's former House minority leader Stacey Abrams, three U.S. Senate candidates (Sarah Riggs Amico, Mayor Teresa Tomlinson, and Jon Ossoff), and state senator Sheikh Rahman.

Today we are over four hundred strong.

Our members have roots in several different countries, faiths, languages, and regions. We are immigrants and U.S.-born. We are learning how to be better allies and accomplices to other communities more marginalized than our own. We are interrogating our anti-Blackness. And we are mobilizing together to help flip Georgia blue.

Despite the risk posed by Covid-19, in the fall leading up to the 2020 presidential election, we worked ourselves to the bone for the Biden-Harris campaign and all down-ticket Democrats. We made thousands of calls, sent thousands of texts, and wrote 7,000 postcards on behalf of Democratic candidates. We hosted virtual forums with candidates. We educated South Asian voters about the voting process and trained to be poll workers and poll monitors. Our labor has paid off. Asian Americans and Pacific Islanders nearly doubled their voter turnout in Georgia from 2016. Approximately three-quarters of AAPI voters voted for Biden. Georgia's sixteen electoral college votes will go to the Democratic presidential candidate for the first time since 1992.

What I am most proud of, though, are the South Asians in Georgia, many of whom had little to no experience with political activism until this election, who found a community in They See Blue Georgia and threw themselves into this work.

This, to me, is the heart of how identity shapes activism. It is the process of engaging people in our communities who have traditionally and intentionally been excluded from political discourse.

It is a movement about solidarity, camaraderie, coalition building, and lifting one another up. It's about how our shared identity can propel us to become agents of social change, whether this takes the form of running for office, volunteering on a campaign, registering voters, or protesting.

It is who we are and where we come from.

I consult a neighbor before I begin. "It will stay longer if you make the rice flour wet," she says. "Turn it into liquid. Then you can paint with your finger."

I watch a few YouTube videos to psyche myself up. I am no artist. I pour some rice flour into a bowl and add water, equal parts. With a fork, I swish the mixture, scraping it from the sides. Eventually it thins evenly. I attempt to paint a design on my countertop with my fingertip, as my neighbor suggested, but my finger makes for a clumsy brush. Instead I roll a sheet of paper into a funnel, pour the wet flour into it, and bend the tip to trap the mixture so it doesn't escape before I'm ready. I practice again, this time forming half of a sloppy circle. Still, it's progress.

I'm no match for my grandmother's dexterous hand. Many years ago, she offered to teach me muggulu when I visited her home. I declined. What I produce now will not measure up. It will fail to honor her legacy. But this no longer matters. She would want me to try.

I sit cross-legged at the base of the sari chest, the door propped wide open, and take a deep breath. When I first unfold the tip of the funnel, the flour mixture rushes out too quickly. I wipe away the excess with a wet paper towel and begin again, squinting to locate my Avva's neat outline. I position my hand over the design, and this time when the flour-ink flows, I'm ready. Curves and angles appear that I hadn't noticed until I reunited them into one.

The image that emerges takes me by surprise. The faint pattern I had assumed these past nine years was a six-pointed star transforms into an eight-petalled jasmine flower, the same sweet-smelling blossoms my grandmother used to string into garlands at her home almost every morning. I would never have recognized her design for what it was if I hadn't tried to restore it to its original state.

When I finish with the rice flour, I set aside the funnel and lean back to take it in. Some of the lines are shaky, too thick or too thin. Certainly, it is imperfect.

But in its very own way, it is beautiful.

Acknowledgments

So many people paved the way for me to write this book. Many thanks to my gracious editor Bethany Snead at the University of Georgia Press and to the rest of the press family for guiding *Southbound* into the world.

Walter Biggins and Valerie Boyd were early champions of the book. Jessica Handler has been my mentor, friend, confidante. Soniah Kamal helped me see the light at the end of the tunnel.

Ebonye Gussine Wilkins and Gayatri Sethi brought great clarity, sensitivity, and focus to the project. Their emotional guidance and frequent check-ins sustained me until the very end.

Special thanks to Cory Howard at Cempa Community Care in Chattanooga and to the reference desk at the downtown Chattanooga Public Library for their generosity.

My New York City support crew, Felice Neals, Kavitha Rajagopalan, Kavita Das, Alison Kinney, Jennifer Baker, Laurie Prendergast, Swati Khurana, Shirleen Robinson, and Pooja Makhijani, cheered me on during the entire journey to publication. Thank you for welcoming me as your Southern Sister.

Deepest gratitude to my family, especially my husband Brian, my three daughters, and my parents Suresh and Patricia. My brother Shanth and his wife Lauren were the first to believe in my writing. They called me a writer long before I called myself one.

Much love and appreciation for Georgia's progressive activists, the kindest, more determined, and most selfless people I know, who have given me the honor of fighting for change alongside them.

Notes

What *Are* You? Where Are You *From?*

1. Asad Haider, *Mistaken Identity: Race and Class in the Age of Trump* (London: Verso, 2018), 2.
2. Anna Brown, "The Changing Categories the U.S. Census Has Used to Measure Race," Pew Research Center, February 25, 2020. www.pewresearch.org/fact-tank/2020/02/25/the-changing-categories -the-u-s-has-used-to-measure-race.

Southbound

1. The Confederama was eventually renovated and renamed the Battles for Chattanooga Museum sometime after I graduated from high school. "Battles for Chattanooga Museum," About North Georgia, www .aboutnorthgeorgia.com/ang/Battles_for_Chattanooga_Museum.
2. Cathy Park Hong, *Minor Feelings: An Asian American Reckoning* (New York: One World, 2020), 9.
3. "Cotton Club," *Chattanooga Times Free Press,* July 1, 2014, www .timesfreepress.com/news/local/story/2014/jul/01/cotton-club /251160/; The Chattanooga Ball, www.thechattanoogaball.com.
4. Sophie Nadeu, "History of Debutante Balls (Also Known as Cotillion): Controversy and Corruption," Solosophie, January 16, 2017, updated June 19, 2020, www.solosophie.com/history-of-debutante -balls/; Jennifer Edson Escalas, "The Consumption of Insignificant Rituals: A Look at Debutante Balls," *Advances in Consumer Research* 20 (1993): 709–16, www.acrwebsite.org/search/view-conference -proceedings.aspx?Id=7547; "High Society: Whatever Happened to the Last of the Debs?" *Independent,* September 24, 2006, www.independent .co.uk/news/uk/this-britain/

high-society-whatever-happened-to-the-last-of-the-debs-417273.html;
Kristen Richardson, *The Season: A Social History of the Debutante* (New York:
W. W. Norton, 2020), 212–38.

5. "Chattanooga's Cotton Ball: The Early Years," Chattanooga Public
Library, chattlibrary.org/meta-exhibits/chattanoogas-cotton-ball-the
-early-years/; Sam Elliott, "Elliott: Zella Armstrong, Named No. 1 Woman
Citizen in Chattanooga," *Chattanooga Times Free Press*, September 27,
2015, www.timesfreepress.com/news/opinion/columns/story/2015
/sep/27/elliott-zellarmstrong-chattanoogas-no-1-womci/326969/.

6. Vijay Prashad, *The Karma of Brown Folk* (Minneapolis: University of
Minnesota Press, 2000), viii.

7. Sarah Begley, "How a Chinese Family's 1927 Law Suit Set a
Precedent for School Segregation," *Time*, October 18, 2016, time.
com/4533476/lum-v-rice-water-tossing-boulders/.

8. Tim Arnold, "Southern Pride?" *Huffington Post*, December 7, 2017,
www.huffpost.com/entry/southern-pride_b_7675370.

9. Tyler Bishop, "Reclaiming Southern Pride: What the Confederate
Flag Means to a Southerner Who Refuses to Embrace It," *Atlantic*,
October 17, 2015, www.theatlantic.com/politics/archive/2015/10
/reclaiming-southern-pride/410965/.

10. Nikita Stewart, "'We Are Committing Educational Malpractice':
Why Slavery Is Mistaught—and Worse—in American Schools," 1619
Project, *New York Times Magazine*, August 19, 2019.

11. Kay Baker Gaston, "John Ross, a Founder of Chattanooga,"
Chattanooga Times Free Press, August 6, 2017, www.timesfreepress.
com/news/opinion/columns/story/2017/aug/06/
gaston-john-ross-founder-chattanooga/441824/.

12. "Walnut Street Bridge," *Atlas Obscura*, February 15, 2016, www.
atlasobscura.com/places/walnut-street-bridge.

13. "Mrs. Blount Sues Chattanooga Over Her Husbands Lynching,"
Cleveland Gazette, July 8, 1893, www.darkfiber.com/tomb/johnson
/alfredblount.html; "EJI Joins Chattanooga Community to Honor
Lynching Victims," *Equal Justice Initiative*, October 19, 2017, eji.org
/chattanooga-honors-lynching-victims; "Lynched: Alfred Blount, a Negro,
Suffers Death," *Chattanooga Times*, February 15, 1893, www.darkfiber.
com/tomb/johnson/blountlynched.html; "The Memorial," Ed Johnson
Project, December 20, 2018, www.edjohnsonproject.com
/the-memorial/.

14. "Photo of Chattanooga Lynching Victim Found as Finalist for His Memorial to Be Announced," WTVC, March 19, 2018, newschannel9. com/news/local/photo-of-chattanooga-lynching-victim-found-as-finalist -for-his-memorial-to-be-announced; "United States v. Shipp, 203 U.S. 563 (1906)," *supreme.justia.com/cases/federal/us/203/563/*; Emily Yellin, "Lynching Victim Is Cleared of Rape, 100 Years Later," *New York Times,* February 27, 2000, www.nytimes.com/2000/02/27/us/lynching-victim -is-cleared-of-rape-100-years-later.html.

15. "The Memorial," Ed Johnson Project (see note 13).

Fraught Feminism

1. See www.youtube.com/watch?v=GyhIsFshd1E, from *Back to the Future,* directed by Robert Zemekis, screenplay by Robert Zemekis and Bob Gale, Amblin Entertainment, 1985.

2. bell hooks, *Talking Back: Thinking Feminist Thinking Black* (Boston: South End Press, 1989), 9.

3. Emily S. Rueb and Niraj Chokshi, "The Violence Against Women Act Is Turning 25: Here's How It Has Ignited Debate," *New York Times,* April 5, 2019, www.nytimes.com/2019/04/04/us/violence-against-women-act -reauthorization.html.

4. Josh Levin, "The Welfare Queen," *Slate,* December 19, 2013, www .slate.com/articles/news_and_politics/history/2013/12/linda_taylor _welfare_queen_ronald_reagan_made_her_a_notorious_american _villain.html.

5. "Aid to Families with Dependent Children (AFDC) and Temporary Assistance with Needy Families (TANF) Overview," Office of the Assistant Secretary for Planning and Evaluation, U.S. Department of Health and Human Services, November 30, 2009, aspe.hhs.gov/aid-families -dependent-children-afdc-and-temporary-assistance-needy-families-tanf -overview-0.

6. "Marian Kramer Interviewed by Loretta Ross," February 1–2, 2014, transcript, Voices of Feminism Oral History Project, Sophia Smith Collection, Smith College, Northampton, MA, www.smith.edu/libraries /libs/ssc/vof/transcripts/Kramer.pdf.

7. "The Black Panther Party's Ten-Point Program," University of California Press blog, February 7, 2020, www.ucpress.edu/blog/25139 /the-black-panther-partys-ten-point-program/.

8. "Education of the Heart: Cesar Chavez in His Own Words," United Farm Workers, ufw.org/research/history/education-heart -cesar-chavez-words/.

9. Jocelyn Y. Stewart, "Champion of Native American Literature," *Los Angeles Times*, June 7, 2008, www.latimes.com/archives/la-xpm-2008 -jun-07-me-allen7-story.html.

10. "The Combahee River Collective Statement," in *How We Get Free: Black Feminism and the Combahee River Collective*, edited by Keeanga-Yamahitta Taylor (Chicago: Haymarket, 2017), 19.

11. Kimberlé Crenshaw, "Demarginalizing the Intersection of Race and Sex: A Black Feminist Critique of Antidiscrimination Doctrine, Feminist Theory and Antiracist Politics," *University of Chicago Legal Forum* no. 1 (1989), art. 8, chicagounbound.uchicago.edu/cgi/viewcontent .cgi?referer=&httpsredir=1&article=1052&context=uclf.

12. Emily Shugarman, "'Don't Forget the White Women!': Members Say Racism Ran Rampant at NOW," *Daily Beast*, June 9, 2020, updated August 12, 2020, www.thedailybeast.com/national-organization-for -women-members-say-racism-ran-rampant.

13. Caroline Kitchener, "'How Many Women of Color Have To Cry?': Top Feminist Organizations Are Plagued by Racism, 20 Former Staffers Say," *The Lily*, July 13, 2020, www.thelily.com/how-many-women-of-color -have-to-cry-top-feminist-organizations-are-plagued-by-racism-20-former -staffers-say/.

14. Faith Evans, interviewed by Leslie D. Farrell, March 17, 1994, *America's War on Poverty*, PBS, streamingvideo.wustl.edu/media_objects /avalon:164.

Anger like Fire

The epigraph quoting Maya Angelou is from *Writing Lives: Conversations between Women Writers*, edited by Mary Chamberlain (London: Virago, 1988), 5.

1. Tillie Olsen, "I Stand Here Ironing," in *Tell Me a Riddle* (Lincoln, Neb.: Bison Books, 2013), 5.

2. August Wilson, *Fences* (New York: Plume, 1986), 96.

3. Alice Walker, *The Color Purple* (New York: Harcourt Brace Jovanovich, 1982), 205.

4. Elena Ferrante, *The Story of a Lost Child* (New York: Europa, 2015), 465–66.

5. Allyson Chiu, "Brett Kavanaugh Likes Beer, but Not Questions about

His Drinking Habits," *Washington Post*, September 28, 2018, www.washingtonpost.com/news/morning-mix/wp/2018/09/28 /brett-kavanaugh-likes-beer-but-not-questions-about-his-drinking-habits/.

6. Audre Lorde, *Sister Outsider: Essays and Speeches* (Trumansburg, N.Y.: Crossing Press, 1984), 127.

7. Emma Brockes, "#MeToo Founder Tarana Burke: 'You Have to Use Your Privilege to Serve Other People,'" *Guardian*, January 15, 2018, www .theguardian.com/world/2018/jan/15/me-too-founder-tarana-burke -women-sexual-assault.

8. Ann-Derrick Gaillot, "The Story Behind #MuteRKelly," *Outline*, May 1, 2018, theoutline.com/post/4379/a-conversation-with-mute-r-kelly -cofounder-kenyette-barnes.

9. Brittney Cooper, *Eloquent Rage: A Black Feminist Discovers Her Superpower* (New York: St. Martin's Press, 2018), 2–3.

10. Mikki Kendall, *Hood Feminism: Notes from the Women That a Movement Forgot* (New York: Viking, 2020), 251.

11. Brockes, "#MeToo Founder Tarana Burke" (see note 7).

Virtual Motherhood

1. Rachel Cusk, *A Life's Work: On Becoming a Mother* (New York: Picador, 2003), 2.

2. Louise Erdrich, *The Blue Jay's Dance: A Birth Year* (New York: HarperCollins, 1995), 4.

Reflecting Jasmine

1. William Grimes, "Bharati Mukherjee, Writer of Immigrant Life, Dies at 76," *New York Times*, February 1, 2017, www.nytimes. com/2017/02/01/books/bharati-mukherjee-dead-author-jasmine.html.

2. Muzaffar Chishti, Faye Hipsman, and Isabel Ball, "Fifty Years On, the 1965 Immigration and Nationality Act Continues to Reshape the United States," Migration Policy Institute, October 15, 2015, www .migrationpolicy.org/article/fifty-years-1965-immigration-and-nationality -act-continues-reshape-united-states.

3. Bharati Mukherjee, *Jasmine* (New York: Grove Weidenfeld, 1989), 214.

4. Bharati Mukherjee, Clark Blaise, Michael Connell, Jessie Grearson, and Tom Grimes, "An Interview with Bharati Mukherjee," *Iowa Review* 20, no. 3 (Fall 1990): 7–32, ir.uiowa.edu/cgi/viewcontent.cgi?referer =&httpsredir=1&article=3908&context=iowareview.

5. Justine Larbalestier, "Ain't That a Shame (updated)," *Justine Larbalestier*, July 23, 2009, justinelarbalestier.com/blog/2009/07/23/aint-that-a-shame/.

6. Maddie Crum, "Sci-Fi Author Nnedi Okorafor Says Publishers Whitewashed Her Book Cover," *Huffington Post*, March 14, 2017, www.huffpost.com/entry/author-nnedi-okorafor-says-publishers-whitewashed-her-book-cover_n_58c83b68e4b022994fa2bb19.

7. Ursula K. Le Guin, "A Whitewashed Earthsea: How the SciFi Channel Wrecked My Books," *Slate*, December 16, 2004, slate.com/culture/2004/12/ursula-k-le-guin-on-the-tv-earthsea.html.

In Memory of Vincent Chin

1. King Rose Archives, "Bashing a Toyota in Detroit," YouTube, September 21, 2016, www.youtube.com/watch?v=CNvWoMrS-m8.

2. Heather Johnson Yu, "35 Years Ago, Vincent Chin Was Murdered in Cold Blood for Being Asian," *NextShark*, June 23, 2017, nextshark.com/vincent-chin-murder-35-years-ago-2017/.

3. Asia Society, "35 Years After Vincent Chin's Murder, How Has America Changed?" Asia Blog, June 16, 2017, asiasociety.org/blog/asia/35-years-after-vincent-chins-murder-how-has-america-changed.

4. Tule Lake Committee, "History," 2012, www.tulelake.org/history.

5. Denshō, "Timeline: Important Moments in Japanese American History Before, During, and After World War II Mass Incarceration," 2019, densho.org/timeline/; U.S. Department of Justice, "Ten Year Program to Compensate Japanese Americans Interned during World War II Closes Its Doors," February 19, 1999, www.justice.gov/archive/opa/pr/1999/February/059cr.htm.

6. Detroit Historical Society, "Uprising of 1967," Encyclopedia of Detroit, detroithistorical.org/learn/encyclopedia-of-detroit/uprising-1967.

7. "Uniroyal Giant Tire, Allen Park, Michigan," *Atlas Obscura*, October 11, 2010, www.atlasobscura.com/places/uniroyal-giant-tire.

8. Micheline Maynard, "O'Neill in Detroit for Auto Talks," UPI, March 8, 1982, www.upi.com/Archives/1982/03/08/ONeill-in-Detroit-for-auto-talks/3545384411600/.

9. "Among All the Horrors of the Jeffrey Dahmer Murders," *Chicago Tribune*, July 30, 1991, www.chicagotribune.com/news/ct-xpm-1991-07-30-9103240096-story.html.

10. Robert Imrie, "Refugee Family's Two Encounters with Dahmer End in Sorrow," Associated Press, July 27, 1991, apnews.com/494ace1a56444 ed99dc3ca3b16e13497.

11. Greg Gardner, "Trump Asks Japanese Automakers to Do Something They've Been Doing for 35 Years," *Detroit Free Press*, November 6, 2017, www.freep.com/story/money/cars/2017/11/06/trump-japan -america-auto-production/835275001/.

12. Stephany Bai, "President Obama Signs Bill Eliminating 'Oriental' from Federal Law," NBC News, May 20, 2016, www.nbcnews.com/news /asian-america/president-obama-signs-bill-eliminating-oriental -federal-law-n577811.

13. "Where 'Asian-American' Came From." KIMT News, May 27, 2018, www.kimt.com/content/national/483779211.html.

14. "Chinese Immigration and the Chinese Exclusion Acts," Office of the Historian, U.S. Department of State, history.state.gov/milestones/ 1866–1898/chinese-immigration.

15. Associated Press, "Mark Wahlberg Victim: Don't Pardon Him," *USA Today*, January 20, 2015, www.usatoday.com/story/life/people/2015 /01/20/wahlberg-victim/22047231/.

16. Samantha Schmidt, "Suspect in Kansas Bar Shooting of Indians Apparently Thought They Were Iranians," *Washington Post*, February 28, 2017, www.washingtonpost.com/news/morning-mix/wp/2017/02/28 /suspect-in-kansas-bar-shooting-of-indians-apparently-thought-they-were -iranians/.

17. Jack London, "The Yellow Peril," in *Revolution, and Other Essays* (New York: Macmillan, 1910), 267–89, www.marxists.org/archive /london/revolution/ch12.htm.

18. Niraj Warikoo, "Michigan Had Highest Number of Bias Crimes in Midwest Post-election," *Detroit Free Press*, December 2, 2016, www.freep .com/story/news/local/michigan/2016/12/01/michigan-bias-crimes -midwest-election/94744196/.

19. Rosana Xia, "Where They Are Now," *Los Angeles Times*, April 20, 2012, graphics.latimes.com/towergraphic-where-they -are-now/.

20. Mari Nakahara, "A War Remembered: Maya Lin's Design for the Vietnam Veterans Memorial," *Medium*, June 22, 2017, medium.com /@librarycongress/a-war-remembered-maya-lins-design-for-the -vietnam-veterans-memorial-ef7a0232e550.

21. Chishti Muzaffar, Faye Hipsman, and Isabel Ball, "Fifty Years On, the 1965 Immigration and Nationality Act Continues to Reshape the United States," Migration Policy Institute, March 2, 2017, www.migrationpolicy.org/article/fifty-years-1965-immigration-and-nationality-act-continues-reshape-united-states.

22. Christina Capatides, "Bullies Attack Asian American Teen at School, Accusing Him of Having Coronovirus," CBS News, February 14, 2020, www.cbsnews.com/news/coronavirus-bullies-attack-asian-teen-los-angeles-accusing-him-of-having-coronavirus/.

23. Julie Hinds, "25 Years Later, 'Roger & Me' Still Packs a Punch," *Detroit Free Press*, October 5, 2014, www.freep.com/story/entertainment/movies/2014/10/04/roger-michael-moore-blu-ray-th-anniverwary/16673457/.

24. Molly Crane-Newman and Leonard Greene, "NYC Hammer Attack Suspect Charged with Murder from Hospital Psych Ward," *New York Daily News*, February 1, 2019, www.nydailynews.com/new-york/brooklyn/ny-metro-hammer-attack-restaurant-20190201-story.html.

25. Brian Flanigan, "Slaying Ends Couple's Dream," *Detroit Free Press*, July 1, 1982.

26. Frank H. Wu, "The Case against Vincent Chin," *HuffPost*, September 24, 2014, www.huffpost.com/entry/the-case-against-vincent_b_5237359; Frank H. Wu, "Why Vincent Chin Matters," *New York Times*, June 22, 2012, www.nytimes.com/2012/06/23/opinion/why-vincent-chin-matters.html; Emil Guillermo, "Ronald Ebens, the Man Who Killed Vincent Chin, Apologizes 30 Years Later," Asian American Legal Defense and Education Fund, June 22, 2012, www.aaldef.org/blog/ronald-ebens-the-man-who-killed-vincent-chin-apologizes-30-years-later/; "Lily Chin Tries to Ease Pain," *Detroit Free Press*, September 9, 1987; Helen Zia, "Lily Chin: The Courage to Speak Out," in *Untold Civil Rights Stories: Asian Americans Speak Out for Justice*, edited by Stewart Kwoh and Russell C. Leong (Los Angeles: Asian Pacific American Legal Center, 2009), 35–41.

27. *Who Killed Vincent Chin?*, directed by Christine Choy and Renee Tajima-Pena, screenplay by Kenneth Chisholm, Film News Now Foundation, 1989.

28. Associated Press, "Civil Rights Charges Dropped in Beating Death of Asian-Indian Physician," *New York Times*, June 19, 1993, www.nytimes.com/1993/06/19/nyregion/civil-rights-charges-dropped-in-beating-of-asian-indian-physician.html; Michael Marriot, "In Jersey City, Indians

Protest Violence," *New York Times*, October 12, 1987, www.nytimes.com
/1987/10/12/nyregion/in-jersey-city-indians-protest-violence.html.

29. *Who Killed Vincent Chin?*, www.youtube.com/
watch?v=1qM1GIgBktE.

30. Emil Guillermo, "Lessons from Vincent Chin Murder 35 Years
After; Podcast Interview with Helen Zia; and Thoughts on My Interview
with Chin's Killer, Ronald Ebens," AALDEF, June 18, 2017, www.aaldef
.org/blog/emil-guillermo-lessons-from-vincent-chin-murder-35-years-ago
-podcast-helen-zia/.

31. Emil Guillermo, "Ronald Ebens, Vincent Chin's Killer, Denies
Financial Windfall, Debt to Chin Estate in New Interview," June 25, 2015,
www.aaldef.org/blog/emil-guillermo-ronald-ebens-vincent-chins
-killer-denies-getting-windfall-in-new-interview-2/.

32. Zia, "Lily Chin: The Courage to Speak Out" (see note 26).

33. Guillermo, "Lessons from Vincent Chin Murder."

34. "Lily Chin Grapples with Her Life," *Detroit Free Press*, September 9,
1987.

35. Judith Cummings, "Detroit Asian-Americans Protest Lenient
Penalties for Murder," *New York Times*, April 26, 1983, www.nytimes.
com/1983/04/26/us/detroit-asian-americans-protest-lenient-penalties
-for-murder.html.

36. "The $3,000 License to Kill," *Washington Post*, April 30, 1983, www
.washingtonpost.com/archive/politics/1983/04/30/the-3000-license-to
-kill/e2c6f8bb-017b-46a1-9fcb-e1766e61291b/.

37. John Holusha, "2 Fined in Detroit Slaying Are Indicted by
Federal Jury," *New York Times*, November 3, 1983, www.nytimes.com
/1983/11/03/us/2-fined-in-detroit-slaying-are-indicted-by-federal
-jury.html.

38. Louis Aguilar, "Estate of Vincent Chin Seeks Millions from His
Killer," *Detroit News*, June 27, 2017, www.detroitnews.com/story/news
/local/oakland-county/2017/06/24/vincent-chin-th-anniversary
/103167672/.

39. Frances Kai-Hwa Wang, "Who Is Vincent Chin? The History and
Relevance of a 1982 Killing," NBC News, June 15, 2017, www.nbcnews
.com/news/asian-america/who-vincent-chin-history-relevance-1982
-killing-n771291.

40. Marissa Marandola, "Reenacting the Vincent Chin Trial," *Harvard
Law Today*, March 21, 2017, today.law.harvard.edu/apalsa-conference
-judge-chin-brings-civil-rights-trial-life/.

41. Don Sherman, "How Toyota Went from a Cotton Weaver's Dream to Global Car Sales Dominance" Hagerty, December 18, 2017, www. hagerty.com/ media/news/sixty-years-of-toyota-usa.

42. Scott Miller, "Transformers: Why Japanese-Nameplate Automakers Became American Manufacturers," Japan Automobile Manufacturers Association, October 4, 2017, www.jama.org/csis-japanese-nameplate-automakers-became-american-manufacturers/; John Holusha, "Japan's Made-in-America Cars," *New York Times*, March 31, 1985, www.nytimes.com/1985/03/31/business/japan-s-made-in-america-cars.html.

43. James Risen, "First Imports, Now Auto Plants in the U.S.: Japanese Stepping Up Pressure on Big 3," *Los Angeles Times*, October 15, 1988, www.latimes.com/archives/la-xpm-1988-10-15-fi-3525-story.html.

44. John Castine, "Probation of Killers Draws Fire," *Detroit Free Press*, May 9, 1983.

45. Lawrence Lan, "'It's Not Fair!': Remembering Vincent Chin, Thirty Years Later," *Discover Nikkei*, June 28, 2012, www.discovernikkei.org/en /journal/2012/6/28/vincent-chin/.

46. Cayden Mak, "In Search of Justice: Another Way to Remember Vincent Chin," *18 Million Rising*, June 29, 2014, 18millionrising.org /2014/06/search-justice-another-way-remember-vincent-chin.html.

Treatment

1. Ninth Street was renamed Martin Luther King Boulevard in January 1982. Derek H. Alderman, "Naming Streets for Martin Luther King, Jr.: No Easy Road," in *Landscape and Race in the United States*, edited by Richard H. Schein (New York: Routledge, 2006), 215–18. artsandsciences.sc.edu/cege/alderman_chapter.pdf.

2. David Cook, "The People's History of Chattanooga," *Chattanooga Times Free Press*, February 21, 2016, www.timesfreepress.com/news /opinion/columns/story/2016/feb/21/peoples-history-chattanooga /351187/.

3. "*Pneumocystis* Pneumonia—Los Angeles," *Morbidity and Mortality Weekly Report* (hereafter *MMWR*, Centers for Disease Control) 30, no. 21 (June 5, 1981): 1–3, www.cdc.gov/mmwr/preview/mmwrhtml/june_5. htm; Lawrence K. Altman, "Rare Cancer Seen in 41 Homosexuals," *New York Times*, July 3, 1981, www.nytimes.com/1981/07/03/us/rare-cancer -seen-in-41-homosexuals.html; "Current Trends Update on Acquired Immune Deficiency Syndrome (AIDS)—United States," *MMWR* 31, no. 37 (September 24, 1982): 507–8, 513–14, www.cdc.gov/mmwr/preview

/mmwrhtml/00001163.htm; Sonja Schmid, "The Discovery of HIV-1," *Nature*, November 28, 2018, www.nature.com/articles/d42859-018 -00003-x; Chris Hardesty, "That's a Fact," *Chattanooga Times*, November 18, 1993. In the early 1980s, particularly in medical literature, the predominant term to describe people with same-sex partners was *gay*.

4. "A Timeline of HIV and AIDS," HIV.gov, March 12, 2019, www.hiv. gov/hiv-basics/overview/history/hiv-and-aids-timeline; Robert C. Gallo and Luc Montagnier, "The Discovery of HIV as the Cause of AIDS," *New England Journal of Medicine* 349, no. 24 (2003): 2283–85, doi:10.1056 /nejmp038194.

5. "First 500,000 AIDS Cases—United States, 1995," *MMWR* 44, no. 46 (November 24, 1995): 848–53, www.cdc.gov/mmwr/preview/mmwrhtml /00039622.htm.

6. German Lopez, "The Reagan Administration's Unbelievable Response to the HIV/AIDS Epidemic," *Vox*, December 1, 2016, www.vox .com/2015/12/1/9828348/ronald-reagan-hiv-aids.

7. CDC, "Epidemiologic Notes and Reports Acquired Immuno-deficiency Syndrome (AIDS) among Blacks and Hispanics—United States," *MMWR* 35, no. 43 (October 24, 1986): 655–58, 663–66, www.cdc .gov/mmwr/preview/mmwrhtml/00039622.htm.

8. Abraham Verghese, *My Own Country: A Doctor's Story of a Town and Its People in the Age of AIDS*. (New York: Simon & Schuster, 1994), 13.

9. Michael Warren, "Woman Who Caught AIDS from Dentist Near Death," Associated Press, June 15, 1991, apnews.com/d1546c6739100 46000ac9fc50ae2ec52.

10. "Majority of Public Favors Same-Sex Marriage, but Divisions Persist," Pew Research Center, May 14, 2019, www.people-press.org/2019 /05/14/majority-of-public-favors-same-sex-marriage-but-divisions -persist/.

On the Unbearable Whiteness of Southern Literature

1. Olive Ann Burns, *Cold Sassy Tree* (New York: Ticknor & Fields, 1984).

2. Harper Lee, *To Kill a Mockingbird* (Philadephia: Lippincott, 1960).

3. Matthew W. Hughey, "Cinethetic Racism: White Redemption and Black Stereotypes in 'Magical Negro' Films," *Social Problems* 56, no. 3 (August 2009): 543–77, academic.oup.com/socpro/article-abstract/56 /3/543/1707611?redirectedFrom=fulltext.

4. John Grisham, *A Time to Kill* (New York: Wynwood, 1989).

5. Melinda Haynes, *Mother of Pearl* (New York: Hyperion, 1999).

6. Kathryn Stockett, *The Help* (New York: Amy Einhorn Books / Putnam, 2009).

7. Roxane Gay, "The Solace of Preparing Fried Foods and Other Quaint Remembrances," *Rumpus*, August 11, 2011, therumpus .net/2011/08/the-solace-of-preparing-fried-foods-and-other-quaint -remembrances-from-1960s-mississippi-thoughts-on-the-help/.

8. "Good 'Help' Isn't Hard to Find, Thanks to Kathryn Stockett," *USA Today*, March 4, 2009, www.usatoday.com/story/life/books/2013 /06/28/good-help-isnt—hard-to-find-thanks-to-kathryn-stockett /2469043/.

9. Elizabeth Day, "Kathryn Stockett: 'I Still Think I'm Going to Get into Trouble for Tackling the Issue of Race in America,'" *Guardian*, October 8, 2011, www.theguardian.com/theobserver/2011/oct/09/kathryn -stockett-help-civil-rights.

10. Day, "Kathryn Stockett."

11. "2010 Census Shows Black Population Has Highest Concentration in the South," United States Census Bureau, September 29, 2011, www .census.gov/newsroom/releases/archives/2010_census/cb11-cn185 .html.

12. Interview with LeAnne Howe, "It's about Story," *About South*, season 1, episode 6, soundcloud.com/about-south/s01-episode-06-its-about -story.

13. Devi S. Laskar, *The Atlas of Reds and Blues* (Berkeley, Calif.: Counterpoint, 2019).

14. Laskar, *The Atlas of Reds and Blues*, 98.

Gun Show

1. Erika Christakis, "Active-Shooter Drills Are Tragically Misguided," *Atlantic*, March 2019, www.theatlantic.com/magazine/archive/2019/03 /active-shooter-drills-erika-christakis/580426/.

2. Ken Curtis, Lisa Sacaccio, and Camille Gayle, "Three Teens Arrested for Making Threat against Dothan School," wtvy, November 17, 2017, www.wtvy.com/content/news/Three-teens-arrested-for-making-threat -against-Dothan-school-458225323.html.

3. Jamila King, "A White Man Shot and Killed Her Only Son: Now Lucy McBath Is Running So It Doesn't Happen to Anyone Else," *Mother Jones*, March/April 2018, www.motherjones.com/politics/2018/02/a-white- man-shot-and-killed-her-only-son-now-lucy-mcbath-is-running-so-it -doesnt-happen-to-anyone-else/.

4. Allyson Chiu and Samantha Schmidt, "Lucy McBath: Moved to Run for Congress by Son's Fatal Shooting, She Just Won Her Primary," *Washington Post*, July 25, 2018, www.washingtonpost.com/news/morning-mix/wp/2018/07/25/lucy-mcbath-moved-to-run-for-congress-by-sons-fatal-shooting-she-just-won-her-primary/.

5. Lucia Kay McBath and Rosemarie Robotham, *Standing Our Ground: The Triumph of Faith over Gun Violence: A Mother's Story* (New York: Atria, 2018), 25–26.

6. Brian Kemp for Governor, "Jake," April 27, 2018, www.youtube.com/watch?v=4ABRz_epvic.

7. Darryl Pinckney, "The American Tradition of Anti-Black Vigilantism," *Literary Hub*, November 18, 2019, lithub.com/the-american-tradition-of-anti-black-vigilantism/.

8. Mike Petchenik, "Family Seeking Answers after Woman Dies in Police-Involved Shooting," WSB-TV, April 30, 2018, www.wsbtv.com/news/local/family-seeking-answers-after-woman-dies-in-police-involved-shooting/741388491/.

9. "CAIR Georgia Releases New Details in Police Shooting after Officers Refuse to Cooperate with Prosecutors," CAIR (Council on American-Islamic Relations) Georgia, April 26, 2019, www.cairgeorgia.com/press-releases/536-cair-georgia-release-new-details-in-police-shooting-after-officers-refuse-to-cooperate-with-prosecutors.html.

10. "What Happened to Shukri Ali Said, a Town Hall," CAIR Georgia, www.youtube.com/watch?v=iT65_DOLgWE&t=954s.

11. Shaddi Abusaid, "Family of Woman Shot, Killed by Johns Creek Police Files Lawsuit against Officers, City," *Atlanta Journal-Constitution*, www.ajc.com/news/crime—law/family-woman-shot-killed-johns-creek-police-files-lawsuit-against-officers-city/9TBvUh5QNoW61dD1CjaWTM/.

12. Jade Abdul-Malik, "911 Dispatcher Doesn't Understand What Arbery Is 'Doing Wrong,'" GPB News, May 8, 2020, www.gpbnews.org/post/listen-911-dispatcher-doesn-t-understand-what-arbery-doing-wrong.

13. "Ahmaud Arbery Shooting: A Timeline of the Case," *New York Times*, June 24, 2020, www.nytimes.com/article/ahmaud-arbery-timeline.html.

14. Tim Stelloh, "Ahmaud Arbery Was Struck Twice in the Chest by Shotgun Blasts, Autopsy Shows," NBC News, May 12, 2020, www.nbcnews.com/news/us-news/ahmaud-arbery-was-struck-twice-chest-shotgun-blasts-autopsy-shows-n1204921.

15. Khushbu Shah, "'Every Stone Will Be Uncovered': How Georgia Officials Failed the Ahmaud Arbery Case," *Guardian*, May 9, 2020, www.theguardian.com/us-news/2020/may/09/every-stone-will-be-uncovered-how-georgia-officials-failed-the-ahmaud-arbery-case; Richard Fausset, "2 Suspects Charged with Murder in Ahmaud Arbery Shooting," *New York Times*, May 7, 2020, updated May 21, 2020, www.nytimes.com/2020/05/07/us/ahmaud-arbery-shooting-arrest.html.

16. "Ahmaud Arbery Murder Investigation," Georgia Bureau of Investigation, May 21, 2020, gbi.georgia.gov/press-releases/2020–05–14/ahmaud-arbery-murder-investigation; Eliott C. McLaughlin, "Ahmaud Arbery Was Hit with a Truck Before He Died, and His Killer Allegedly Used a Racial Slur, Investigator Testifies," CNN, June 4, 2020, *www.cnn.com/2020/06/04/us/mcmichaels-hearing-ahmaud-arbery/index.html.*

17. Rebecca M. Cunningham, Maureen A. Walton, and Patrick M. Carter, "The Major Causes of Death in Children and Adolescents in the United States," *New England Journal of Medicine*, December 20, 2018, www.nejm.org/doi/full/10.1056/NEJMsr1804754; Joanne Silberner, "Study: Kids More Likely to Die from Cars and Guns in U.S. than Elsewhere," NPR, December 19, 2018, www.npr.org/sections/goatsandsoda/2018/12/19/678193620/study-kids-more-likely-to-die-from-cars-and-guns-in-u-s-than-elsewhere.

18. Mikki Kendall, *Hood Feminism* (New York: Viking, 2020), 17.

19. Moms Demand Action, "Our Victories," momsdemandaction.org/about/victories/.

20. Everytown for Gun Safety, "Victory for Gun Sense: Louisiana Moms Demand Action, Everytown Applaud Defeat of Dangerous Bills This Session," June 6, 2019, everytown.org/press/victory-for-gun-sense-louisiana-moms-demand-action-everytown-applaud-defeat-of-dangerous-bills-this-session/.

21. Everytown for Gun Safety, "Victory for Gun Sense: Nevada Moms Demand Action, Everytown Applaud Nevada Legislature for Passing Gun Violence Prevention Policies This Session," June 5, 2019, everytown.org/press/victory-for-gun-sense-nevada-moms-demand-action-everytown-applaud-nevada-legislature-for-passing-gun-violence-prevention-policies-this-session/.

22. Rhonda Cook, "Georgia Gun Laws Differ from Florida's," *Atlanta Journal-Constitution*, February 15, 2018, www.ajc.com/news/georgia-gun-laws-like-nevada-are-among-weakest-the-nation/Eh4S74DXDoph H5bpqMb5XL/.

23. Erin Schumaker, "Congress Agrees on Historic Deal to Fund $25 Million in Gun Violence Research," ABC News, December 16, 2019, abcnews.go.com/Health/congress-approves-unprecedented-25-million -gun-violence-research/story?id=67762555.

24. "McBath Secures $25 Million for Gun Violence Prevention Research, Applauds First Funding Allocation in Two Decades," press release, U.S. Representative Lucy McBath, December 16, 2019, mcbath.house.gov/2019/12/mcbath-secures-25-million-for-gun -violence-prevention-research-applauds-first-funding-allocation-in-two- decades.

25. Hannah Fry, Marisa Gerber, James Queally, Brittny Mejia, Richard Winton, and Sarah Parvini, "Saugus High Shooter Opened Fire on Crowded Quad in 16-Second Attack That Left 2 Dead and 3 Wounded, Sheriff Says," *Los Angeles Times*, November 14, 2019, www.latimes.com /california/story/2019-11-14/shooting-reported-at-saugus-high-school -in-santa-clarita-police-searching-for-teen-suspect.

To the Extreme

1. Frances FitzGerald, *The Evangelicals: The Struggle to Shape America* (New York: Simon & Schuster, 2017).

2. Daniel K. Williams, *God's Own Party: The Making of the Christian Right* (New York: Oxford University Press, 2010), 1–9.

3. Nate Silver, "The Comey Letter Probably Cost Clinton the Election," FiveThirtyEight, May 3, 2017, fivethirtyeight.com/features/the-comey -letter-probably-cost-clinton-the-election/.

4. Abdullah Shihipar, "Why Americans Must Stop Talking about Trump's Mythical 'White Working Class' Voters," Quartz, July 4, 2017, qz.com/991072/why-americans-must-stop-talking-about-the-mythical -homogenous-white-working-class/.

5. Hannah Arendt, *The Origins of Totalitarianism* (1951; New York: Harcourt Brace Jovanovich, 1973), 333.

6. "WWII: German Camera Captures Nazi Troops at Rest," BBC, January 5, 2015, www.bbc.com/news/uk-england-kent-30613338.

7. Éric Vuillard, *The Order of the Day*, translated by Mark Polizzotti (New York: Other Press, 2018).

8. Vuillard, *The Order of the Day*, 2.

9. Vuillard, *The Order of the Day*, 46.

10. Steven Perlberg, "Rick Santelli Started the Tea Party with a Rant Exactly 5 Years Ago Today—Here's How He Feels about It Now," *Business*

Insider, February 19, 2014, www.businessinsider.com xrick-santelli -tea-party-rant-2014-2.

11. Theda Skocpol and Vanessa Williamson, *The Tea Party and the Remaking of Republican Conservatism* (New York: Oxford University Press, 2012), 3–7.

12. John Nichols, "You Say Sarah Palin's Just Not Extreme Enough? How about Michele Bachmann for President?" *Nation*, January 8, 2011, www.thenation.com/article/you-say-sarah-palins-just-not-extreme -enough-how-about-michele-bachmann-president/.

13. Jeff Nesbit, "The Secret Origins of the Tea Party," *Time*, April 5, 2016, time.com/secret-origins-of-the-tea-party/.

14. Frank Bajak, "Georgia Election Server Wiped after Suit Filed," Associated Press, October 26, 2017, apnews.com/ article/877ee1015f1c43f1965f63538b035d3f.

"Armchair" Activism in the Real World

1. Adi Robertson, "Trump's White House Website Is One Year Old: It's Still Ignoring LGBT Issues, Climate Change, and a Lot More," *Verge*, January 20, 2018, www.theverge.com/2018/1/20/16909218 /trump-white-house-website-update-lgbt-climate-change-disabilities -one-year-anniversary.

2. Brian Stelter, "Trump Says He Has 'Running War' with Media, Gets Facts Wrong, in CIA Speech," CNN Business, January 21, 2017, money .cnn.com/2017/01/21/media/donald-trump-war-with-the-media/.

3. Jessica Taylor, "Yes, All This Happened: Trump's First 2 Weeks as President," NPR, February 4, 2017, www.npr.org/2017/02/04 /513473827/yes-all-this-happened-trumps-first-2-weeks-as-president.

4. "Introduction to the Guide," Indivisible Project, 2020, indivisible .org/guide.

5. Jordan Wilkie, "Exclusive: High Rate of Absentee Ballot Rejection Reeks of Voter Suppression," *WhoWhatWhy*, October 16, 2018, whowhatwhy.org/2018/10/12/exclusive-high-rate-of-absentee-ballot -rejection-reeks-of-voter-suppression/.

6. Anjali Enjeti (@anjalienjeti), Twitter, October 12, 2018, twitter.com /anjalienjeti/status/1050891910133501952.

7. Anjali Enjeti (@anjalienjeti), Twitter, October 13, 2018, twitter .com/anjalienjeti/status/1051283441726164993.

8. Tyler Estep, "Federal Judge Mulling Action over Georgia Absentee Ballots," *Atlanta Journal-Constitution*, October 24, 2018, www.ajc.com

/news/local-govt—politics/federal-judge-mulling-action-over-georgia
-absentee-ballots/JS3hXmCTpowiI6ZOJui47L/.

9. Alexis Okeowo, "Fighting for Abortion Access in the South," *New Yorker*, October 7, 2019, www.newyorker.com/magazine/2019/10/14
/fighting-for-abortion-access-in-the-south.

Unnewsworthy

1. Shawn Langois, "How Biased Is Your News Source? You Probably Won't Agree with This Chart," *MarketWatch*, April 21, 2018, www.marketwatch.
com/story/how-biased-is-your-news-source-you-probably-wont-agree
-with-this-chart-2018–02–28.

2. Katie Kilkenny, "Michelle Wolf Blasts Trump and Media at White House Correspondents' Dinner," *Hollywood Reporter*, April 28, 2018, www
.hollywoodreporter.com/news/michelle-wolf-blasts-trump-congress
-at-white-house-correspondents-dinner-1106353.

3. Katie McLaughlin, "5 Surprising Things That 1960s TV Changed," CNN, August 25, 2014, www.cnn.com/2014/05/29/showbiz/tv/sixties
-five-things-television/index.html.

4. Colin Marshall, "Famed Art Critic Robert Hughes Hosts the Premiere of 20/20, Where Tabloid TV News Began (1978)," *Open Culture*, January 6, 2017, www.openculture.com/2017/01/robert-hughes
-hosts-the-premiere-of-2020.html.

5. David Folkenflik, "The Birth of Fox News," *Salon*, October 21, 2013, www.salon.com/2013/10/19/the_birth_of_fox_news/.

6. "H.J. Res. 114 (107th): Authorization for Use of Military Force against Iraq Resolution of 2002," Senate Vote #237, October 11, 2002, GovTrack, www.govtrack.us/congress/votes/107-2002/s237; Charles Lane, "We Expected the War on Terror to Unite Us: What Went Wrong?" *Washington Post*, September 10, 2018, www.washingtonpost.com
/opinions/we-expected-the-war-on-terror-to-unite-us-what-went-wrong
/2018/09/10/5fb58c38-b4ff-11e8-a7b5-adaaa5b2a57f_story.html.

7. "The War in Iraq: 10 Years and Counting," Iraq Body Count, March 19, 2013, www.iraqbodycount.org/analysis/numbers/ten-years/.

8. Brent Cunningham, "Re-thinking Objectivity." *Columbia Journalism Review*, July/August 2003, archives.cjr.org/feature/rethinking_objectivity
.php.

9. Michiko Kakutani, *The Death of Truth: Notes on Falsehood in the Age of Trump* (New York: Tim Duggan Books/Penguin Random House, 2018), 17.

10. Michael J. Socolow, "American Broadcasting Has Always Been Closely Intertwined with American Politics," *Conversation*, April 5, 2018, theconversation.com/amp/american-broadcasting-has-always-been-closely-intertwined-with-american-politics-94392.

11. The Radio Act of 1927, Public Law No. 632, 69th Congress, February 23, 1927, www.americanradiohistory.com/Archive-FCC/Federal%20Radio%20Act%201927.pdf; Sharon L. Morrison, "Radio Act of 1927." *The First Amendment Encyclopedia* (Middle Tennessee State University), 2009, www.mtsu.edu/first-amendment/article/1091/radio-act-of-1927.

12. Dylan Matthews, "Everything You Need to Know about the Fairness Doctrine in One Post," *Washington Post*, August 23, 2011, www.washingtonpost.com/blogs/ezra-klein/post/everything-you-need-to-know-about-the-fairness-doctrine-in-one-post/2011/08/23/gIQAN8CXZJ_blog.html; Kathleen Ann Ruane, *Fairness Doctrine: History and Constitutional Issues* (Washington, D.C.: Congressional Research Service, 2011).

13. Ruane, *Fairness Doctrine*.

14. Kristen Hare, "ASNE's Latest Diversity Survey Shows Some Progress, but Newsrooms Are Still Mostly White and Male," *Poynter*, October 10, 2017, www.poynter.org/business-work/2017/asnes-latest-diversity-survey-shows-some-progress-but-newsrooms-are-still-mostly-white-and-male/.

15. Michael Kunzelman, "Report: Tree of Life Massacre Led to a String of Attack Plots," *Pittsburgh Post-Gazette*, October 21, 2019, www.post-gazette.com/news/crime-courts/2019/10/21/Report-tree-life-synagogue-Pittsburgh-massacre-led-to-string-attack-plots/stories/201910210087.

16. American Society of News Editors, "The ASNE Newsroom Diversity Survey," October 10, 2017, www.asne.org/diversity-survey-2017; "ASNE, Google News Lab Release 2017 Diversity Survey Results with Interactive Website," myemail.constantcontact.com/ASNE-2017-diversity-survey-results-with-Google-News-Lab-s-interactive-website.html?soid=1110653940249&aid=9uB8mnp4pMY; Emily Sullivan, "Women of Color Are Severely Underrepresented in Newsrooms, Study Says," NPR, March 7, 2018, www.npr.org/sections/thetwo-way/2018/03/07/591513558/women-of-color-are-severely-underrepresented-in-newsrooms-study-says.

17. Brian Mann, "As Protests Emerge, Brothers Agree to Give Trump Administration a Chance," NPR, January 29, 2017, www.npr.org/2017 /01/29/512336574/as-protests-emerge-brothers-agree-to-give-trump -administration-a-chance.

18. Nina Shapiro, "A Washington County That Went for Trump Is Shaken as Immigrant Neighbors Start Disappearing," *Seattle Times*, November 15, 2017.

19. Jennifer Percy, "The Life of an American Boy at 17," *Esquire*, February 12, 2019, www.esquire.com/news-politics/a26016236/the -american-boy-at-17/.

20. Percy, "The Life of an American Boy."

21. Phillip Atiba Goff, Matthew Christian Jackson, Brooke Allison Lewis Di Leone, Carmen Marie Culotta, and Natalie Ann DiTomasso, "The Essence of Innocence: Consequences of Dehumanizing Black Children," *Journal of Personality and Social Psychology* 106, no. 4 (2014): 526–45, psycnet.apa.org/record/2014-06238-001.

22. Jenny Jarvie, "He Survived COVID-19. He's Broke. But He Thinks America Is Over-Reacting." *Los Angeles Times*, March 26, 2020, www .latimes.com/world-nation/story/2020-03-26/ coronavirus-suburbs-trump-supporters-georgia-waffle-house.

23. Lyz Lenz, "You Should Care That Richard Spencer's Wife Says He Abused Her," *HuffPost*, January 13, 2019, www.huffpost.com/entry /richard-spencer-nina-kouprianova-divorce-abuse_n_5c2fc90ee4bod75a9 830ab69.

24. Isaac Chotiner, "Bret Easton Ellis Thinks You're Overreacting to Donald Trump," *New Yorker*, April 11, 2019, www.newyorker.com/news/ q-and-a/bret-easton-ellis-thinks-youre-overreacting-to-donald-trump.

One Nation

1. "Remarks by President Trump and Prime Minister Modi of India at 'Howdy, Modi: Shared Dreams, Bright Futures' Event," September 22, 2019, www.whitehouse.gov/briefings-statements/remarks-president- trump-prime-minister-modi-india-howdy-modi-shared-dreams-bright -futures-event/.

2. Joanna Slater and Niha Masih "India Passes Controversial Citizenship Law Excluding Muslim Migrants," *Washington Post*, December 11, 2019, www.washingtonpost.com/world/asia_pacific/india-poised-to -pass-controversial-citizenship-law-excluding-muslim-migrants

/2019/12/11/ebda6a7e-1b71-11ea-977a-15a6710ed6da_story
.html; "Kashmir under Lockdown," Al Jazeera, October 27, 2019, www
.aljazeera.com/news/2019/08/india-revokes-kashmir-special-status-latest
-updates-190806134011673.html.

3. Stef W. Kight, "The Evolution of Trump's Muslim Ban," *Axios*,
February 10, 2020, www.axios.com/trump-muslim-travel-ban
-immigration-6ce8554f-05bd-467b-b3c2-ea4876f7773a.html.

4. Jordyn Phelps and Serena Marshall, "Trump's Executive Orders on
Immigration Explained," ABC News, January 26, 2017, abcnews.go.com
/Politics/president-trumps-executive-orders-immigration-explained
/story?id=45062485; Kristen Bialik, "ICE Arrests Went Up in 2017, with
Biggest Increases in Florida, Northern Texas, Oklahoma," Pew Research
Center, February 8, 2018, www.pewresearch.org/fact-tank/2018/02/08
/ice-arrests-went-up-in-2017-with-biggest-increases-in-florida
-northern-texas-oklahoma/.

5. John B. Judis, *The Nationalist Revival: Trade, Immigration, and the Revolt
Against Globalization* (New York: Columbia Global Reports, 2018), 15.

6. James Meek, *Dreams of Leaving and Remaining* (London: Verso,
2019), 3.

7. Adam Gopnik, *A Thousand Small Sanities: The Moral Adventure of
Liberalism* (New York: Basic Books, 2019), 2–3.

8. Vanessa Maria de Castro, "Why Did Bolsonaro's Supporters Vote for
Him?" in *In Spite of You: Bolsonaro and the New Brazilian Resistance*, edited
by Conor Foley (New York: OR Books, 2019), 71.

9. "Uruguayan Dictator Guilty of Murder," Al Jazeera, October 23,
2009, www.aljazeera.com/news/americas/2009/10/200910
22224639667740.html.

10. Carolina De Robertis, *Cantoras* (New York: Knopf, 2019), 17.
Cantora means "songstress" or "songbird."

11. De Robertis, *Cantoras*, 3–4.

12. De Robertis, *Cantoras*, 12.

13. De Robertis, *Cantoras*, 23–24.

14. De Robertis, *Cantoras*, 6.

15. De Robertis, *Cantoras*, 41.

16. Lomi Kriel and Dug Begley, "Trump Administration Still
Separating Hundreds of Migrant Children at the Border through Often
Questionable Claims of Danger," *Houston Chronicle*, June 22, 2019. www
.houstonchronicle.com/news/houston-texas/houston/article/Trump
-administration-still-separating-hundreds-of-14029494.php.

17. Valeria Luiselli, *Lost Children Archive* (New York: Knopf, 2019), 145.

18. Luiselli, *Lost Children Archive*, 82.

19. Valeria Luiselli, *Tell Me How It Ends: An Essay in Forty Questions* (Minneapolis: Coffee House Press, 2017).

20. Luiselli, *Lost Children Archive*, 146.

21. Yoko Ogawa, *The Memory Police*, translated by Stephen Snyder (New York: Pantheon, 2019), 8.

22. Ogawa, *The Memory Police*, 53.

23. Ogawa, *The Memory Police*, 95.

24. Nick Estes, *Our History Is the Future: Standing Rock versus the Dakota Access Pipeline, and the Long Tradition of Indigenous Resistance* (New York: Verso, 2019), 10–11, 20–21.

25. Estes, *Our History Is the Future*, 10–11.

26. Arelis R. Hernández and Laurie McGinley, "Harvard Study Estimates Thousands Died in Puerto Rico Because of Hurricane Maria," *Washington Post*, May 20, 2018, www.washingtonpost.com/national /harvard-study-estimates-thousands-died-in-puerto-rico-due-to-hurricane -maria/2018/05/29/1a82503a-6070-11e8-a4a4-c070ef53f315_story.html.

27. Bianca Padró Ocasio, "Puerto Ricans Who Fled to Orlando after Hurricane María Struggled More than Those in South Florida, Study Finds," *Orlando Sentinel*, February 1, 2019. www.orlandosentinel.com /weather/hurricane/puerto-rico-hurricane-recovery/os-ne-study-puerto -ricans-florida-mental-health-20190201-story.html.

28. Ed Morales, *Fantasy Island: Colonialism, Exploitation, and the Betrayal of Puerto Rico* (New York: Bold Type Books, 2019), 23.

29. Morales, *Fantasy Island*, 14.

30. Patrice Nganang, *When the Plums Are Ripe*, translated by Amy B. Reid (New York: Farrar, Straus and Giroux, 2019), 336.

31. Maaza Mengiste, *The Shadow King* (New York: W. W. Norton, 2019), 36.

32. Mengiste, *The Shadow King*, 87.

33. Mengiste, *The Shadow King*, 114.

34. Keith Bradsher, "Hong Kong Election Landslide Signals More Frictions with Beijing," *New York Times*, November 25, 2019, www.nytimes .com/2019/11/25/world/asia/hong-kong-election-protests.html.

35. "Gotabaya Rajapaksa Sworn In as Sri Lanka's New President," Al Jazeera, November 18, 2019, www.aljazeera.com/news/2019/11 /gotabaya-rajapaksa-sworn-sri-lanka-president-191118072535784.html.

36. Nganang, *When the Plums Are Ripe*, 18.

The Little Sanctuary in the Shadow of ICE

This article was originally published by *The Nation* magazine and is republished here with permission. It originally appeared at www .thenation.com/article/archive/the-little-yellow-sanctuary-in-the-shadow -of-ice/.

1. In December 2018 they moved to their new location, a white brick house three miles from the detention center. Martha Dalton, "Georgia Hospitality House Gets an Upgrade for Christmas," WABE, December 20, 2018, www.wabe.org/georgia-hospitality-house-gets-an -upgrade-for-christmas/.

2. Shane Bauer, "Today It Locks Up Immigrants. But CoreCivic's Roots Lie in the Brutal Past of America's Prisons," *Mother Jones*, September /October 2018, www.motherjones.com/crime-justice/2018/09/ corecivic-private-prison-shane-bauer-book/.

3. Dara Lind, "Fear Itself: Donald Trump's Real Immigration Policy," *Vox*, September 29, 2017, www.vox.com/policy-and-politics/2017 /9/14/16293906/trump-immigration-deportation.

4. "Immigration Detainers," American Civil Liberties Union, www.aclu .org/issues/immigrants-rights/ice-and-border-patrol-abuses/ immigration-detainers.

5. Vivian Yee, "A Marriage Used to Prevent Deportation. Not Anymore," *New York Times*, April 19, 2018, www.nytimes. com/2018/04/19/us/immigration-marriage-green-card.html.

6. Catherine E. Shoichet, "A Cell Became His Cemetery," CNN, 2020, www.cnn.com/interactive/2018/08/us/ice-detention-stewart -georgia/.

7. "Detention by the Numbers," Freedom for Immigrants, 2018, www .freedomforimmigrants.org/detention-statistics.

8. "Imprisoned Justice: Inside Two Georgia Immigrant Detention Centers," Penn State Law Center for Immigrants' Rights Clinic, May 2017, projectsouth.org/wp-content/uploads/2017/06/Imprisoned _Justice_Report-1.pdf.

9. "Concerns about ICE Detainee Treatment and Care at Detention Facilities," Office of Inspector General, Department of Homeland Security, December 11, 2017, www.oig.dhs.gov/sites/default/files /assets/2017-12/OIG-18-32-Dec17.pdf.

10. "ICE Detainee Passes Away at Georgia Hospital," U.S. Immigration

and Customs Enforcement, July 12, 2018, www.ice.gov/news/releases|
/ice-detainee-passes-away-georgia-hospital-1.

11. José Olivares, "ICE Detainee Diagnosed With Schizophrenia Spent
21 Days in Solitary Confinement, Then Took His Own Life," *Intercept*, July
27, 2018, theintercept.com/2018/07/27/
immigrant-detention-suicides-ice-corecivic/.

12. Catherine E. Shoichet, "The Death Toll in ICE Custody Is the
Highest It's Been in 15 Years," CNN, September 30, 2020, www.cnn.
com/2020/09/30/us/ice-deaths-detention-2020/index.html.

Reckoning with Georgia's Increasing Suppression
of Asian American Voters

1. Angela Chen, "A Snapshot of How Asian-Americans Are Changing
the South," *HuffPost*, March 28, 2018, www.huffpost.com/entry/asian
-american-growth-south_n_5a948133e4b0699553cb5834.

2. "Asian Quick Facts: Georgia—Atlanta." AARP, 2013, www.aarp.org
/content/dam/aarp/research/surveys_statistics/general/2013/Asian
-Quick-Facts-Sheet-Atlanta-Georgia-AARP-rsa-gen.pdf.

3. Karthick Ramakrishnan, "The Asian American Vote in 2016: Record
Gains, but Also Gaps," *Data Bits*, May 19, 2017, aapidata.com/blog
/voting-gains-gaps/.

4. David Leonhardt, "Asian-Americans, a Sleeping Political Giant," *New
York Times*, April 5, 2018, www.nytimes.com/2018/04/05/opinion/asian
-americans-a-sleeping-political-giant.html.

5. "Organizing & Civic Engagement," Asian Americans Advancing
Justice—Atlanta, 2020, advancingjustice-atlanta.org/page/12.

6. Ibid.

7. Adam Liptak, "Supreme Court Invalidates Key Part of Voting Rights
Act," *New York Times*, June 25, 2013, *www.nytimes.com/2013/06/26/us
/supreme-court-ruling.html.*

8. Tim Reid and Grant Smith, "Missing Hyphens Will Make It Hard for
Some People to Vote in U.S. Election," Reuters, April 11, 2018, www
.reuters.com/article/us-usa-election-laws/missing-hyphens-will-make-it
-hard-for-some-people-to-vote-in-u-s-election-idUSKBN1HI1PX.

9. Brentin Mock, "How Dismantling the Voting Rights Act Helped
Georgia Discriminate Again," *Bloomberg CityLab*, October 15, 2018, www.
citylab.com/equity/2018/10/how-dismantling-voting-rights-act-helped
-georgia-discriminate-again/572899/.

10. Jordan Wilkie, "Exclusive: High Rate of Absentee Ballot Rejection Reeks of Voter Suppression," *WhoWhatWhy*, October 16, 2018, whowhatwhy.org/2018/10/12/exclusive-high-rate-of-absentee-ballot-rejection-reeks-of-voter-suppression/.

11. Kristina Torres, "Georgia Settles Suit Alleging It Blocked Thousands of Minority Voters," *Atlanta Journal-Constitution*, February 10, 2017, www.ajc.com/news/state—regional-govt—politics/georgia-settles-suit-alleging-blocked-thousands-minority-voters/g9sJf2f9yDGxtVe Oo8FDhI/.

12. Geoff Hing, Angela Caputo, and Johnny Kauffman, "Georgia Purged About 107,000 People from Voter Rolls: Report," WABE, October 19, 2018, www.wabe.org/georgia-purged-about-107000-people-from-voter-rolls-report/; Johnny Kauffman, "6 Takeaways from Georgia's 'Use It or Lose It' Voter Purge Investigation," WABE, October 22, 2018, www.wabe.org/6-takeaways-from-georgias-use-it-or-lose-it-voter-purge-investigation/; Matthew Charles Cardinale, "Stacey Hopkins, ACLU Preserve 160,000 Voter Registrations in State Settlement (Update 1)," *Atlanta Progressive News*, February 21, 2018, atlantaprogressivenews.com/2018/02/21/stacey-hopkins-aclu-preserve-130000-voter-registrations-in-state-settlement/.

13. Erin Durkin, "GOP Candidate Improperly Purged 340,000 from Georgia Voter Rolls, Investigation Claims," *Guardian*, October 19, 2018, www.theguardian.com/us-news/2018/oct/19/georgia-governor-race-voter-suppression-brian-kemp.

14. Don Owens, "Civil Rights Groups Sue Georgia Secretary of State Brian Kemp to Cease Discriminatory 'No Match, No Vote' Registration Protocol," Lawyers' Committee for Civil Rights Under Law, October 11, 2018, lawyerscommittee.org/civil-rights-groups-sue-georgia-secretary-of-state-brian-kemp-to-cease-discriminatory-no-match-no-vote-registration-protocol/.

15. Torres, "Georgia Settles Suit " (see note 11); Lauren Padgett, "Federal Judge Orders Georgia to Allow New U.S. Citizens to Vote, Clarify Process at Polls," 11 Alive, November 2, 2018, www.11alive.com/article/news/politics/elections/federal-judge-orders-georgia-to-allow-new-us-citizens-to-vote-clarify-process-at-polls/85-610750250.

16. Mark Niesse and Tyler Estep, "High Rate of Absentee Ballots Thrown out in Gwinnett," *Atlanta Journal-Constitution*, October 16, 2018, https://www.ajc.com/news/state—regional-govt—politics/georgia-election-officials-settle-lawsuit-over-interpreters-for-voters

/ZASWN4OnabHQaONEZazUoJ/; Doug Richards, "Lawsuit Says Gwinnett County Rejects Too Many Absentee Ballots," 11 Alive, October 16, 2018, www.11alive.com/article/news/local/lawsuit-says-gwinnett -county-rejects-too-many-absentee-ballots/85-604931314.

17. Brentin Mock, "In Georgia, Registration Restrictions Disproportionately Affect Urban Voters," *Pacific Standard*, October 22, 2018, psmag.com/social-justice/ georgia-voter-suppression-targets-urban-areas.

18. Alan Blinder, "Brian Kemp Resigns as Georgia Secretary of State, with Governor's Race Still Disputed," *New York Times*, November 08, 2018, www.nytimes.com/2018/11/08/us/georgia-brian-kemp-resign-stacey -abrams.html.

19. Amy Gardner, Beth Reinhard, and Aaron C. Davis, "Brian Kemp's Lead over Stacey Abrams Narrows amid Voting Complaints in Georgia Governor's Race," *Washington Post*, November 7, 2018, www .washingtonpost.com/politics/brian-kemps-lead-over-stacey-abrams -narrows-amid-voting-complaints-in-georgia-governors-race/2018/11/07 /39cf25f2-e2b7-11e8-b759-3d88a5cege19_story.html?utm_term =.5d6f8e44097e.

20. Mark Niesse, "Lawsuit Settlement Gives Georgia Voters Greater Access to Interpreters," *Atlanta Journal-Constitution*, December 4, 2018, www.ajc.com/news/state—regional-govt—politics/georgia-election -officials-settle-lawsuit-over-interpreters-for-voters/ZASWN4Onab HQaONEZazUoJ/.

21. "The Asian American Vote: A Report on the Multilingual Exit Poll from the 2012 Presidential Election, Georgia," Asian American Legal Defense and Education Fund, 2013, www.aaldef.org/uploads/pdf /Georgia%20Exit%20Poll%20Presentation.pdf.

22. "AALDEF Exit Poll of 7,600 Asian American Voters in 2018 Midterm Elections: Preliminary Results," AALDEF, November 8, 2018, www.aaldef.org/press-release/aaldef-exit-poll-of-7-600-asian-american -voters-in-2018-midterm-elections-preliminary-results/.

23. Karthick Ramakrishnan, "How Asian Americans Became Democrats," *American Prospect*, July 26, 2016, prospect.org/article /how-asian-americans-became-democrats-0.

24. "APA Elected Judges in GA," GAPABA Judiciary Committee, gapabajudiciary.weebly.com/apa-elected-judges-in-ga.html.

25. "Charlice Byrd," Georgia House of Representatives, 2011, www.house .ga.gov/representatives/en-US/member.aspx?Member=75&Session=18.

26. Craig Schneider, "Asian Americans Edging into the Political Arena," *Atlanta Journal-Constitution*, January 2, 2014, https://www.ajc.com/news/state—regional-govt—politics/asian-americans-edging-into-the-political-arena/LhGBccBXBClkEpWv4mTgiI/.

27. "One Asian American Candidate Wins Election, and Two Candidates Head to a Run-Off," Asian Americans Advancing Justice—Atlanta, November 4, 2015, advancingjustice-atlanta.org/story/48.

28. Greg Bluestein, "Georgia 2018: After Shotgun Ad, Kemp Features Explosions and Chainsaws," *Atlanta Journal-Constitution*, May 9, 2018, www.ajc.com/blog/politics/georgia-2018-after-shotgun-kemp-leads-with-explosions-and-chainsaws/tXnZ9AiDUAlPZjXzbLBtTP/.

29. Nurith Aizenman, "Gun Violence: How The U.S. Compares with Other Countries," NPR, October 6, 2017, www.npr.org/sections/goatsandsoda/2017/10/06/555861898/gun-violence-how-the-u-s-compares-to-other-countries.

30. Ramakrishnan, "How Asian Americans Became Democrats" (see note 23).

31. Charles Bethea, "How 'Religious Freedom' Laws Became a Flash Point in the Georgia Governor's Race," *New Yorker*, October 31, 2018, www.newyorker.com/news/news-desk/how-religious-freedom-laws-became-a-flash-point-in-the-georgia-governors-race; Russ Bynum, "Rivals for Georgia Governor Clash on 'Religious Freedom' Law," Associated Press, September 21, 2018, www.apnews.com/55607ef861d24fdb8506d9c1a97ae29c.

Crux, the Georgia Series in Literary Nonfiction